PEN

AH, WILDERNESS!

THE HAIRY APE

ALL GOD'S CHILLUN GOT WINGS

THE EMPEROR JONES

DESIRE UNDER THE ELMS

EUGENE O'NEILL

Ah, Wilderness!
The Hairy Ape
All God's Chillun Got Wings
The Emperor Jones
Desire Under the Elms

INTRODUCED AND EDITED BY

E. MARTIN BROWNE

PENGUIN BOOKS

Penguin Books Ltd, Harmondsworth, Middlesex, England
Penguin Books Pty Ltd, Ringwood, Victoria, Australia

—

First published in Penguin Plays 1960
This collection first published in Penguin Plays 1966

—

Ah, Wilderness! first produced 1933
First published 1933
First published in Great Britain by Cape 1934

The Hairy Ape first produced 1922
First published 1922
First published in Great Britain by Cape 1923

All God's Chillun Got Wings first produced 1924
First published 1924
First published in Great Britain by Cape 1925

The Emperor Jones first produced 1920
First published 1921
First published in Great Britain by Cape 1922

Desire Under the Elms first produced 1924
First published 1924
First published in Great Britain by Cape 1925

—

Made and printed in Great Britain
by Western Printing Services Ltd, Bristol
Set in Monotype Bembo

CONTENTS

INTRODUCTION

Eugene O'Neill was born in New York on 16 October 1888. He was little more than thirty when he was recognized as America's leading dramatist. In the 1920s, that position was more significant than at any time before or since: for it was in those years that America achieved for the first time a drama truly her own. Up to the First World War, American writing for the stage was largely based upon European models; but after her great leap forward into power in that war, she produced a generation of writers who dramatized American life in an idiom and a language that belonged to it. Sidney Howard, George Kaufman, Robert Sherwood, Elmer Rice, Paul Green, Lilian Hellman are a few of the distinguished names among them. But Eugene O'Neill has a genius which places him above them all.

To European readers, this genius has certain forbidding aspects. It is violent, seldom relieved by humour. It is almost always concerned with life in the raw. His writing can appear turgid, even morbid. But a deeper acquaintance with it will prove this impression to be false. The low-life in O'Neill's plays is drawn from experience; for until he was twenty-four, when the threat of tuberculosis and five months in a sanatorium changed his way of life and gave him time to discover that writing was his vocation, he had 'bummed' his way round much of the world by sea and land, living hard and desperately.

But this life in his plays is not only authentic; it is also continually touched with poetry. As a social rebel, O'Neill girded at those who were bound by convention and aimed at climbing the social ladder; they were blind, while those who lived at the bottom of the ladder were simple enough to look up through their misery and see the stars.

O'Neill was constantly experimenting with new forms of drama. By this means he made a further and very important contribution to the growth of the American theatre.

He was a voracious reader:

I read about everything I could lay my hands on: the Greeks, the Elizabethans – practically all the classics – and of course all the moderns. Ibsen and Strindberg, especially Strindberg.

This is his own account at the time when he was beginning in earnest to write plays. The two Scandinavians and the German Wedekind were the most powerful influences on his mind. It is often said that he followed the German Expressionists of the early twenties – Toller and Kaiser; but in fact he had found for himself certain of their ideas. He always kept what they surrendered, the human individual as the mainspring of his drama; for him, man never became an abstract or a mechanical being.

In fact, his effort to free the theatre from outworn conventions of form took him in the opposite direction. Already, in one of his early one-act plays, *The Moon of the Caribbees*, he dispenses almost entirely with plot, in order to allow his principal character to reveal himself by speaking his dreams aloud.

Here also we can already listen to that strongly rhythmic prose which he develops as he gains confidence. It is the right vehicle to convey the universalized characters who march through the following plays. *The Emperor Jones*, *The Hairy Ape*, *The Great God Brown*, each becomes more boldly experimental, until as the twenties draw to a close the marathon *Strange Interlude* raises the old convention of the 'aside' to its *n*th power.

Like all good rebels, O'Neill started with a first-hand knowledge of what he was rebelling against. His father, James O'Neill, was an accomplished actor of the old school. By the time Eugene was grown up, James had found in *Monte Cristo* a 'surefire' vehicle which ruined his art by allowing it to become a routine. Eugene occasionally toured with him and played small parts, and when in 1913 he knew his destiny as a playwright he had soaked himself in the ways and tricks of the old-fashioned theatre. (His own account of the family's life is given with masterly power in *Long Day's Journey into Night*.)

So anti-conventional a dramatist could not find his way directly on to Broadway. It was to the Provincetown Players under George Cram Cook that he owed his first productions. Most of his plays until the middle twenties had their first showing in Greenwich Village under Cook. Since then, he has come to occupy a position in America not unlike that of G.B.S. in England: the young rebel has become the Old Master. Of the plays written in the years immediately preceding his death in 1953, two very long ones, *The Iceman Cometh* and *Long Day's Journey*, have made the most sustained impact.

This volume of O'Neill's plays begins with one which was written several years later than the others we have included, and which reveals a side of O'Neill not seen elsewhere. *Ah, Wilderness!* is his only domestic comedy. The family life is subtly and tenderly studied, with careful detail and loving understanding. The characters emerge in greater depth than many of those in other plays whose emotions are raised to greater intensity. The autumnal close of *Ah, Wilderness!* denotes a maturity in its author.

The Hairy Ape (1922), like *The Emperor Jones*, has often been called an Expressionist play. Both concentrate upon an outsize figure, and focus their action on him, seeing life through his eyes. It would be truer to call these plays Impressionist: Fifth Avenue on a Sunday morning, for instance, is seen in *The Hairy Ape* as an impression in Yank's distracted head. In this play, too, 'dat ole davil sea' (as Chris in *Anna Christie* calls it) seems to exist not outside but inside the stinking hold of the ship in which Yank works. It is a simple, angry, and extremely powerful play.

All God's Chillun Got Wings (1924) created a great storm when it was first produced, because it deals with the marriage of a white girl to a Negro man. For O'Neill it was not the sociological problem that prejudiced people made out of it, but a tragic story of human relationships, between two simple and God-fearing people whose natural impulses ran contrary to the current social pattern. It is a moving play because of its warm humanity, the quality which one misses in *The Hairy Ape*, and will survive after the stresses which produced its situation have been relaxed.

The Emperor Jones is the first major example of that simplification on to a single theme which we have noted as O'Neill's brand of Expressionism. It exhibits the power of O'Neill's rhythm, with the drums as ground-bass; the evocation of the noble savage, and of the effect of primitive terror upon him, is haunting. It is a short play, confined to one cumulative effect; but it does superbly what it sets out to do.

Desire Under the Elms (1924) is a much subtler work, one of the playwright's finest creations. It is a tragedy, according to the strict definition of that word, and has the cathartic effect that Aristotle associated with tragedy. Ephraim, the father and owner of the farm, is a figure of tragic stature, breeding his downfall by his own pride, yet expressing in himself the permanent values for which he stands.

Against him are set the young and passionate lovers, whose love is bound up with the land-hunger which motivates Ephraim, but is finally released from it. The play is firmly constructed, and unified within a multiple set showing the whole of the house which is the symbol of possession; one is reminded of Hauptmann's *The Weavers* by this experiment. This play may be reckoned one of the first classics to be produced by the American theatre.

Complete list of O'Neill plays and years in which they were written

—

1913

THE WEB

1914

THIRST – RECKLESSNESS – WARNING

BOUND EAST FOR CARDIFF

FOG – SERVITUDE – A WIFE FOR A LIFE

THE MOVIE MAN – ABORTION

1915

A KNOCK AT THE DOOR – THE SNIPER

BELTHAZAR – THE DEAR DOCTOR

THE SECOND ENGINEER

1916

THE LONG VOYAGE HOME

IN THE ZONE – ILE

THE MOON OF THE CARIBBEES (S.S. GLENCAIRN)

BEFORE BREAKFAST

1918

BEYOND THE HORIZON – THE STRAW

WHERE THE CROSS IS MADE – THE DREAMY KID

SHELL SHOP – TILL WE MEET – THE ROPE

1919

HONOUR AMONG THE BRADLEYS – THE TRUMPET

EXORCISM – CHRIS CHRISTOPHERSON

1920

DIFF'RENT – THE EMPEROR JONES

GOLD – ANNA CHRISTIE

1921

THE FIRST MAN – THE HAIRY APE – THE FOUNTAIN

1923

WELDED – ALL GOD'S CHILLUN GOT WINGS

1924

DESIRE UNDER THE ELMS – THE ANCIENT MARINER

1925

THE GREAT GOD BROWN – MARCO MILLIONS

1926

STRANGE INTERLUDE – LAZARUS LAUGHED

1928

DYNAMO

1930

MOURNING BECOMES ELECTRA

(Homecoming, The Hunted, The Haunted)

1932

NINE PLAYS

1933

AH, WILDERNESS!

1934

DAYS WITHOUT END

1940

LONG DAY'S JOURNEY INTO NIGHT

1943

MOON FOR THE MISBEGOTTEN

1946

THE ICEMAN COMETH

Found at O'Neill's death

A TOUCH OF THE POET – HUGHIE

MORE STATELY MANSIONS

AH, WILDERNESS!

CHARACTERS

NAT MILLER, owner of the *Evening Globe*
ESSIE his wife
ARTHUR, RICHARD, MILDRED, TOMMY — their children
SID DAVIS, Essie's brother
LILY MILLER, Nat's sister
DAVID MCCOMBER
MURIEL MCCOMBER, his daughter
WINT SELBY, a classmate of Arthur's at Yale
BELLE
NORAH
BARTENDER
SALESMAN

ACT ONE

Sitting-room of the Miller home in a large small-town in Connecticut – about 7.30 in the morning of 4 July 1906.

The room is fairly large, homely looking and cheerful in the morning sunlight, furnished with scrupulous medium-priced tastelessness of the period. Beneath the two windows at left, front, a sofa with silk and satin cushions stands against the wall. At rear of sofa, a bookcase with glass doors, filled with cheap sets, extends along the remaining length of wall. In the rear wall, left, is a double doorway with sliding doors and portières, leading into a dark, windowless, back parlour. At right of this doorway, another bookcase, this time a small, open one, crammed with boys' and girls' books and the best-selling novels of many past years – books the family really have read. To the right of this bookcase is the mate of the double doorway at its left, with sliding doors and portières, this one leading to a well-lighted front parlour. In the right wall, rear, a screen door opens on a porch. Farther forward in this wall are two windows, with a writing-desk and a chair between them. At centre is a big, round table with a green-shaded reading-lamp, the cord of the lamp running up to one of five sockets in the chandelier above. Five chairs are grouped about the table – three rockers at left, right, and right rear of it, two armchairs at rear and left rear. A medium-priced, inoffensive rug covers most of the floor. The walls are papered white with a cheerful, ugly blue design.

[*Voices are heard in a conversational tone from the dining-room beyond the back parlour, where the family are just finishing breakfast. Then* MRS MILLER's *voice, raised commandingly:* 'Tommy! Come back here and finish your milk!' *At the same moment* TOMMY *appears in the doorway from the back parlour – a chubby, sunburnt boy of eleven with dark eyes, blond hair wetted and plastered down in a parting, and a shiny, good-natured face, a rim of milk visible about his lips. Bursting with bottled-up energy and a longing to get started on the Fourth, he nevertheless has hesitated obediently at his mother's call.*]

TOMMY [*calls back pleadingly*]: Aw, I'm full, Ma. And I said excuse me and you said all right. [*His father's voice is heard speaking to his mother. Then she calls:* 'All right, Tommy,' *and* TOMMY *asks eagerly*] Can I go out now?

MOTHER'S VOICE [*correctingly*]: May I!

TOMMY [*fidgeting, but obediently*]: May I, Ma?

MOTHER'S VOICE: Yes. [TOMMY *jumps for the screen door to the porch at right like a sprinter released by the starting-shot.*]

FATHER'S VOICE [*shouts after him*]: But you set off your crackers away from the house, remember! [*But* TOMMY *is already through the screen door, which he leaves open behind him.*]

[*A moment later the family appear from the back parlour, coming from the dining-room. First are* MILDRED *and* ARTHUR. MILDRED *is fifteen, tall and slender, with big, irregular features, resembling her father to the complete effacing of any pretence at prettiness. But her big, grey eyes are beautiful; she has vivacity and a fetching smile, and everyone thinks of her as an attractive girl. She is dressed in blouse and skirt in the fashion of the period.*

ARTHUR, *the eldest of the Miller children who are still living at home, is nineteen. He is tall, heavy, barrel-chested and muscular, the type of football linesman of that period, with a square, stolid face, small blue eyes and thick sandy hair. His manner is solemnly collegiate. He is dressed in the latest college fashion of that day, which has receded a bit from the extreme of preceding years, but still runs to padded shoulders and trousers half pegged at the top, and so small at their wide-cuffed bottoms that they cannot be taken off with shoes on.*]

MILDRED [*as they appear – inquisitively*]: Where are you going today, Art?

ARTHUR [*with superior dignity*]: That's my business. [*He ostentatiously takes from his pocket a tobacco pouch with a big 'Y' and class numerals stamped on it, and a heavy bulldog briar pipe with silver 'Y' and numerals, and starts filling the pipe.*]

MILDRED [*teasingly*]: Bet I know, just the same! Want me to tell you her initials? E.R.! [*She laughs.*]

[ARTHUR, *pleased by this insinuation at his lady-killing activities, yet finds it beneath his dignity to reply. He goes to the table, lights his pipe and picks up the local morning paper, and slouches back into the armchair at left rear of table, beginning to whistle 'Oh, Waltz Me Around Again, Willie' as he scans the headlines.* MILDRED *sits on the sofa at left, front. Meanwhile, their mother and their* AUNT LILY, *their father's. sister, have appeared, following them from the back parlour* MRS MILLER *is around fifty, a short, stout woman with fading light-brown hair sprinkled with grey, who must have been decidedly pretty as a girl in a round-faced, cute, small-featured, wide-eyed fashion. She has big brown eyes, soft and maternal – a bustling, mother-of-a-family manner. She is dressed in blouse and skirt.*

LILY MILLER, *her sister-in-law, is forty-two, tall, dark, and thin. She conforms outwardly to the conventional type of old-maid school teacher, even to wearing glasses. But behind the glasses her grey eyes are gentle and tired, and her whole atmosphere is one of shy kindliness. Her voice presents the greatest contrast to her appearance – soft and full of sweetness. She, also, is dressed in a blouse and skirt.*]

MRS MILLER [*as they appear*]: Getting milk down him is like – [*Suddenly she is aware of the screen door standing half open.*] Goodness, look at that door he's left open! The house will be alive with flies! [*Rushing out to shut it*] I've told him again and again – and that's all the good it does! It's just a waste of breath! [*She slams the door shut.*]

LILY [*smiling*]: Well, you can't expect a boy to remember to shut doors – on the Fourth of July. [*She goes diffidently to the straight-backed chair before the desk at right, front, leaving the comfortable chairs to the others.*]

MRS MILLER: That's you all over, Lily – always making excuses for him. You'll have him spoiled to death in spite of me. [*She sinks in rocker at right of table.*] Phew, I'm hot, aren't you? This is going to be a scorcher. [*She picks up a magazine from the table and begins to rock, fanning herself.*]

[*Meanwhile, her husband and her brother have appeared from the back parlour, both smoking cigars.* NAT MILLER *is in his late fifties, a tall, dark, spare man, a little stoop-shouldered, more than a little bald, dressed with an awkward attempt at sober respectability imposed upon an innate heedlessness of clothes. His long face has large, irregular, undistinguished features, but he has fine, shrewd, humorous grey eyes.*

SID DAVIS, *his brother-in-law, is forty-five, short and fat, bald-headed, with the Puckish face of a Peck's Bad Boy who has never grown up. He is dressed in what had once been a very natty loud light suit but is now a shapeless and faded nondescript in cut and colour.*]

SID [*as they appear*]: Oh, I like the job first rate, Nat. Waterbury's a nifty old town with the lid off, when you get to know the ropes. I rang in a joke in one of my stories that tickled the folks there pink. Waterwagon – Waterbury – Waterloo!

MILLER [*grinning*]: Darn good!

SID [*pleased*]: I thought it was pretty fair myself. [*Goes on a bit ruefully, as if oppressed by a secret sorrow*] Yes, you can see life in Waterbury, all right – that is, if you're looking for life in Waterbury!

MRS MILLER: What's that about Waterbury, Sid?

SID: I was saying it's all right in its way – but there's no place like home.

[*As if to punctuate this remark, there begins a series of bangs from just beyond the porch outside, as* TOMMY *inaugurates his celebration by setting off a package of firecrackers. The assembled family jump in their chairs.*]

MRS MILLER: That boy! [*She rushes to the screen door and out on the porch, calling*] Tommy! You mind what your Pa told you! You take your crackers out in the back-yard, you hear me!

ARTHUR [*frowning scornfully*]: Fresh kid! He did it on purpose to scare us.

MILLER [*grinning through his annoyance*]: Darned youngster! He'll have the house afire before the day's out.

SID [*grins and sings*]:

'Dunno what ter call 'im
But he's mighty like a Rose – velt.'

[*They all laugh.*]

LILY: Sid, you Crazy!

[*Sid beams at her.* MRS MILLER *comes back from the porch, still fuming.*]

MRS MILLER: Well, I've made him go out back at last. Now we'll have a little peace.

[*As if to contradict this, the bang of firecrackers and torpedoes begins from the rear of the house, left, and continues at intervals throughout the scene, not nearly so loud as the first explosion, but sufficiently emphatic to form a disturbing punctuation to the conversation.*]

MILLER: Well, what's on the tappee for all of you today? Sid, you're coming to the Sachem Club picnic with me, of course.

SID [*a bit embarrassedly*]: You bet. I mean I'd like to, Nat – that is, if –

MRS MILLER [*regarding her brother with smiling suspicion*]: Hmm! I know what that Sachem Club picnic's always meant!

LILY [*breaks in in a forced joking tone that conceals a deep earnestness*]: No, not this time, Essie. Sid's a reformed character since he's been on the paper in Waterbury. At least, that's what he swore to me last night.

SID [*avoiding her eyes, humiliated – joking it off*]: Pure as the driven snow, that's me. They're running me for president of the W.C.T.U.

[*They all laugh.*]

MRS MILLER: Sid, you're a caution. You turn everything into a joke. But you be careful, you hear? We're going to have dinner in the evening tonight, you know – the best shore dinner you ever tasted and I don't want you coming home – well, not able to appreciate it.

LILY: Oh, I know he'll be careful today. Won't you, Sid?

SID [*more embarrassed than ever – joking it off melodramatically*]: Lily, I swear to you if any man offers me a drink, I'll kill him – that is, if he changes his mind!

[*They all laugh except* LILY, *who bites her lip and stiffens.*]:

MRS MILLER: No use talking to him, Lily. You ought to know better by this time. We can only hope for the best.

MILLER: Now, you women stop picking on Sid. It's the Fourth of July and even a downtrodden newspaperman has a right to enjoy himself when he's on his holiday.

MRS MILLER: I wasn't thinking only of Sid.

MILLER [*with a wink at the others*]: What, are you insinuating I ever – ?

MRS MILLER: Well, to do you justice, no, not what you'd really call – But I've known you to come back from this darned Sachem Club picnic – Well, I didn't need any little bird to whisper that you'd been some place besides to the well! [*She smiles good-naturedly.* MILLER *chuckles.*]

SID [*after a furtive glance at the stiff and silent* LILY *– changes the subject abruptly by turning to* ARTHUR]: How are you spending the festive Fourth, Boola-Boola?

[*Arthur stiffens dignifiedly.*]

MILDRED [*teasingly*]: I can tell you, if he won't.

MRS MILLER [*smiling*]: Off to the Rands', I suppose.

ARTHUR [*with dignity*]: I and Bert Turner are taking Elsie and Ethel Rand canoeing. We're going to have a picnic lunch on Strawberry Island. And this evening I'm staying at the Rands' for dinner.

MILLER: You're accounted for, then. How about you, Mid?

MILDRED: I'm going to the beach to Anne Culver's.

ARTHUR [*sarcastically*]: Of course, there won't be any boys present! Johnny Dodd, for example?

MILDRED [*giggles – then with a coquettish toss of her head*]: Pooh! What do I care for him? He's not the only pebble on the beach.

MILLER: Stop your everlasting teasing, you two. How about you and Lily, Essie?

MRS MILLER: I don't know. I haven't made any plans. Have you, Lily?

LILY [*quietly*]: No. Anything you want to do.

MRS MILLER: Well, I thought we'd just sit around and rest and talk.

MILLER: You can gossip any day. This is the Fourth. Now, I've got a better suggestion than that. What do you say to an automobile ride? I'll get out the Buick and we'll drive around town and out to the lighthouse and back. Then Sid and I will let you off here, or anywhere you say, and we'll go on to the picnic.

MRS MILLER: I'd love it. Wouldn't you, Lily?

LILY: It would be nice.

MILLER: Then, that's all settled.

SID [*embarrassedly*]: Lily, want to come with me to the fireworks display at the beach tonight?

MRS MILLER: That's right, Sid. You take her out. Poor Lily never has any fun, always sitting home with me.

LILY [*flustered and grateful*]: I – I'd like to, Sid, thank you. [*Then an apprehensive look comes over her face.*] Only not if you come home – you know.

SID [*again embarrassed and humiliated – again joking it off, solemnly*]: Evil-minded, I'm afraid, Nat. I hate to say it of your sister.

[*They all laugh. Even* LILY *cannot suppress a smile.*]

ARTHUR [*with heavy jocularity*]: Listen, Uncle Sid. Don't let me catch you and Aunt Lily spooning on a bench tonight – or it'll be my duty to call a cop!

[SID *and* LILY *both look painfully embarrassed at this, and the joke falls flat, except for* MILDRED *who can't restrain a giggle at the thought of these two ancients spooning.*]

MRS MILLER [*rebukingly*]: Arthur!

MILLER [*dryly*]: That'll do you. Your education in kicking a football around Yale seems to have blunted your sense of humour.

MRS MILLER [*suddenly – startledly*]: But where's Richard? We're forgetting all about him. Why, where is that boy? I thought he came in with us from breakfast.

MILDRED: I'll bet he's off somewhere writing a poem to Muriel McComber, the silly! Or pretending to write one. I think he just copies –

ARTHUR [*looking back toward the dining-room*]: He's still in the dining-room, reading a book. [*Turning back – scornfully*] Gosh, he's always reading now. It's not my idea of having a good time in vacation.

MILLER [*caustically*]: He reads his school books, too, strange as that may seem to you. That's why he came out top of his class. I'm hoping before you leave New Haven they'll find time to teach you reading is a good habit.

MRS MILLER [*sharply*]: That reminds me, Nat. I've been meaning to speak to you about those awful books Richard is reading. You've got to give him a good talking to – [*She gets up from her chair.*] I'll go up and get them right now. I found them where he'd hid them on the shelf in his wardrobe. You just wait till you see what –

[*She bustles off, rear right, through the front parlour.*]

MILLER [*plainly not relishing whatever is coming – to* SID *grum-*

blingly]: Seems to me she might wait until the Fourth is over before bringing up – [*Then with a grin*] I know there's nothing to it, anyway. When I think of the books I used to sneak off and read when I was a kid.

SID: Me, too. I suppose Dick is deep in Nick Carter or Old Cap Collier.

MILLER: No, he passed that period long ago. Poetry's his red meat nowadays, I think – love poetry – and socialism, too, I suspect, from some dire declarations he's made. [*Then briskly*] Well, might as well get him on the carpet. [*He calls.*] Richard. [*No answer – louder*] Richard. [*No answer – then in a bellow*] Richard!

ARTHUR [*shouting*]: Hey, Dick, wake up! Pa's calling you.

RICHARD'S VOICE [*from the dining-room*]: All right. I'm coming.

MILLER: Darn him! When he gets his nose in a book, the house could fall down and he'd never –

[RICHARD *appears in the doorway from the back parlour, the book he has been reading in one hand, a finger marking his place. He looks a bit startled still, reluctantly called back to earth from another world.*

He is going on seventeen, just out of high school. In appearance he is a perfect blend of father and mother, so much so that each is convinced he is the image of the other. He has his mother's light-brown hair, his father's grey eyes; his features are neither large nor small; he is of medium height, neither fat nor thin. One would not call him a handsome boy; neither is he homely. But he is definitely different from both of his parents, too. There is something of extreme sensitiveness added – a restless, apprehensive, defiant, shy, dreamy selfconscious intelligence about him. In manner he is alternately plain simple boy and a posy actor solemnly playing a role. He is dressed in prep. school reflection of the college style of Arthur.]

RICHARD: Did you want me, Pa?

MILLER: I'd hoped I'd made that plain. Come and sit down a

while. [*He points to the rocking chair at the right of table near his.*]

RICHARD [*coming forward – seizing on the opportunity to play up his preoccupation – with apologetic superiority*]: I didn't hear you, Pa. I was off in another world.

[MILDRED *slyly shoves her foot out so that he trips over it, almost falling. She laughs gleefully. So does* ARTHUR.]

ARTHUR: Good for you, Mid! That'll wake him up!

RICHARD [*grins sheepishly – all boy now*]: Darn you, Mid! I'll show you!

[*He pushes her back on the sofa and tickles her with his free hand, still holding the book in the other. She shrieks.*]

ARTHUR: Give it to her, Dick!

MILLER: That's enough, now. No more rough-house. You sit down here, Richard.

[RICHARD *obediently takes the chair at right of table, opposite his father.*]

What were you planning to do with yourself today? Going out to the beach with Mildred?

RICHARD [*scornfully superior*]: That silly skirt party! I should say not!

MILDRED: He's not coming because Muriel isn't. I'll bet he's got a date with her somewheres.

RICHARD [*flushing bashfully*]: You shut up! [*Then to his father*] I thought I'd just stay home, Pa – this morning, anyway.

MILLER: Help Tommy set off firecrackers, eh?

RICHARD [*drawing himself up – with dignity*]: I should say not. [*Then frowning portentously*] I don't believe in this silly celebrating the Fourth of July – all this lying talk about liberty – when there is no liberty!

MILLER [*a twinkle in his eye*]: Hmm.

RICHARD [*getting warmed up*]: The land of the free and the home of the brave! Home of the slave is what they ought to call it – the wage slave ground under the heel of the capitalist class, starving, crying for bread for his children, and all he gets is a stone! The Fourth of July is a stupid farce!

MILLER [*putting a hand to his mouth to conceal a grin*]: Hmm. Them are mighty strong words. You'd better not repeat such sentiments outside the bosom of the family or they'll have you in jail.

SID: And throw away the key.

RICHARD [*darkly*]: Let them put me in jail. But how about the freedom of speech in the Constitution, then? That must be a farce, too. [*Then he adds grimly*] No, you can celebrate your Fourth of July. I'll celebrate the day the people bring out the guillotine again and I see Pierpont Morgan being driven by in a tumbril!

[*His father and* SID *are greatly amused;* LILY *is shocked but, taking her cue from them, smiles.* MILDRED *stares at him in puzzled wonderment, never having heard this particular line before. Only* ARTHUR *betrays the outraged reaction of a patriot.*]

ARTHUR: Aw say, you fresh kid, tie that bull outside! You ought to get a punch in the nose for talking that way on the Fourth!

MILLER [*solemnly*]: Son, if I didn't know it was you talking, I'd think we had Emma Goldman with us.

ARTHUR: Never mind, Pa. Wait till we get him down to Yale. We'll take that out of him!

RICHARD [*with high scorn*]: Oh, Yale! You think there's nothing in the world besides Yale. After all, what is Yale?

ARTHUR: You'll find out what!

SID [*provocatively*]: Don't let them scare you, Dick. Give 'em hell!

LILY [*shocked*]: Sid! You shouldn't swear before –

RICHARD: What do you think I am, Aunt Lily – a baby? I've heard worse than anything Uncle Sid says.

MILDRED: And said worse himself, I bet.

MILLER [*with a comic air of resignation*]: Well, Richard, I've always found I've had to listen to at least one stump speech every Fourth. I only hope getting your extra strong one right after breakfast will let me off for the rest of the day. [*They all laugh now, taking this as a cue.*]

RICHARD [*sombrely*]: That's right, laugh! After you, the deluge, you think! But look out! Supposing it comes before? Why shouldn't the workers of the world unite and rise? They have nothing to lose but their chains! [*He recites threateningly*] 'The days grow hot, O Babylon! 'Tis cool beneath thy willow trees!'

MILLER: Hmm. That's good. But where's the connexion, exactly? Something from that book you're reading?

RICHARD [*superior*]: No. That's poetry. This is prose.

MILLER: I've heard there was a difference between 'em. What is the book?

RICHARD [*importantly*]: Carlyle's *French Revolution.*

MILLER: Hmm. So that's where you drove the tumbril from and piled poor old Pierpont in it. [*Then seriously*] Glad you're reading it, Richard. It's a darn fine book.

RICHARD [*with unflattering astonishment*]: What, have you read it?

MILLER: Well, you see, even a newspaper owner can't get out of reading a book every now and again.

RICHARD [*abashed*]: I – I didn't mean – I know you – [*Then enthusiastically*] Say, isn't it a great book, though – that part about Mirabeau – and about Marat and Robespierre –

MRS MILLER [*appears from the front parlour in a great state of flushed annoyance*]: Never you mind Robespierre, young man! You tell me this minute where you've hidden those books! They were on the shelf in your wardrobe and now you've gone and hid them somewheres else. You go right up and bring them to your father!

[RICHARD, *for a second, looks suddenly guilty and crushed. Then he bristles defensively.*]

MILLER [*after a quick understanding glance at him*]: Never mind his getting them now. We'll waste the whole morning over those darned books. And anyway, he has a right to keep his library to himself – that is, if they're not too – What books are they, Richard?

RICHARD [*selfconsciously*]: Well – there's –

MRS MILLER: I'll tell you, if he won't – and you give him a good talking to. [*Then, after a glance at* RICHARD, *mollifiedly*] Not that I blame Richard. There must be some boy he knows who's trying to show off as advanced and wicked, and he told him about –

RICHARD: No! I read about them myself, in the papers and in other books.

MRS MILLER: Well, no matter how, there they were on his shelf. Two by that awful Oscar Wilde they put in jail for heaven knows what wickedness.

ARTHUR [*suddenly – solemnly authoritative*]: He committed bigamy. [*Then as* SID *smothers a burst of ribald laughter.*] What are you laughing at? I guess I ought to know. A fellow at college told me. His father was in England when this Wilde was pinched – and he said he remembered once his mother asked his father about it and he told her he'd committed bigamy.

MILLER [*hiding a smile behind his hand*]: Well then, that must be right, Arthur.

MRS MILLER: I wouldn't put it past him, nor anything else. One book was called the Picture of something or other.

RICHARD: *The Picture of Dorian Gray*. It's one of the greatest novels ever written!

MRS MILLER: Looked to me like cheap trash. And the second book was poetry. The Ballad of I forget what.

RICHARD: 'The Ballad of Reading Gaol', one of the greatest poems ever written. [*He pronounces it Reading Goal (as in goalpost).*]

MRS MILLER: All about someone who murdered his wife and got hung, as he richly deserved, as far as I could make out. And then there were two books by that Bernard Shaw –

RICHARD: The greatest playwright alive today!

MRS MILLER: To hear him tell it, maybe! You know, Nat, the one who wrote a play about – well, never mind – that was so vile they wouldn't even let it play in New York!

MILLER: Hmm. I remember.

MRS MILLER: One was a book of his plays and the other had a long title I couldn't make head or tail of, only it wasn't a play.

RICHARD [*proudly*]: *The Quintessence of Ibsenism.*

MILDRED: Phew! Good gracious, what a name! What does it mean, Dick? I'll bet he doesn't know.

RICHARD [*outraged*]: I do, too, know! It's about Ibsen, the greatest playwright since Shakespeare!

MRS MILLER: Yes, there was a book of plays by that Ibsen there, too! And poems by Swin something –

RICHARD: *Poems and Ballads by Swinburne*, Ma. The greatest poet since Shelley! He tells the truth about real love!

MRS MILLER: Love! Well, all I can say is, from reading here and there, that if he wasn't flung in jail along with Wilde, he should have been. Some of the things I simply couldn't read, they were so indecent – All about – well, I can't tell you before Lily and Mildred.

SID [*with a wink at* RICHARD – *jokingly*]: Remember, I'm next on that one, Dick. I feel the need of a little poetical education.

LILY [*scandalized, but laughing*]: Sid! Aren't you ashamed?

MRS MILLER: This is no laughing matter. And then there was Kipling – but I suppose he's not so bad. And last there was a poem – a long one – the Rubay – What is it, Richard?

RICHARD: *The Rubaiyat of Omar Khayyám.* That's the best of all!

MILLER: Oh, I've read that, Essie – got a copy down at the office.

SID [*enthusiastically*]: So have I. It's a pippin!

LILY [*with shy excitement*]: I – I've read it, too – at the library. I like – some parts of it.

MRS MILLER [*scandalized*]: Why, Lily!

MILLER: Everybody's reading that now, Essie – and it don't seem to do them any harm. There's fine things in it, seems to me – true things.

MRS MILLER [*a bit bewildered and uncertain now*]: Why, Nat, I don't see how you – It looked terrible blasphemous – parts I read.

SID: Remember this one: [*he quotes rhetorically*] 'Oh Thou, who didst with pitfall and gin beset the path I was to wander in – ' Now, I've always noticed how beset my path was with gin – in the past, you understand!

[*He casts a joking side glance at* LILY. *The others laugh. But* LILY *is in a melancholy dream and hasn't heard him.*]

MRS MILLER [*tartly, but evidently suppressing her usual smile where he is concerned*]: You would pick out the ones with liquor in them!

LILY [*suddenly – with a sad pathos, quotes awkwardly and shyly*]: I like – because it's true:

'The Moving Finger writes, and having writ,
Moves on: nor all your Piety nor Wit
Shall lure it back to cancel half a Line,
Nor all your Tears wash out a Word of it.'

MRS MILLER [*astonished, as are all the others*]: Why, Lily, I never knew you to recite poetry before!

LILY [*immediately guilty and apologetic*]: I – it just stuck in my memory somehow.

RICHARD [*looking at her as if he had never seen her before*]: Good for you, Aunt Lily! [*Then enthusiastically*] But that isn't the best. The best is:

'A Book of Verses underneath the Bough,
A Jug of Wine, A Loaf of Bread – and Thou
Beside me singing in the Wilderness – '

ARTHUR [*who, bored to death by all this poetry-quoting, has wandered over to the window at rear of desk, right*]: Hey! Look who's coming up the walk – Old Man McComber!

MILLER [*irritably*]: Dave? Now what in thunder does that damned old – Sid, I can see where we never are going to get to that picnic.

MRS MILLER [*vexatiously*]: He'll know we're in this early, too. No use lying. [*Then appalled by another thought*] That Norah – she's that thick, she never can answer the front door right unless I tell her each time. Nat, you've got to talk to Dave. I'll have her show him in here. Lily, you run up the back stairs and get your things on. I'll be up in a second. Nat, you get rid of him the first second you can! Whatever can the old fool want –

[*She and* LILY *hurry out through the back parlour.*]

ARTHUR: I'm going to beat it – just time to catch the eight-twenty trolley.

MILDRED: I've got to catch that, too. Wait till I get my hat, Art!

[*She rushes into the back parlour.*]

ARTHUR [*shouts after her*]: I can't wait. You can catch up with me if you hurry. [*He turns at the back-parlour door – with a grin.*] McComber may be coming to see if your intentions toward his daughter are dishonourable, Dick! You'd better beat it while your shoes are good!

[*He disappears through the back-parlour door, laughing.*]

RICHARD [*a bit shaken, but putting on a brave front*]: Think I'm scared of him?

MILLER [*gazing at him – frowning*]: Can't imagine what – But it's to complain about something, I know that. I only wish I didn't have to be pleasant with the old buzzard – but he's about the most valuable advertiser I've got.

SID [*sympathetically*]: I know. But tell him to go to hell, anyway. He needs that ad more than you.

[*The sound of the bell comes from the rear of the house, off left from back parlour.*]

MILLER: There he is. You clear out, Dick – but come right back as soon as he's gone, you hear? I'm not through with you, yet.

RICHARD: Yes, Pa.

MILLER: You better clear out, too, Sid. You know Dave doesn't approve jokes.

SID: And loves me like poison! Come on, Dick, we'll go out and help Tommy celebrate.

[*He takes* RICHARD'S *arm and they also disappear through the back-parlour door.* MILLER *glances through the front parlour toward the front door, then calls in a tone of strained heartiness.*]

MILLER: Hello, Dave. Come right in here. What good wind blows you around on this glorious Fourth?

A flat, brittle voice answers him: 'Good morning,' *and a moment later* DAVID MCCOMBER *appears in the doorway from the front parlour. He is a thin, dried-up little man with a head too large for his body perched on a scrawny neck, and a long solemn horse face with deep-set little black eyes, a blunt formless nose, and a tiny slit of a mouth. He is about the same age as* MILLER *but is entirely bald, and looks ten years older. He is dressed with a prim neatness in shiny old black clothes.*]

Here, sit down and make yourself comfortable. [*Holding out the cigar-box*] Have a cigar?

MCCOMBER [*sitting down in the chair at the right of table – acidly*]: You're forgetting. I never smoke.

MILLER [*forcing a laugh at himself*]: That's so. So I was. Well, I'll smoke alone then. [*He bites off the end of the cigar viciously, as if he wished it were McComber's head, and sits down opposite him.*]

MCCOMBER: You asked me what brings me here, so I'll come to the point at once. I regret to say it's something disagreeable – disgraceful would be nearer the truth – and it concerns your son, Richard!

MILLER [*beginning to bristle – but calmly*]: Oh, come now, Dave, I'm sure Richard hasn't –

MCCOMBER [*sharply*]: And I'm positive he has. You're not accusing me of being a liar, I hope.

MILLER: No one said anything about liar. I only meant you're surely mistaken if you think –

MCCOMBER: I'm not mistaken. I have proof of everything in his own handwriting!

MILLER [*sharply*]: Let's get down to brass tacks. Just what is it you're charging him with?

MCCOMBER: With being dissolute and blasphemous – with deliberately attempting to corrupt the morals of my young daughter Muriel.

MILLER: Then I'm afraid I will have to call you a liar, Dave!

MCCOMBER [*without taking offence – in the same flat, brittle voice*]: I thought you'd get around to that, so I brought some of the proofs with me. I've a lot more of 'em at home. [*He takes a wallet from his inside coat pocket, selects five or six slips of paper, and holds them out to* MILLER.] These are good samples of the rest. My wife discovered them in one of Muriel's bureau drawers hidden under the underwear. They're all in his handwriting, you can't deny it. Anyway, Muriel's confessed to me he wrote them. You read them and then say I'm a liar.

[MILLER *has taken the slips and is reading them frowningly.* MCCOMBER *talks on.*]

Evidently you've been too busy to take the right care about Richard's bringing up or what he's allowed to read – though I can't see why his mother failed in her duty. But that's your misfortune, and none of my business. But Muriel is my business and I can't and I won't have her innocence exposed to the contamination of a young man whose mind, judging from his choice of reading matter, is as foul –

MILLER [*making a tremendous effort to control his temper*]: Why, you damned old fool! Can't you see Richard's only a fool kid who's just at the stage when he's out to rebel against all authority, and so he grabs at everything radical to read and wants to pass it on to his elders and his girl and boy friends to show off what a young hellion he is! Why, at heart you'd find Richard is just as innocent and as big a kid as Muriel is! [*He pushes the slips of paper across the table contemptuously.*] This stuff doesn't mean anything to me – that is, nothing of what you think it means. If you believe this would corrupt Muriel, then you must believe she's easily corrupted! But I'll bet you'd find she knows a lot more about life than you give her credit for – and can guess a stork didn't bring her down your chimney!

MCCOMBER: Now you're insulting my daughter. I won't forget that.

MILLER: I'm not insulting her. I think Muriel is a darn nice girl. That's why I'm giving her credit for ordinary good sense. I'd say the same about my own Mildred, who's the same age.

MCCOMBER: I know nothing about your Mildred except that she's known all over as a flirt. [*Then more sharply*] Well, I knew you'd prove obstinate, but I certainly never dreamed you'd have the impudence, after reading those papers, to claim your son was innocent of all wrongdoing!

MILLER: And what did you dream I'd do?

MCCOMBER: Do what it's your plain duty to do as a citizen to protect other people's children! Take and give him a hiding he'd remember to the last day of his life! You'd ought to do it for his sake, if you had any sense – unless you want him to end up in jail!

MILLER [*his fists clenched, leans across the table*]: Dave, I've stood all I can stand from you! You get out! And get out quick, if you don't want a kick in the rear to help you!

MCCOMBER [*again in his flat, brittle voice, slowly getting to his feet*]: You needn't lose your temper. I'm only demanding you do your duty by your own as I've already done by mine. I'm punishing Muriel. She's not to be allowed out of the house for a month and she's to be in bed every night by eight sharp. And yet she's blameless, compared to that –

MILLER: I said I'd had enough out of you, Dave! [*He makes a threatening movement.*]

MCCOMBER: You needn't lay hands on me. I'm going. But there's one thing more. [*He takes a letter from his wallet.*] Here's a letter from Muriel for your son. [*Puts it on the table.*] It makes clear, I think, how she's come to think about him, now that her eyes have been opened. I hope he heeds what's inside – for his own good and yours – because if I ever catch him hanging about my place again I'll have him arrested! And don't think I'm not going to make you regret the insults you've heaped on me. I'm taking the advertisement for my store out of your paper – and it won't go in again, I tell you, not unless you apologize in writing and promise to punish –

MILLER: I'll see you in hell first! As for your damned old ad, take it out and go to hell!

MCCOMBER: That's plain bluff. You know how badly you need it. So do I. [*He starts stiffly for the door.*]

MILLER: Here! Listen a minute! I'm just going to call *your* bluff and tell you that, whether you want to reconsider your decision or not, I'm going to refuse to print your damned ad after tomorrow! Put that in your pipe and smoke it! Furthermore, I'll start a campaign to encourage outside capital to open a dry-goods store in opposition to you that won't be the public swindle I can prove yours is!

MCCOMBER [*a bit shaken by this threat – but in the same flat tone*]: I'll sue you for libel.

MILLER: When I get through, there won't be a person in town will buy a dish-rag in your place!

MCCOMBER [*more shaken, his eyes shifting about furtively*]: That's all bluff. You wouldn't dare – [*Then finally he says uncertainly*] Well, good day. [*And turns and goes out.*]

[NAT *stands looking after him. Slowly the anger drains from his face and leaves him looking a bit sick and disgusted.* SID *appears from the back parlour. He is nursing a burn on his right hand, but his face is one broad grin of satisfaction.*]

SID: I burned my hand with one of Tommy's damned fire-crackers and came in to get some vaseline. I was listening to the last of your scrap. Good for you, Nat! You sure gave him hell!

MILLER [*dully*]: Much good it'll do. He knows it was all talk.

SID: That's just what he don't know, Nat. The old skinflint has a guilty conscience.

MILLER: Well, anyone who knows me knows I wouldn't use my paper for a dirty, spiteful trick like that – no matter what he did to me.

SID: Yes, everyone knows you're an old sucker, Nat, too decent for your own good. But McComber never saw you like this before. I tell you you scared the pants off him. [*He chuckles.*]

MILLER [*still dejectedly*]: I don't know what made me let go like that. The hell of skunks like McComber is that after being with them ten minutes you become as big skunks as they are.

SID [*notices the slips of paper on the table*]: What's this? Something he brought? [*He picks them up and starts to read.*]

MILLER [*grimly*]: Samples of the new freedom – from those books Essie found – that Richard's been passing on to Muriel to educate her. They're what started the rumpus. [*Then frowning*] I've got to do something about that young anarchist or he'll be getting me, and himself, in a peck of trouble. [*Then pathetically helpless*] But what can I do? Putting the curb bit on would make him worse. Then he'd have a harsh tyrant to defy. He'd love that, darn him!

SID [*has been reading the slips, a broad grin on his face – suddenly he whistles*]: Phew! This is a warm lulu for fair! [*He recites with a joking intensity:*]

> 'My life is bitter with thy love; thine eyes
> Blind me, thy tresses burn me, thy sharp sighs
> Divide my flesh and spirit with soft sound –'

MILLER [*with a grim smile*]: Hmm. I missed that one. That must be Mr Swinburne's copy. I've never read him, but I've heard something like that was the matter with him.

SID: Yes, it's labelled Swinburne – 'Anactoria'. Whatever that is. But wait, watch and listen! The worst is yet to come! [*He recites with added comic intensity:*]

'That I could drink thy veins as wine, and eat
Thy breasts like honey, that from face to feet
Thy body were abolished and consumed,
And in my flesh thy very flesh entombed!'

MILLER [*an irrepressible boyish grin coming to his face*]: Hell and hallelujah! Just picture old Dave digesting that for the first time! Gosh, I'd give a lot to have seen his face! [*Then a trace of shocked reproof showing in his voice*] But it's no joking matter. That stuff *is* warm – too damned warm, if you ask me! I don't like this a damned bit, Sid. That's no kind of thing to be sending a decent girl. [*More worriedly*] I thought he was really stuck on her – as one gets stuck on a decent girl at his age – all moonshine and holding hands and a kiss now and again. But this looks – I wonder if he is hanging around her to see what he can get! [*Angrily*] By God, if that's true, he deserves that licking McComber says it's my duty to give him! I've got to draw the line somewhere!

SID: Yes, it won't do to have him getting any decent girl in trouble.

MILLER: The only thing I can do is put it up to him straight. [*With pride*] Richard'll stand up to his guns, no matter what. I've never known him to lie to me.

SID [*at a noise from the back parlour, looks that way – in a whisper*]: Then now's your chance. I'll beat it and leave you alone – see if the women folk are ready upstairs. We ought to get started soon – if we're ever going to make that picnic.

[*He is half-way to the entrance to the front parlour as* RICHARD *enters from the back parlour, very evidently nervous about McComber's call.*]

RICHARD [*adopting a forced, innocent tone*]: How's your hand, Uncle Sid?

SID: All right, Dick, thanks – only hurts a little.

[*He disappears.* MILLER *watches his son frowningly.* RICHARD *gives him a quick side glance and grows more guiltily self-conscious.*]

RICHARD [*forcing a snicker*]: Gee, Pa, Uncle Sid's a bigger kid than Tommy is. He was throwing firecrackers in the air and catching them on the back of his hand and throwing 'em off again just before they went off – and one came and he wasn't quick enough, and it went off almost on top of –

MILLER: Never mind that. I've got something else to talk to you besides firecrackers.

RICHARD [*apprehensively*]: What, Pa?

MILLER [*suddenly puts both hands on his shoulders – quietly*]: Look here, Son. I'm going to ask you a question, and I want an honest answer. I warn you beforehand if the answer is 'yes' I'm going to punish you and punish you hard because you'll have done something no boy of mine ought to do. But you've never lied to me before, I know, and I don't believe, even to save yourself punishment, you'd lie to me now, would you?

RICHARD [*impressed – with dignity*]: I won't lie, Pa.

MILLER: Have you been trying to have something to do with Muriel – something you shouldn't – you know what I mean.

RICHARD [*stares at him for a moment, as if he couldn't comprehend – then, as he does, a look of shocked indignation comes over his face*]: No! What do you think I am, Pa? I never would! She's not that kind! Why, I – I love her! I'm going to marry her – after I get out of college! She's said she would! We're engaged!

MILLER [*with great relief*]: All right. That's all I wanted to know. We won't talk any more about it. [*He gives him an approving pat on the back.*]

RICHARD: I don't see how you could think – Did that old idiot McComber say that about me?

MILLER [*joking now*]: Shouldn't call your future father-in-law names, should you? 'Tain't respectful. [*Then after a glance at* RICHARD'S *indignant face – points to the slips of paper on the table.*] Well, you can't exactly blame old Dave, can you, when you read through that literature you wished on his innocent daughter?

RICHARD [*sees the slips for the first time and is overcome by embarrassment, which he immediately tries to cover up with a superior carelessness*]: Oh, so that's why. He found those, did he? I told her to be careful – Well, it'll do him good to read the truth about life for once and get rid of his old-fogy ideas.

MILLER: I'm afraid I've got to agree with him, though, that they're hardly fit reading for a young girl. [*Then with subtle flattery*] They're all well enough, in their way, for you who're a man, but – Think it over, and see if you don't agree with me.

RICHARD [*embarrassedly*]: Aw, I only did it because I liked them – and I wanted her to face life as it is. She's so darned afraid of life – afraid of her Old Man – afraid of people saying this or that about her – afraid of being in love – afraid of everything. She's even afraid to let me kiss her. I thought, maybe, reading those things – they're beautiful, aren't they, Pa? – I thought they would give her the spunk to lead her own life, and not be – always thinking of being afraid.

MILLER: I see. Well, I'm afraid she's still afraid. [*He takes the letter from the table.*] Here's a letter from her he said to give you.

[RICHARD *takes the letter from him uncertainly, his expression changing to one of apprehension.*]

[MILLER *adds with a kindly smile:*] You better be prepared for a bit of a blow. But never mind. There's lots of other fish in the sea.

[RICHARD *is not listening to him, but staring at the letter with a sort of fascinated dread.* MILLER *looks into his son's face a second, then turns away, troubled and embarrassed.*]

Darn it! I better go upstairs and get rigged out or I never will get to that picnic.

[*He moves awkwardly and selfconsciously off through the front parlour.* RICHARD *continues to stare at the letter for a moment – then girds up his courage and tears it open and begins to read swiftly. As he reads, his face grows more and more wounded and tragic, until at the end his mouth draws down at the corners, as if he were about to break into tears. With an effort he forces them back and his face grows flushed with humiliation and wronged anger.*]

RICHARD [*blurts out to himself*]: The little coward! I hate her! She can't treat me like that! I'll show her!

[*At the sound of voices from the front parlour, he quickly shoves the letter into the inside pocket of his coat and does his best to appear calm and indifferent, even attempting to whistle 'Waiting at the Church'. But the whistle peters out miserably as his mother,* LILY, *and* SID *enter from the front parlour. They are dressed in all the elaborate paraphernalia of motoring at that period – linen dusters, veils, goggles,* SID *in a snappy cap.*]

MRS MILLER: Well, we're about ready to start at last, thank goodness! Let's hope no more callers are on the way. What did that McComber want, Richard, do you know? Sid couldn't tell us.

RICHARD: You can search me. Ask Pa.

MRS MILLER [*immediately sensing something 'down' in his manner – going to him worriedly*]: Why, whatever's the matter with you, Richard? You sound as if you'd lost your last friend! What is it?

RICHARD [*desperately*]: I – I don't feel so well – my stomach's sick.

MRS MILLER [*immediately all sympathy – smoothing his hair back from his forehead*]: You poor boy! What a shame – on the Fourth, too, of all days! [*Turning to the others*] Maybe I better stay home with him, if he's sick.

LILY: Yes, I'll stay, too.

RICHARD [*more desperately*]: No! You go, Ma! I'm not really sick. I'll be all right. You go. I want to be alone! [*Then, as a louder bang comes from in back as* TOMMY *sets off a cannon cracker, he jumps to his feet.*] Darn Tommy and his darned firecrackers! You can't get any peace in this house with that darned kid around! Darn the Fourth of July, anyway! I wish we still belonged to England! [*He strides off in an indignant fury of misery through the front parlour.*]

MRS MILLER [*stares after him worriedly – then sighs philosophically*]: Well, I guess he can't be so very sick – after that. [*She shakes her head.*] He's a queer boy. Sometimes I can't make head or tail of him.

MILLER [*calls from the front door beyond the back parlour*]: Come along, folks. Let's get started.

SID: We're coming, Nat.

[*He and the two women move off through the front parlour.*]

CURTAIN

ACT TWO

Dining-room of the Miller home – a little after six o'clock in the evening of the same day.

The room is much too small for the medium-priced, formidable dining-room set, especially now when all the leaves of the table are in. At left, toward rear, is a double doorway with sliding doors and portières leading into the back parlour. In the rear wall, left, is the door to the pantry. At the right of door is the china closet with its display of the family cut glass and fancy china. In the right wall are two windows looking out on a side lawn. In front of the windows is a heavy, ugly sideboard with three pieces of old silver on its top. In the left wall, extreme front, is a screen door opening on a side porch. A dark rug covers most of the floor. The table, with a chair at each end, left and right, three chairs on the far side, facing front, and two on the near side, their backs to front, takes up most of the available space. The walls are papered in a sombre brown and dark-red design.

[MRS MILLER *is supervising and helping the second girl,* NORAH, *in the setting of the table.* NORAH *is a clumsy, heavy-handed, heavy-footed, long-jawed, beamingly good-natured young Irish girl – a 'greenhorn'.*]

MRS MILLER: I really think you better put on the lights, Norah. It's getting so cloudy out, and this pesky room is so dark, anyway.

NORAH: Yes, Mum. [*She stretches awkwardly over the table to reach the chandelier that is suspended from the middle of the ceiling and manages to turn one light on – scornfully.*] Arrah, the contraption!

MRS MILLER [*worriedly*]: Careful!

NORAH: Careful as can be, Mum. [*But in moving around to reach the next bulb she jars heavily against the table.*]

MRS MILLER: There! I knew it! I do wish you'd watch – !

NORAH [*a flustered appeal in her voice*]: Arrah, what have I done wrong now?

MRS MILLER [*draws a deep breath – then sighs helplessly*]: Oh, nothing. Never mind the rest of the lights. You might as well go out in the kitchen and wait until I ring.

NORAH [*relieved and cheerful again*]: Yes, Mum. [*She starts for the pantry.*]

MRS MILLER: But there's one thing – [NORAH *turns apprehensively*] No, two things – things I've told you over and over, but you always forget. Don't pass the plates on the wrong side at dinner tonight, and do be careful not to let that pantry door slam behind you. Now you will try to remember, won't you?

NORAH: Yes, Mum.

[*She goes into the pantry and shuts the door behind her with exaggerated care as* MRS MILLER *watches her apprehensively.* MRS MILLER *sighs and reaches up with difficulty and turns on another of the four lights in the chandelier. As she is doing so,* LILY *enters from the back parlour.*]

LILY: Here, let me do that, Essie. I'm taller. You'll only strain yourself. [*She quickly lights the other two bulbs.*]

MRS MILLER [*gratefully*]: Thank you, Lily. It's a stretch for me, I'm getting so fat.

LILY: But where's Norah? Why didn't she – ?

MRS MILLER [*exasperatedly*]: Oh, that girl! Don't talk about her! She'll be the death of me! She's that thick, you honestly wouldn't believe it possible.

LILY [*smiling*]: Why, what did she do now?

MRS MILLER: Oh, nothing. She means all right.

LILY: Anything else I can do, Essie?

MRS MILLER: Well, she's got the table all wrong. We'll have to reset it. But you're always helping me. It isn't fair to ask you – in your vacation. You need your rest after teaching a pack of wild Indians of kids all year.

LILY [*beginning to help with the table*]: You know I love to help. It makes me feel I'm some use in this house instead of just sponging –

MRS MILLER [*indignantly*]: Sponging! You pay, don't you?

LILY: Almost nothing. And you and Nat only take that little to make me feel better about living with you. [*Forcing a smile*] I don't see how you stand me – having a cranky old maid around all the time.

MRS MILLER: What nonsense you talk! As if Nat and I weren't only too tickled to death to have you! Lily Miller, I've no patience with you when you go on like that. We've been over this a thousand times before, and still you go on! Crazy, that's what it is! [*She changes the subject abruptly.*] What time's it getting to be?

LILY [*looking at her watch*]: Quarter past six.

MRS MILLER: I do hope those men folks aren't going to be late for dinner. [*She sighs.*] But I suppose with that darned Sachem Club picnic it's more likely than not. [LILY *looks worried, and sighs.* MRS MILLER *gives her a quick side glance.*] I see you've got your new dress on.

LILY [*embarrassedly*]: Yes, I thought – if Sid's taking me to the fireworks – I ought to spruce up a little.

MRS MILLER [*looking away*]: Hmm. [*A pause – then she says with an effort to be casual:*] You mustn't mind if Sid comes home feeling a bit – gay. I expect Nat to – and we'll have to listen to all those old stories of his about when he was a boy. You know what those picnics are, and Sid'd be running into all his old friends.

LILY [*agitatedly*]: I don't think he will – this time – not after his promise.

MRS MILLER [*avoiding looking at her*]: I know. But men are weak. [*Then quickly*] That was a good notion of Nat's, getting Sid the job on the Waterbury *Standard*. All he ever needed was to get away from the rut he was in here. He's the kind that's the victim of his friends. He's easily led – but there's no real harm in him, you know that. [LILY *keeps silent, her eyes downcast.* MRS MILLER *goes on meaningly:*] He's making good money in Waterbury, too – thirty-five a week. He's in a better position to get married than he ever was.

LILY [*stiffly*]: Well, I hope he finds a woman who's willing – though after he's through with his betting on horse-races, and dice, and playing Kelly pool, there won't be much left for a wife – even is there was nothing else he spent his money on.

MRS MILLER: Oh, he'd give up all that – for the right woman. [*Suddenly she comes directly to the point.*] Lily, why don't you change your mind and marry Sid and reform him? You love him and always have –

LILY [*stiffly*]: I can't love a man who drinks.

MRS MILLER: You can't fool me. I know darned well you love him. And he loves you and always has.

LILY: Never enough to stop drinking for. [*Cutting off Mrs Miller's reply*] No, it's no good in your talking, Essie. We've been over this a thousand times before and I'll always feel the same as long as Sid's the same. If he gave me proof he'd – but even then I don't believe I could. It's sixteen years since I broke off our engagement, but what made me break it off is as clear to me today as it was then. It was what he'd be liable to do now to anyone who married him – his taking up with bad women.

MRS MILLER [*protests half-heartedly*]: But he's always sworn he got raked into that party and never had anything to do with those harlots.

LILY: Well, I don't believe him – didn't then and don't now. I do believe he didn't deliberately plan to, but – Oh, it's no good talking, Essie. What's done is done. But you know how much I like Sid – in spite of everything. I know he was just born to be what he is – irresponsible, never meaning to harm but harming in spite of himself. But don't talk to me about marrying him – because I never could.

MRS MILLER [*angrily*]: He's a dumb fool – a stupid dumb fool, that's what he is!

LILY [*quietly*]: No. He's just Sid.

MRS MILLER: It's a shame for you – a measly shame – you that would have made such a wonderful wife for any man – that ought to have your own home and children!

LILY [*winces but puts her arm around her affectionately – gently*]: Now don't you go feeling sorry for me. I won't have that. Here I am, thanks to your and Nat's kindness, with the best home in the world; and as for the children, I feel the same love for yours as if they were mine, and I didn't have the pain of bearing them. And then there are all the boys and girls I teach every year. I like to feel I'm a sort of second mother to them and helping them to grow up to be good men and women. So I don't feel such a useless old maid, after all.

MRS MILLER [*kisses her impulsively – her voice husky*]: You're a good woman, Lily – too good for the rest of us. [*She turns away, wiping a tear furtively – then abruptly changing the subject.*] Good gracious, if I'm not forgetting one of the most important things! I've got to warn that Tommy against giving me away to Nat about the fish. He knows, because I had to send him to market for it, and he's liable to burst out laughing –

LILY: Laughing about what?

MRS MILLER [*guiltily*]: Well, I've never told you, because it seemed sort of a sneaking trick, but you know how Nat carries on about not being able to eat bluefish.

LILY: I know he says there's a certain oil in it that poisons him.

MRS MILLER [*chuckling*]: Poisons him, nothing! He's been eating bluefish for years – only I tell him each time it's weakfish. We're having it tonight – and I've got to warn that young imp to keep his face straight.

LILY [*laughing*]: Aren't you ashamed, Essie!

MRS MILLER: Not much, I'm not! I like bluefish! [*She laughs.*] Where is Tommy? In the sitting-room?

LILY: No, Richard's there alone. I think Tommy's out on the piazza with Mildred.

[MRS MILLER *bustles out through the back parlour. As soon as she is gone, the smile fades from* LILY'S *lips. Her face grows sad and she again glances nervously at her watch.* RICHARD *appears from the back parlour, moving in an aimless way. His face wears a set expression of bitter gloom; he exudes tragedy. For* RICHARD, *after his first outburst of grief and humiliation, has begun to take a masochistic satisfaction in his great sorrow, especially in the concern which it arouses in the family circle. On seeing his aunt, he gives her a dark look and turns and is about to stalk back toward the sitting-room when she speaks to him pityingly.*]

Feel any better, Richard?

RICHARD [*sombrely*]: I'm all right, Aunt Lily. You mustn't worry about me.

LILY [*going to him*]: But I do worry about you. I hate to see you so upset.

RICHARD: It doesn't matter. Nothing matters.

LILY [*puts her arm around him sympathetically*]: You really mustn't let yourself take it so seriously. You know, something happens and things like that come up, and we think there's no hope –

RICHARD: Things like what come up?

LILY: What's happened between you and Muriel.

RICHARD [*with disdain*]: Oh, her! I wasn't even thinking about her. I was thinking about life.

LILY: But then – if we really, *really* love – why, then something else is bound to happen soon that changes everything again, and it's all as it was before the misunderstanding, and everything works out all right in the end. That's the way it is with life.

RICHARD [*with a tragic sneer*]: Life! Life is a joke! And everything comes out all wrong in the end!

LILY [*a little shocked*]: You mustn't talk that way. But I know you don't mean it.

RICHARD: I do too mean it! You can have your silly optimism, if you like, Aunt Lily. But don't ask me to be so blind. I'm a pessimist! [*Then with an air of cruel cynicism*] As for Muriel, that's all dead and past. I was only kidding her, anyway, just to have a little fun, and she took it seriously, like a fool. [*He forces a cruel smile to his lips.*] You know what they say about women and trolley cars, Aunt Lily: there's always another one along in a minute.

LILY [*really shocked this time*]: I don't like you when you say such horrible, cynical things. It isn't nice.

RICHARD: Nice! That's all you women think of! I'm proud to be a cynic. It's the only thing you can be when you really face life. I suppose you think I ought to be heart-broken about Muriel – a little coward that's afraid to say her soul's her own, and keeps tied to her father's apron strings! Well, not for mine! There's plenty of other fish in the sea! [*As he is finishing, his mother comes back through the back parlour.*]

MRS MILLER: Why, hello. You here, Richard? Getting hungry, I suppose?

RICHARD [*indignantly*]: I'm not hungry a bit! That's all you think of, Ma – food!

MRS MILLER: Well, I must say I've never noticed you to hang back at mealtimes. [*To Lily*] What's that he was saying about fish in the sea?

LILY [*smiling*]: He says he's through with Muriel now.

MRS MILLER [*tartly – giving her son a rebuking look*]: She's through with him, he means! The idea of your sending a nice girl like her things out of those indecent books!

[*Deeply offended,* RICHARD *disdains to reply but stalks woundedly to the screen door at left, front, and puts a hand on the knob.*]

Where are you going?

RICHARD [*quotes from* Candida *in a hollow voice*]: 'Out, then, into the night with me!'

[*He stalks out, slamming the door behind him.*]

MRS MILLER [*calls*]: Well, don't you go far, 'cause dinner'll be ready in a minute, and I'm not coming running after you! [*She turns to* LILY *with a chuckle.*] Goodness, that boy! He ought to be on the stage! [*She mimics.*] 'Out – into the night' – and it isn't even dark yet! He got that out of one of those books, I suppose. Do you know, I'm actually grateful to old Dave McComber for putting an end to his nonsense with Muriel. I never did approve of Richard getting so interested in girls. He's not old enough for such silliness. Why, seems to me it was only yesterday he was still a baby. [*She sighs – then matter-of-factly*] Well, nothing to do now till those men turn up. No use standing here like gawks. We might as well go in the sitting-room and be comfortable.

LILY [*the nervous, worried note in her voice again*]: Yes, we might as well. [*They go out through the back parlour. They have no sooner disappeared than the screen door is opened cautiously and* RICHARD *comes back in the room.*]

RICHARD [*stands inside the door, looking after them – quotes bitterly*]: 'They do not know the secret in the poet's heart.' [*He comes nearer the table and surveys it, especially the cut-glass dish containing olives, with contempt and mutters disdainfully.*] Food!

[*But the dish of olives seems to fascinate him and presently he has approached nearer, and stealthily lifts a couple and crams them into his mouth. He is just reaching out for more when the pantry door is opened slightly and* NORAH *peers in.*]

NORAH: Mister Dick, you thief, lave them olives alone, or the missus'll be swearing it was me at them!

RICHARD [*draws back his hand as if he had been stung – too flustered to be anything but guilty boy for a second*]: I – wasn't eating –

NORAH: Oho, no, of course not, divil fear you, you was only feeling their pulse! [*Then warningly*] Mind what I'm saying now, or I'll have to tell on you to protect me good name!

[*She draws back into the pantry, closing the door.* RICHARD *stands, a prey to feelings of bitterest humiliation and seething revolt against everyone and everything. A low whistle comes from just outside the porch door. He starts. Then a masculine voice calls:* 'Hey, Dick.' *He goes over to the screen door grumpily – then as he recognizes the owner of the voice, his own as he answers becomes respectful and admiring.*]

RICHARD: Oh, hello, Wint. Come on in.

[*He opens the door and* WINT SELBY *enters and stands just inside the door.* SELBY *is nineteen, a classmate of Arthur's at Yale. He is a typical, good-looking college boy of the period, not the athletic but the hell-raising sport type. He is tall, blond, dressed in extreme collegiate cut.*]

WINT [*as he enters – warningly, in a low tone*]: Keep it quiet, Kid. I don't want the folks to know I'm here. Tell Art I want to see him a second – on the Q.T.

RICHARD: Can't. He's up at the Rands' – won't be home before ten, anyway.

WINT [*irritably*]: Damn! I thought he'd be here for dinner. [*More irritably*] Hell, that gums the works for fair!

RICHARD [*ingratiatingly*]: What is it, Wint? Can't I help?

WINT [*gives him an appraising glance*]: I might tell you, if you can keep your face shut.

RICHARD: I can.

WINT: Well, I ran into a couple of swift babies from New Haven this after. and I dated them up for tonight, thinking I could catch Art. But now it's too late to get anyone else and I'll have to pass it up. I'm nearly broke and I can't afford to blow them both to drinks.

RICHARD [*with shy eagerness*]: I've got eleven dollars saved up. I could loan you some.

WINT [*surveys him appreciatively*]: Say, you're a good sport. [*Then shaking his head*] Nix, Kid, I don't want to borrow your money. [*Then getting an idea*] But say, have you got anything on for tonight?

RICHARD: No.

WINT: Want to come along with me? [*Then quickly*] I'm not trying to lead you astray, understand. But it'll be a help if you would just sit around with Belle and feed her a few drinks while I'm off with Edith. [*He winks.*] See what I mean? You don't have to do anything, not even take a glass of beer – unless you want to.

RICHARD [*boastfully*]: Aw, what do you think I am – a rube?

WINT: You mean you're game for anything that's doing?

RICHARD: Sure I am!

WINT: Ever been out with any girls – I mean, real swift ones that there's something doing with, not these dead Janes around here?

RICHARD [*lies boldly*]: Aw, what do you think? Sure I have!

WINT: Ever drink anything besides sodas?

RICHARD: Sure. Lots of times. Beer and sloe-gin fizz and – Manhattans.

WINT [*impressed*]: Hell, you know more than I thought. [*Then considering*] Can you fix it so your folks won't get wise? I don't want your old man coming after me. You can get back by half past ten or eleven, though, all right. Think you can cook up some lie to cover that? [*As* RICHARD *hesitates – encouraging him*] Ought to be easy – on the Fourth.

RICHARD: Sure. Don't worry about that.

WINT: But you've got to keep your face closed about this, you hear? – to Art and everybody else. I tell you straight, I wouldn't ask you to come if I wasn't in a hole – and if I didn't know you were coming down to Yale next year, and didn't think you're giving me the straight goods about having been around before. I don't want to lead you astray.

RICHARD [*scornfully*]: Aw, I told you that was silly.

WINT: Well, you be at the Pleasant Beach Hotel at half past nine then. Come in the back room. And don't forget to grab some cloves to take the booze off your breath.

RICHARD: Aw, I know what to do.

WINT: See you later, then. [*He starts out and is just about to close the door when he thinks of something.*] And say, I'll say you're a Harvard freshman, and you back me up. They don't know a damn thing about Harvard. I don't want them thinking I'm travelling around with any high school kid.

RICHARD: Sure. That's easy.

WINT: So long, then. You better beat it right after your dinner while you've got a chance, and hang around until it's time. Watch your step, Kid.

RICHARD: So long. [*The door closes behind* WINT. RICHARD *stands for a moment, a look of bitter, defiant rebellion coming over his face, and mutters to himself.*] I'll show her she can't treat me the way she's done! I'll show them all!

[*Then the front door is heard slamming, and a moment later* TOMMY *rushes in from the back parlour.*]

TOMMY: Where's Ma?

RICHARD [*surlily*]: In the sitting-room. Where did you think, Bonehead?

TOMMY: Pa and Uncle Sid are coming. Mid and I saw them from the front piazza. Gee, I'm glad. I'm awful hungry, ain't you? [*He rushes out through the back parlour, calling*] Ma! They're coming! Let's have dinner quick! [*A moment later* MRS MILLER *appears from the back parlour accompanied by* TOMMY, *who keeps insisting urgently*] Gee, but I'm awful hungry, Ma!

MRS MILLER: I know. You always are. You've got a tape-worm, that's what I think.

TOMMY: Have we got lobsters, Ma? Gee, I love lobsters.

MRS MILLER: Yes, we've got lobsters. And fish. You remember what I told you about that fish. [*He snickers.*] Now, do be quiet, Tommy! [*Then with a teasing smile at* RICHARD] Well, I'm glad to see you've got back out of the night, Richard.

[*He scowls and turns his back on her.* LILY *appears through the back parlour, nervous and apprehensive. As she does so, from the front yard* SID'S *voice is heard singing 'Poor John!'*

MRS MILLER *shakes her head forebodingly – but, so great is the comic spell for her even in her brother's voice, a humorous smile hovers at the corners of her lips.*]

Mmm! Mmm! Lily, I'm afraid –

LILY [*bitterly*]: Yes, I might have known.

[MILDRED *runs in through the back parlour. She is laughing to herself a bit shamefacedly. She rushes to her mother.*]

MILDRED: Ma, Uncle Sid's – [*She whispers in her ear.*]

MRS MILLER: Never mind! You shouldn't notice such things – at your age! And don't you encourage him by laughing at his foolishness, you hear!

TOMMY: You needn't whisper, Mid. Think I don't know? Uncle Sid's soused again.

MRS MILLER [*shakes him by the arm indignantly*]: You be quiet! Did I ever! You're getting too smart! [*Gives him a push.*] Go to your place and sit right down and not another word out of you!

TOMMY [*aggrieved – rubbing his arm as he goes to his place*]: Aw, Ma!

MRS MILLER: And you sit down, Richard and Mildred. You better, too, Lily. We'll get him right in here and get some food in him. He'll be all right then.

[RICHARD, *preserving the pose of the bitter, disillusioned pessimist, sits down in his place in the chair at right of the two whose backs face front.* MILDRED *takes the other chair facing back, at his left.* TOMMY *has already slid into the end chair at right of those at the rear of table facing front.* LILY *sits in the one of those at left, by the head of the table, leaving the middle one (Sid's) vacant. While they are doing this, the front screen door is heard slamming and* MILLER *and* SID'S *laughing voices, raised as they come in and for a moment after, then suddenly cautiously lowered.* MRS MILLER *goes to the entrance to the back parlour and calls peremptorily.*]

You come right in here! Don't stop to wash up or anything. Dinner's coming right on the table.

MILLER'S VOICE [*jovially*]: All right, Essie. Here we are! Here we are!

MRS MILLER [*goes to the pantry door, opens it, and calls*]: All right, Norah. You can bring in the soup.

[*She comes back to the back-parlour entrance just as* MILLER *enters. He isn't drunk by any means. He is just mellow and benignly ripened. His face is one large, smiling, happy beam of utter appreciation of life. All's right with the world, so satisfyingly right that he becomes sentimentally moved even to think of it.*]

MILLER: Here we are, Essie! Right on the dot! Here we are!

[*He pulls her to him and gives her a smacking kiss on the ear as she jerks her head away.* MILDRED *and* TOMMY *giggle.* RICHARD *holds rigidly aloof and disdainful, his brooding gaze fixed on his plate.* LILY *forces a smile.*]

MRS MILLER [*pulling away – embarrassedly, almost blushing*]: Don't, you Crazy! [*Then recovering herself – tartly*] So I see, you're here! And if I didn't, you've told me four times already!

MILLER [*beamingly*]: Now, Essie, don't be critical. Don't be carpingly critical. Good news can stand repeating, can't it? 'Course it can!

[*He slaps her jovially on her fat buttocks.* TOMMY *and* MILDRED *roar with glee. And* NORAH, *who has just entered from the pantry with a huge tureen of soup in her hands, almost drops it as she explodes in a merry guffaw.*]

MRS MILLER [*scandalized*]: Nat! Aren't you ashamed!

MILLER: Couldn't resist it! Just simply couldn't resist it!

[NORAH, *still standing with the soup tureen held out stiffly in front of her, again guffaws.*]

MRS MILLER [*turns on her with outraged indignation*]: Norah! Bring that soup here this minute! [*She stalks with stiff dignity toward her place at the foot of the table, right.*]

NORAH [*guiltily*]: Yes, Mum. [*She brings the soup around the head of the table, passing* MILLER.]

MILLER [*jovially*]: Why, hello, Norah!

MRS MILLER: Nat! [*She sits down stiffly at the foot of the table.*]

NORAH [*rebuking him familiarly*]: Arrah now, don't be making me laugh and getting me into trouble!

MRS MILLER: Norah!

NORAH [*a bit resentfully*]: Yes, Mum. Here I am. [*She sets the soup tureen down with a thud in front of* MRS MILLER *and passes around the other side, squeezing with difficulty between the china closet and the backs of chairs at the rear of the table.*]

MRS MILLER: Tommy! Stop spinning your napkin ring! How often have I got to tell you? Mildred! Sit up straight in your chair! Do you want to grow up a humpback? Richard! Take your elbows off the table!

MILLER [*coming to his place at the head of the table, rubbing his hands together genially*]: Well, well, well. Well, well, well. It's good to be home again.

[NORAH *exits into the pantry and lets the door slam with a bang behind her.*]

MRS MILLER [*jumps*]: Oh! [*Then exasperatedly*] Nat, I do wish you wouldn't encourage that stupid girl by talking to her, when I'm doing my best to train –

MILLER [*beamingly*]: All right, Essie. Your word is law! [*Then laughingly*] We did have the darndest fun today! And Sid was the life of that picnic! You ought to have heard him! Honestly, he had that crowd just rolling on the ground and splitting their sides! He ought to be on the stage.

MRS MILLER [*as* NORAH *comes back with a dish of saltines – begins ladling soup into the stack of plates before her*]: He ought to be at this table eating something to sober him up, that's what he ought to be! [*She calls.*] Sid! You come right in here! [*Then to* NORAH, *handing her a soup plate*] Here, Norah. [NORAH *begins passing soup.*] Sit down, Nat, for goodness' sakes. Start eating, everybody. Don't wait for me. You know I've given up soup.

MILLER [*sits down but bends forward to call to his wife in a con-*

fidential tone]: Essie – Sid's sort of embarrassed about coming – I mean I'm afraid he's a little bit – not too much, you understand – but he met such a lot of friends and – well, you know, don't be hard on him. Fourth of July is like Christmas – comes but once a year. Don't pretend to notice, eh? And don't you kids, you hear! And don't you, Lily. He's scared of you.

LILY [*with stiff meekness*]: Very well, Nat.

MILLER [*beaming again – calls*]: All right, Sid. The coast's clear. [*He begins to absorb his soup ravenously.*] Good soup, Essie! Good soup!

[*A moment later* SID *makes his entrance from the back parlour. He is in a condition that can best be described as blurry. His movements have a hazy uncertainty about them. His shiny fat face is one broad, blurred, Puckish, naughty-boy grin; his eyes have a blurred, wondering vagueness. As he enters he makes a solemnly intense effort to appear casual and dead, cold sober. He waves his hand aimlessly and speaks with a silly gravity.*]

SID: Good evening. [*They all answer* 'Good evening', *their eyes on their plates. He makes his way vaguely toward his place, continuing his grave effort at conversation.*] Beautiful evening. I never remember seeing – more beautiful sunset. [*He bumps vaguely into* LILY'S *chair as he attempts to pass behind her – immediately he is all grave politeness.*] Sorry – sorry, Lily – deeply sorry.

LILY [*her eyes on her plate – stiffly*]: It's all right.

SID [*manages to get into his chair at last – mutters to himself*]: Wha' was I sayin'? Oh, sunsets. But why butt in? Hasn't sun – perfect right to set? Mind y'r own business. [*He pauses thoughtfully, considering this – then looks around from face to face, fixing each with a vague, blurred, wondering look, as if some deep puzzle were confronting him. Then suddenly he grins mistily and nods with satisfaction.*] And there you are! Am I right?

MILLER [*humouring him*]: Right.

SID: Right! [*He is silent, studying his soup plate, as if it were some strange enigma. Finally he looks up and regards his sister and asks with wondering amazement*] Soup?

MRS MILLER: Of course, it's soup. What did you think it was? And you hurry up and eat it.

SID [*again regards his soup with astonishment*]: Well! [*Then suddenly*] Well, all right then! Soup be it! [*He picks up his spoon and begins to eat, but after two tries in which he finds it difficult to locate his mouth, he addresses the spoon plaintively.*] Spoon, is this any way to treat a pal? [*Then suddenly comically angry, putting the spoon down with a bang*] Down with spoons! [*He raises his soup plate and declaims:*] 'We'll drink to the dead already, and hurrah for the next who dies.' [*Bowing solemnly to right and left*] Your good health, ladies *and* gents.

[*He starts drinking the soup.* MILLER *guffaws and* MILDRED *and* TOMMY *giggle. Even* RICHARD *forgets his melancholy and snickers, and* MRS MILLER *conceals a smile. Only* LILY *remains stiff and silent.*]

MRS MILLER [*with forced severity*]: Sid!

SID [*peers at her muzzily, lowering the soup plate a little from his lips*]: Eh?

MRS MILLER: Oh, nothing. Never mind.

SID [*solemnly offended*]: Are you – publicly rebuking me before assembled – ? Isn't soup liquid? Aren't liquids drunk? [*Then considering this to himself*] What if they are drunk? It's a good man's failing. [*He again peers mistily about at the company.*] Am I right or wrong?

MRS MILLER: Hurry up and finish your soup, and stop talking nonsense!

SID [*turning to her – again offendedly*]: Oh, no, Essie, if I ever so far forget myself as to drink a leg of lamb, then you might have some – excuse for – Just think of waste effort eating soup with spoons – fifty gruelling lifts per plate – billions of soup-eaters on globe – why, it's simply staggering! [*Then darkly to himself*] No more spoons for me! If I want to develop my biceps, I'll buy Sandow Exerciser! [*He drinks the rest of his soup in a gulp and beams around at the company, suddenly all happiness again.*] Am I right, folks?

MILLER [*who has been choking with laughter*]: Haw, haw! You're right, Sid.

SID [*peers at him blurredly and shakes his head sadly*]: Poor old Nat! Always wrong – but heart of gold, heart of purest gold. And drunk again, I regret to note. Sister, my heart bleeds for you and your poor fatherless chicks!

MRS MILLER [*restraining a giggle – severely*]: Sid! Do shut up for a minute! Pass me your soup plates, everybody. If we wait for that girl to take them, we'll be here all night.

[*They all pass their plates, which* MRS MILLER *stacks up and then puts on the sideboard. As she is doing this,* NORAH *appears from the pantry with a platter of broiled fish. She is just about to place these before* MILLER *when* SID *catches her eye mistily and rises to his feet, making her a deep, uncertain bow.*]

SID [*rapidly*]: Ah, Sight for Sore Eyes, my beautiful Macushla, my star-eyed Mavourneen –

MRS MILLER: Sid!

NORAH [*immensely pleased – gives him an arch, flirtatious glance*]: Ah sure, Mister Sid, it's you that have kissed the Blarney Stone, when you've a drop taken!

MRS MILLER [*outraged*]: Norah! Put down that fish!

NORAH [*flusteredly*]: Yes, Mum. [*She attempts to put the fish down hastily before* MILLER, *but her eyes are fixed nervously on* MRS MILLER *and she gives* MILLER *a nasty swipe on the side of the head with the edge of the dish.*]

MILLER: Ouch!

[*The children, even* RICHARD, *explode into laughter.*]

NORAH [*almost lets the dish fall*]: Oh, glory be to God! Is it hurted you are?

MILLER [*rubbing his head – good-naturedly*]: No, no harm done. Only careful, Norah, careful.

NORAH [*gratefully*]: Yes, sorr. [*She thumps down the dish in front of him with a sigh of relief.*]

SID [*who is still standing – with drunken gravity*]: Careful, Mavourneen, careful! You might have hit him some place besides the head. Always aim at his head, remember – so as not to worry us.

[*Again the children explode. Also* NORAH. *Even* LILY *suddenly lets out a hysterical giggle and is furious with herself for doing so.*]

LILY: I'm so sorry, Nat. I didn't mean to laugh. [*Turning on* SID *furiously*] Will you please sit down and stop making a fool of yourself!

[SID *gives her a hurt, mournful look and then sinks meekly down on his chair.*]

NORAH [*grinning cheerfully, gives* LILY *a reassuring pat on the back*]: Ah, Miss Lily, don't mind him. He's only under the influence. Sure, there's no harm in him at all.

MRS MILLER: Norah!

[NORAH *exits hastily into the pantry, letting the door slam with a crash behind her. There is silence for a moment as* MILLER *serves the fish and it is passed around.* NORAH *comes back with the vegetables and disappears again, and these are dished out.*]

MILLER [*is about to take his first bite – stops suddenly and asks his wife*]: This isn't, by any chance, bluefish, is it, my dear?

MRS MILLER [*with a warning glance at Tommy*]: Of course not. You know we never have bluefish, on account of you.

MILLER [*addressing the table now with the gravity of a man confessing his strange peculiarities*]: Yes, I regret to say, there's a certain peculiar oil in bluefish that invariably poisons me.

[*At this,* TOMMY *cannot stand it any more but explodes into laughter.* MRS MILLER, *after a helpless glance at him, follows suit; then* LILY *goes off into uncontrollable, hysterical laughter, and* RICHARD *and* MILDRED *are caught in the contagion.* MILLER *looks around at them with a weak smile, his dignity now ruffled a bit.*]

Well, I must say I don't see what's so darned funny about my being poisoned.

SID [*peers around him – then with drunken cunning*]: Aha! Nat, I suspect – plot! This fish looks blue to me – very blue – in fact despondent, desperate, and – [*He points his fork dramatically, at* MRS MILLER.] See how guilty she looks – a ver – veritable Lucretia Georgia! Can it be this woman has been slowly poisoning you all these years? And how well – you've stood it! What iron constitution! Even now, when you are invariably at death's door, I can't believe –

[*Everyone goes off into uncontrollable laughter.*]

MILLER [*grumpily*]: Oh, give us a rest, you darned fool! A joke's a joke, but – [*He addresses his wife in a wounded tone.*] Is this true, Essie?

MRS MILLER [*wiping the tears from her eyes – defiantly*]: Yes, it is true, if you must know, and you'd never have suspected it, if it weren't for that darned Tommy, and Sid poking his nose in. You've eaten bluefish for years and thrived on it and it's all nonsense about that peculiar oil.

MILLER [*deeply offended*]: Kindly allow me to know my own constitution! Now I think of it, I've felt upset afterwards every damned time we've had fish! [*He pushes his plate away from him with proud renunciation.*] I can't eat this.

MRS MILLER [*insultingly matter-of-fact*]: Well, don't then. There's lots of lobster coming and you can fill up on that.

[RICHARD *suddenly bursts out laughing again.*]

MILLER [*turns to him caustically*]: You seem in a merry mood, Richard. I thought you were the original of the Heart Bowed Down today.

SID [*with mock condolence*]: Never mind, Dick. Let them – scoff! What can they understand about girls whose hair sizzchels, whose lips are fireworks, whose eyes are red-hot sparks –

MILDRED [*laughing*]: Is that what he wrote to Muriel? [*Turning to her brother*] You silly goat, you!

RICHARD [*surlily*]: Aw, shut up, Mid. What do I care about her? I'll show all of you how much I care!

MRS MILLER: Pass your plates as soon as you're through, everybody. I've rung for the lobster. And that's all. You don't get any dessert or tea after lobster, you know.

[NORAH *appears bearing a platter of cold boiled lobsters which she sets before* MILLER, *and disappears.*]

TOMMY: Gee, I love lobster!

[MILLER *puts one on each plate, and they are passed around and everyone starts in pulling the cracked shells apart.*]

MILLER [*feeling more cheerful after a couple of mouthfuls – determining to give the conversation another turn, says to his daughter*]: Have a good time at the beach, Mildred?

MILDRED: Oh, fine, Pa, thanks. The water was wonderful and warm.

MILLER: Swim far?

MILDRED: Yes, for me. But that isn't so awful far.

MILLER: Well, you ought to be a good swimmer, if you take after me. I used to be a regular water-rat when I was a boy. I'll have to go down to the beach with you one of these days – though I'd be rusty, not having been in in all these years. [*The reminiscent look comes into his eyes of one about to embark on an oft-told tale of childhood adventure.*] You know, speaking of swimming, I never go down to that beach but what it calls to mind the day I and Red Sisk went in swimming there and I saved his life.

[*By this time the family are beginning to exchange amused, guilty glances. They all know what is coming.*]

SID [*with a sly, blurry wink around*]: Ha! Now we – have it again!

MILLER [*turning on him*]: Have what?

SID: Nothing – go on with your swimming – don't mind me.

MILLER [*glares at him – but immediately is overcome by the reminiscent mood again*]: Red Sisk – his father kept a blacksmith shop where the Union Market is now – we kids called him Red because he had the darndest reddest crop of hair –

SID [*as if he were talking to his plate*]: Remarkable! – the curious imagination – of little children.

MRS MILLER [*as she sees* MILLER *about to explode – interposes tactfully*]: Sid! Eat your lobster and shut up! Go on, Nat.

MILLER [*gives* SID *a withering look – then is off again*]: Well, as I was saying, Red and I went swimming that day. Must have been – let me see – Red was fourteen, bigger and older than me, I was only twelve – forty-five years ago – wasn't a single house down there then – but there was a stake out where the whistling buoy is now, about a mile out.

[TOMMY, *who has been having difficulty restraining himself, lets out a stifled giggle.* MILLER *bends a frowning gaze on him.*]

One more sound out of you, young man, and you'll leave the table!

MRS MILLER [*quickly interposing, trying to stave off the story*]: Do eat your lobster, Nat. You didn't have any fish, you know.

MILLER [*not liking the reminder – pettishly*]: Well, if I'm going to be interrupted every second anyway – [*He turns to his lobster and chews in silence for a moment.*]

MRS MILLER [*trying to switch the subject*]: How's Anne's mother's rheumatism, Mildred?

MILDRED: Oh, she's much better, Ma. She was in wading today. She says salt water's the only thing that really helps her bunion.

MRS MILLER: Mildred! Where are your manners? At the table's no place to speak of –

MILLER [*fallen into the reminiscent obsession again*]: Well, as I was saying, there was I and Red, and he dared me to race him out to the stake and back. Well, I didn't let anyone dare me in those days. I was a spunky kid. So I said all right and we started out. We swam and swam and were pretty evenly matched; though, as I've said, he was bigger and older than me, but finally I drew ahead. I was going along easy, with lots of reserve, not a bit tired, when suddenly I heard a sort of gasp from behind me – like this – 'help!' [*He imitates. Everyone's eyes are firmly fixed on their plates, except* SID's.] And I turned and there was Red, his face all pinched and white, and he says weakly: 'Help, Nat! I got a cramp in my leg!' Well, I don't mind telling you I got mighty scared. I didn't know what to do. Then suddenly I thought of the pile. If I could pull him to that, I could hang on to him till someone'd notice us. But the pile was still – well, I calculate it must have been two hundred feet away.

SID: Two hundred and fifty!

MILLER [*in confusion*]: What's that?

SID: Two hundred *and* fifty! I've taken down the distance every time you've saved Red's life for thirty years and the mean average to that pile is two hundred and fifty feet! [*There is a burst of laughter from around the table.* SID *continues complainingly.*] Why didn't you let that Red drown, anyway, Nat? I never knew him but I know I'd never have liked him.

MILLER [*really hurt, forces a feeble smile to his lips and pretends to be a good sport about it*]: Well, guess you're right, Sid. Guess I have told that one too many times and bored everyone. But it's a good true story for kids because it illustrates the danger of being foolhardy in the water –

MRS MILLER [*sensing the hurt in his tone, comes to his rescue*]: Of course it's a good story – and you tell it whenever you've a mind to. And you, Sid, if you were in any responsible state, I'd give you a good piece of my mind for teasing Nat like that.

MILLER [*with a sad, self-pitying smile at his wife*]: Getting old, I guess, Mother – getting to repeat myself. Someone ought to stop me.

MRS MILLER: No such thing! You're as young as you ever

were. [*She turns on* SID *again angrily.*] You eat your lobster and maybe it'll keep your mouth shut!

SID [*after a few chews – irrepressibly*]: Lobster! Did you know, Tommy, your Uncle Sid is the man invented lobster? Fact! One day – when I was building the Pyramids – took a day off and just dashed off lobster. He was bigger'n' older than me and he had the darndest reddest crop of hair but I dashed him off just the same! Am I right, Nat? [*Then suddenly in the tones of a sideshow barker*] Ladies *and* Gents –

MRS MILLER: Mercy sakes! Can't you shut up?

SID: In this cage you see the lobster. You will not believe me, ladies *and* gents, but it's a fact that this interesting bivalve only makes love to his mate once in every thousand years – but, dearie me, how he does enjoy it!

[*The children roar.* LILY *and* MRS MILLER *laugh in spite of themselves – then look embarrassed.* MILLER *guffaws – then suddenly grows shocked.*]

MILLER: Careful, Sid, careful. Remember you're at home.

TOMMY [*suddenly in a hoarse whisper to his mother, with an awed glance of admiration at his uncle*]: Ma! Look at him! He's eating that claw, shells and all!

MRS MILLER [*horrified*]: Sid, do you want to kill yourself? Take it away from him, Lily!

SID [*with great dignity*]: But I prefer the shells. All famous epicures prefer the shells – to the less delicate coarser meat. It's the same with clams. Unless I eat the shells there is a certain, peculiar oil that invariably poisons – Am I right, Nat?

MILLER [*good-naturedly*]: You seem to be getting a lot of fun kidding me. Go ahead, then. I don't mind.

MRS MILLER: He better go right up to bed for a while, that's what he better do.

SID [*considering this owlishly*]: Bed? Yes, maybe you're right. [*He gets to his feet.*] I am not at all well – in very delicate condition – we are praying for a boy. Am I right, Nat?

Nat, I kept telling you all day I was in delicate condition and yet you kept forcing demon chowder on me, although you knew full well – even if you were full – that there is a certain, peculiar oil in chowder that invariably – [*They are again all laughing* – LILY, *hysterically*.]

MRS MILLER: *Will* you get to bed, you idiot!

SID [*mutters graciously*]: Immediately – if not sooner [*He turns to pass behind* LILY, *then stops, staring down at her*.] But wait. There is still a duty I must perform. No day is complete without it. Lily, answer once and for all, will you marry me?

LILY [*with a hysterical giggle*]: No, I won't – never!

SID [*nodding his head*]: Right! And perhaps it's all for the best. For how could I forget the pre – precepts taught me at mother's dying knee. 'Sidney,' she said, 'never marry a woman who drinks! Lips that touch liquor shall never touch yours!' [*Gazing at her mournfully*] Too bad! So fine a woman once – and now such a slave to rum! [*Turning to* MILLER] What can we do to save her, Nat? [*In a hoarse, confidential whisper*] Better put her in institution where she'll be removed from temptation! The mere smell of it seems to drive her frantic!

MRS MILLER [*struggling with her laughter*]: You leave Lily alone, and go to bed!

SID: Right! [*He comes around behind* LILY'S *chair and moves toward the entrance to the back parlour – then suddenly turns and says with a bow*.] Good night, ladies – and gents. We will meet – by and by! [*He gives an imitation of a Salvation Army drum*.] Boom! Boom! Boom! Come and be saved, Brothers! [*He starts to sing the old Army hymn*.]

'In the sweet
By and by
We will meet on that beautiful shore.'

[*He turns and marches solemnly out through the back parlour, singing*.]

'Work and pray
While you may.
We will meet in the sky by and by.'

[MILLER *and his wife and the children are all roaring with laughter.* LILY *giggles hysterically*]

MILLER [*subsiding at last*]: Haw, haw. He's a case, if ever there was one! Darned if you can help laughing at him – even when he's poking fun at you!

MRS MILLER: Goodness, but he's a caution! Oh, my sides ache, I declare! I was trying so hard not to – but you can't help it, he's so silly! But I suppose we really shouldn't. It only encourages him. But, my lands – !

LILY [*suddenly gets up from her chair and stands rigidly, her face working – jerkily*]: That's just it – you shouldn't – even I laughed – it does encourage – that's been his downfall – everyone always laughing, everyone always saying what a card he is, what a case, what a caution, so funny – and he's gone on – and we're all responsible – making it easy for him – we're all to blame – and all we do is laugh!

MILLER [*worriedly*]: Now, Lily, now, you mustn't take on so. It isn't as serious as all that.

LILY [*bitterly*]: Maybe – it is – to me. Or was – once. [*Then contritely*] I'm sorry, Nat. I'm sorry, Essie. I didn't mean to – I'm not feeling myself tonight. If you'll excuse me, I'll go in the front parlour and lie down on the sofa awhile.

MRS MILLER: Of course, Lily. You do whatever you've a mind to.

[LILY *goes out.*]

MILLER [*frowning – a little shamefaced*]: Hmm. I suppose she's right. Never knew Lily to come out with things that way before. Anything special happened, Essie?

MRS MILLER: Nothing I know – except he'd promised to take her to the fireworks.

MILLER: That's so. Well, supposing I take her. I don't want her to feel disappointed.

MRS MILLER [*shaking her head*]: Wild horses couldn't drag her there now.

MILLER: Hmm. I thought she'd got completely over her foolishness about him long ago.

MRS MILLER: She never will.

MILLER: She'd better. He's got fired out of that Waterbury job – told me at the picnic after he'd got enough Dutch courage in him.

MRS MILLER: Oh, dear! Isn't he the fool!

MILLER: I knew something was wrong when he came home. Well, I'll find a place for him on my paper again, of course. He always was the best news-getter this town ever had. But I'll tell him he's got to stop his damn nonsense.

MRS MILLER [*doubtfully*]: Yes.

MILLER: Well, no use sitting here mourning over spilt milk.

[*He gets up, and* RICHARD, MILDRED, TOMMY, *and* MRS MILLER *follow his example, the children quiet and a bit awed.*]

You kids go out in the yard and try to keep quiet for a while, so's your Uncle Sid'll get to sleep and your Aunt Lily can rest.

TOMMY [*mournfully*]: Ain't we going to set off the sky rockets and Roman candles, Pa?

MILLER: Later, Son, later. It isn't dark enough for them yet anyway.

MILDRED: Come on, Tommy. I'll see he keeps quiet, Pa.

MILLER: That's a good girl.

[MILDRED *and* TOMMY *go out through the screen door.* RICHARD *remains standing, sunk in bitter, gloomy thoughts.*]

[MILLER *glances at him – then irritably*] Well, Melancholy Dane, what are you doing?

RICHARD [*darkly*]: I'm going out – for a while. [*Then suddenly*] Do you know what I think? It's Aunt Lily's fault, Uncle Sid's going to ruin. It's all because he loves her, and she keeps him dangling after her, and eggs him on and ruins his life – like all women love to ruin men's lives! I don't blame him for drinking himself to death! What does he care if he dies, after the way she's treated him! I'd do the same thing myself if I were in his boots!

MRS MILLER [*indignantly*]: Richard! You stop that talk.

RICHARD [*quotes bitterly*]:

'Drink! for you know not whence you come nor why.
Drink! for you know not why you go nor where!'

MILLER [*losing his temper – harshly*]: Listen here, young man! I've had about all I can stand of your nonsense for one day! You're growing a lot too big for your size, seems to me! You keep that damn fool talk to yourself, you hear me – or you're going to regret it! Mind, now! [*He strides angrily away through the back parlour.*]

MRS MILLER [*still indignant*]: Richard, I'm ashamed of you, that's what I am.

[*She follows her husband.* RICHARD *stands for a second, bitter, humiliated, wronged, even his father turned enemy, his face growing more and more rebellious. Then he forces a scornful smile to his lips.*]

RICHARD: Aw, what the hell do I care? I'll show them! [*He turns and goes out the screen door.*]

CURTAIN

ACT THREE

SCENE 1

The back room of a bar in a small hotel – a small, dingy room, dimly lighted by two fly-specked globes in a fly-specked gilt chandelier suspended from the middle of the ceiling. At left, front, is the swinging door leading to the bar. At rear of door, against the wall, is a nickel-in-the-slot player-piano. In the rear wall, right, is a door leading to the 'Family Entrance' and the stairway to the upstairs rooms. In the middle of the right wall is a window with closed shutters. Three tables with stained tops, four chairs around each table, are placed at centre, front, at right, toward rear, and at rear, centre. A brass cuspidor is on the floor by each table. The floor is unswept, littered with cigarette and cigar-butts. The hideous saffron-coloured wallpaper is blotched and spotted.

[*It is about ten o'clock the same night.* RICHARD *and* BELLE *are discovered sitting at the table at centre,* BELLE *at left of it,* RICHARD *in the next chair at the middle of table, rear, facing front.*

BELLE *is twenty, a rather pretty peroxide blonde, a typical college 'tart' of the period, and of the cheaper variety, dressed with tawdry flashiness. But she is a fairly recent recruit to the ranks, and is still a bit remorseful behind her make-up and defiantly careless manner.*

BELLE *has an empty gin-rickey glass before her,* RICHARD *a half-empty glass of beer. He looks horribly timid, embarrassed and guilty, but at the same time thrilled and proud of at last mingling with the pace that kills.*

The player-piano is grinding out 'Bedelia'. The BARTENDER, *a stocky young Irishman with a foxily cunning, stupid face, and a cynically wise grin, stands just inside the bar entrance, watching them over the swinging door.*]

BELLE [*with an impatient glance at her escort – rattling the ice in her empty glass*]: Drink up your beer, why don't you? It's getting flat.

RICHARD [*embarrassedly*]: I let it get that way on purpose. I like it better when it's flat.

[*But he hastily gulps down the rest of his glass, as if it were some nasty-tasting medicine. The* BARTENDER *chuckles audibly.* BELLE *glances at him.*]

BELLE [*nodding at the player-piano scornfully*]: Say, George, is 'Bedelia' the latest to hit this hick burg? Well, it's only a couple of years old! You'll catch up in time! Why don't you get a new roll for that old box?

BARTENDER [*with a grin*]: Complain to the boss, not me. We're not used to having Candy Kiddoes like you around – or maybe we'd get up to date.

BELLE [*with a professionally arch grin at him*]: Don't kid me, please. I can't bear it. [*Then she sings to the music from the piano, her eyes now on* RICHARD.] 'Bedelia, I'd like to feel yer.' [*The* BARTENDER *laughs. She smirks at* RICHARD.] Ever hear those words to it, Kid?

RICHARD [*who has heard them but is shocked at hearing a girl say them – putting on a blasé air*]: Sure, lots of times. That's old.

BELLE [*edging her chair closer and putting a hand over one of his*]: Then why don't you act as if you knew what they were all about?

RICHARD [*terribly flustered*]: Sure, I've heard that old parody lots of times. What do you think I am?

BELLE: I don't know, Kid. Honest to God, you've got me guessing.

BARTENDER [*with a mocking chuckle*]: He's a hot sport, can't you tell it? I never seen such a spender. My head's dizzy bringing you in drinks!

BELLE [*laughs irritably – to* RICHARD]: Don't let him kid you. You show him. Loosen up and buy another drink, what say?

RICHARD [*humiliated – manfully*]: Sure. Excuse me. I was thinking of something else. Have anything you like. [*He turns to the* BARTENDER *who has entered from the bar.*] See what the lady will have – and have one on me yourself.

BARTENDER [*coming to the table – with a wink at* BELLE]: That's talking! Didn't I say you were a sport? I'll take a cigar on you. [*To* BELLE] What's yours, Kiddo – the same?

BELLE: Yes. And forget the house rules this time and remember a rickey is supposed to have gin in it.

BARTENDER [*grinning*]: I'll try to – seeing it's you. [*Then to* RICHARD] What's yours – another beer?

RICHARD [*shyly*]: A small one, please. I'm not thirsty.

BELLE [*calculatedly taunting*]: Say, honest, are things that slow up at Harvard? If they had you down at New Haven, they'd put you in a kindergarten! Don't be such a dead one! Filling up on beer will only make you sleepy. Have a man's drink!

RICHARD [*shamefacedly*]: All right. I was going to. Bring me a sloe-gin fizz.

BELLE [*to* BARTENDER]: And make it a real one.

BARTENDER [*with a wink*]: I get you. Something that'll warm him up, eh? [*He goes into the bar, chuckling.*]

BELLE [*looks around the room – irritably*]: Christ, what a dump! [RICHARD *is startled and shocked by this curse and looks down at the table.*] If this isn't the deadest burg I ever struck! Bet they take the side-walks in after nine o'clock! [*Then turning on him*] Say, honestly, Kid, does your mother know you're out?

RICHARD [*defensively*]: Aw, cut it out, why don't you – trying to kid me!

BELLE [*glances at him – then resolves on a new tack – patting his hand*]: All right. I didn't mean to, Dearie. Please don't get sore at me.

RICHARD: I'm not sore.

BELLE [*seductively*]: You see, it's this way with me. I think you're one of the sweetest kids I've ever met – and I could like you such a lot if you'd give me half a chance – instead of acting so cold and indifferent.

RICHARD: I'm not cold and indifferent. [*Then solemnly tragic*] It's only that I've got – a weight on my mind.

BELLE [*impatiently*]: Well, get it off your mind and give something else a chance to work.

[*The* BARTENDER *comes in, bringing the drinks.*]

BARTENDER [*setting them down – with a wink at* BELLE]: This'll warm him for you. Forty cents, that is – with the cigar.

RICHARD [*pulls out his roll and hands a dollar bill over – with exaggerated carelessness*]: Keep the change.

[BELLE *emits a gasp and seems about to protest, then thinks better of it. The* BARTENDER *cannot believe his luck for a moment – then pockets the bill hastily, as if afraid* RICHARD *will change his mind.*]

BARTENDER [*respect in his voice*]: Thank you, sir.

RICHARD [*grandly*]: Don't mention it.

BARTENDER: I hope you like the drink. I took special pains with it. [*The voice of the* SALESMAN, *who has just come in the bar, calls* 'Hey! Anybody here?' *and a coin is rapped on the bar.*] I'm coming. [*The* BARTENDER *goes out.*]

BELLE [*remonstrating gently, a new appreciation for her escort's possibilities in her voice*]: You shouldn't be so generous, Dearie. Gets him in bad habits. A dime would have been plenty.

RICHARD: Ah, that's all right. I'm no tightwad.

BELLE: That's the talk I like to hear. [*With a quick look toward the bar, she stealthily pulls up her dress – to* RICHARD's *shocked fascination – and takes a package of cheap cigarettes from her stocking.*] Keep an eye out for that bartender, Kid, and tell me if you see him coming. Girls are only allowed to smoke upstairs in the rooms, he said.

RICHARD [*embarrassedly*]: All right. I'll watch.

BELLE [*having lighted her cigarette and inhaled deeply, holds the package out to him*]: Have a Sweet? You smoke, don't you?

RICHARD [*taking one*]: Sure! I've been smoking for the last two years – on the sly. But next year I'll be allowed – that is, pipes and cigars. [*He lights his cigarette with elaborate nonchalance, puffs, but does not inhale – then, watching her, with shocked concern.*] Say, you oughtn't to inhale like that! Smoking's awful bad for girls, anyway, even if they don't –

BELLE [*cynically amused*]: Afraid it will stunt my growth? Gee, Kid, you are a scream! You'll grow up to be a minister yet! [RICHARD *looks shamefaced. She scans him impatiently – then holds up her drink.*] Well, here's how! Bottoms up, now! Show me you really know how to drink. It'll take that load off your mind.

[RICHARD *follows her example, and they both drink the whole contents of their glasses before setting them down.*]

There! That's something like! Feel better?

RICHARD [*proud of himself – with a shy smile*]: You bet.

BELLE: Well, you'll feel still better in a minute – and then maybe you won't be so distant and unfriendly, eh?

RICHARD: I'm not.

BELLE: Yes, you are. I think you just don't like me.

RICHARD [*more manfully*]: I do too like you.

BELLE: How much? A lot?

RICHARD: Yes, a lot.

BELLE: Show me how much! [*Then as he fidgets embarrassedly*] Want me to come sit on your lap?

RICHARD: Yes – I – [*She comes and sits on his lap. He looks desperately uncomfortable, but the gin is rising to his head and he feels proud of himself and devilish, too.*]

BELLE: Why don't you put your arm around me? [*He does so awkwardly.*] No, not that dead way. Hold me tight. You needn't be afraid of hurting me. I like to be held tight, don't you?

RICHARD: Sure I do.

BELLE: 'Specially when it's by a nice handsome kid like you. [*Ruffling his hair*] Gee, you've got pretty hair; do you know it? Honest, I'm awfully strong for you! Why can't you be about me? I'm not so awfully ugly, am I?

RICHARD: No, you're – you're pretty.

BELLE: You don't say it as if you meant it.

RICHARD: I do mean it – honest.

BELLE: Then why don't you kiss me? [*She bends down her lips toward his. He hesitates, then kisses her and at once shrinks back.*] Call that kissing? Here. [*She holds his head and fastens her lips on his and holds them there. He starts and struggles. She laughs.*] What's the matter, Honey Boy? Haven't you ever kissed like that before?

RICHARD: Sure. Lots of times.

BELLE: Then why did you jump as if I'd bitten you? [*Squirming around on his lap*] Gee, I'm getting just crazy about you! What shall we do about it, eh? Tell me.

RICHARD: I – don't know. [*Then boldly*] I – I'm crazy about you, too.

BELLE [*kissing him again*]: Just think of the wonderful time Edith and your friend, Wint, are having upstairs – while we sit down here like two dead ones. A room only costs two dollars. And, seeing I like you so much, I'd only take five dollars – from you. I'd do it for nothing – for you – only I've got to live and I owe my room rent in New Haven – and you know how it is. I get ten dollars from everyone else. Honest! [*She kisses him again, then gets up from his lap – briskly.*] Come on. Go out and tell the bartender you want a room. And hurry. Honest, I'm so strong for you I can hardly wait to get you upstairs!

RICHARD [*starts automatically for the door to the bar – then hesitates, a great struggle going on in his mind – timidity, disgust at the money element, shocked modesty, and the guilty thought of Muriel, fighting it out with the growing tipsiness that makes him want to be a hell of a fellow and go in for all forbidden fruit, and makes this tart a romantic, evil vampire in his eyes. Finally, he stops and mutters in confusion*]: I can't.

BELLE: What, are you too bashful to ask for a room? Let me do it, then.

[*She starts for the door.*]

RICHARD [*desperately*]: No – I don't want you to – I don't want to.

BELLE [*surveying him, anger coming into her eyes*]: Well, if you aren't the lousiest cheap skate!

RICHARD: I'm not a cheap skate!

BELLE: Keep me around here all night fooling with you when I might be out with some real live one – if there is such a thing in this burg! – and now you quit on me! Don't be such a piker! You've got five dollars! I seen it when you paid for the drinks, so don't hand me any lies!

RICHARD: I – Who said I hadn't? And I'm not a piker. If you need the five dollars so bad – for your room rent – you can have it without – I mean, I'll be glad to give – [*He has been fumbling in his pocket and pulls out his nine-dollar roll and holds out the five to her.*]

BELLE [*hardly able to believe her eyes, almost snatches it from his hand – then laughs and immediately becomes sentimentally grateful*]: Thanks, Kid. Gee – oh, thanks – Gee, forgive me for losing my temper and bawling you out, will you? Gee, you're a regular peach! You're the nicest kid I've ever met! [*She kisses him and he grins proudly, a hero to himself now on many counts.*] Gee, you're a peach! Thanks, again!

RICHARD [*grandly – and quite tipsily*]: It's – nothing – only too glad. [*Then boldly*] Here – give me another kiss, and that'll pay me back.

BELLE [*kissing him*]: I'll give you a thousand, if you want 'em. Come on, let's sit down, and we'll have another drink – and this time I'll blow you just to show my appreciation. [*She calls.*] Hey, George! Bring us another round – the same!

RICHARD [*a remnant of caution coming to him*]: I don't know as I ought to –

BELLE: Oh, another won't hurt you. And I want to blow you, see.

[*They sit down in their former places.*]

RICHARD [*boldly draws his chair closer and puts an arm around her – tipsily*]: I like you a lot – now I'm getting to know you. You're a darned nice girl.

BELLE: Nice is good! Tell me another! Well, if I'm so nice, why didn't you want to take me upstairs? That's what I don't get.

RICHARD [*lying boldly*]: I did want to – only I – [*Then he adds solemnly*] I've sworn off.

[*The* BARTENDER *enters with the drinks.*]

BARTENDER [*setting them on the table*]: Here's your pleasure. [*Then regarding* RICHARD'S *arm about her waist*] Ho-ho, we're coming on, I see.

[RICHARD *grins at him muzzily.*]

BELLE [*digs into her stocking and gives him a dollar*]: Here. This is mine. [*He gives her change and she tips him a dime, and he goes out. She puts the five* RICHARD *had given her in her stocking and picks up her glass.*] Here's how – and thanks again. [*She sips.*]

RICHARD [*boisterously*]: Bottoms up! Bottoms up! [*He drinks all of his down and sighs with exaggerated satisfaction.*] Gee, that's good stuff, all right. [*Hugging her*] Give me another kiss, Belle.

BELLE [*kisses him*]: What did you mean a minute ago when you said you'd sworn off?

RICHARD [*solemnly*]: I took an oath I'd be faithful.

BELLE [*cynically*]: Till death do us part, eh? Who's the girl?

RICHARD [*shortly*]: Never mind.

BELLE [*bristling*]: I'm not good enough to talk about her, I suppose?

RICHARD: I didn't – mean that. You're all right. [*Then with tipsy gravity*] Only you oughtn't to lead this kind of life. It isn't right – for a nice girl like you. Why don't you reform?

BELLE [*sharply*]: Nix on that line of talk! Can it, you hear! You can do a lot with me for five dollars – but you can't reform me, see. Mind your own business, Kid, and don't butt in where you're not wanted!

RICHARD: I – I didn't mean to hurt your feelings.

BELLE: I know you didn't mean. You're only like a lot of people who mean well, to hear them tell it. [*Changing the subject*] So you're faithful to your one love, eh? [*With an ugly sneer*] And how about her? Bet you she's out with a guy under some bush this minute, giving him all he wants. Don't be a sucker, Kid! Even the little flies do it!

RICHARD [*starting up in his chair – angrily*]: Don't you say that. Don't you dare!

BELLE [*unimpressed – with a cynical shrug of her shoulders*]: All right. Have it your own way and be a sucker! It cuts no ice with me.

RICHARD: You don't know her or –

BELLE: And don't want to. Shut up about her, can't you?

[*She stares before her bitterly.* RICHARD *subsides into scowling gloom. He is becoming perceptibly more intoxicated with each moment now. The* BARTENDER *and the* SALESMAN *appear just inside the swinging door. The* BARTENDER *nods toward* BELLE, *giving the* SALESMAN *a drink. The* SALESMAN *grins and comes into the room, carrying his highball in his hand. He is a stout, jowly-faced man in his late thirties, dressed with cheap nattiness, with the professional breeziness and jocular, kid-'em-along manner of his kind.* BELLE *looks up as he enters and he and she exchange a glance of complete recognition. She knows his type by heart and he knows hers.*]

SALESMAN [*passes by her to the table at right – grinning genially*]: Good evening.

BELLE: Good evening.

SALESMAN [*sitting down*]: Hope I'm not butting in on your

party – but my dogs were giving out standing at that bar.

BELLE: All right with me. [*Giving* RICHARD *a rather contemptuous look*] I've got no party on.

SALESMAN: That sounds hopeful.

RICHARD [*suddenly recites sentimentally*]:

'But I wouldn't do such, 'cause I loved her too much,
But I learned about women from her.'

[*Turns to scowl at the* SALESMAN – *then to* BELLE] Let's have 'nother drink!

BELLE: You've had enough.

[RICHARD *subsides, muttering to himself.*]

SALESMAN: What is it – a child poet or a child actor?

BELLE: Don't know. Got me guessing.

SALESMAN: Well, if you could shake the cradle-robbing act, maybe we could do a little business.

BELLE: That's easy. I just pull my freight. [*She shakes* RICHARD *by the arm.*] Listen, Kid. Here's an old friend of mine, Mr Smith of New Haven, just come in. I'm going over and sit at his table for a while, see. And you better go home.

RICHARD [*blinking at her and scowling*]: I'm never going home! I'll show them!

BELLE: Have it your own way – only let me up.

[*She takes his arm from around her and goes to sit by the* SALESMAN. RICHARD *stares after her offendedly.*]

RICHARD: Go on. What do I care what you do? [*He recites scornfully:*] 'For a woman's only a woman, but a good cigar's a smoke.'

SALESMAN [*as* BELLE *sits beside him*]: Well, what kind of beer will you have, Sister?

BELLE: Mine's a gin rickey.

SALESMAN: You've got extravagant tastes, I'm sorry to see.

RICHARD [*begins to recite sepulchrally*]:

'Yet each man kills the thing he loves,
By each let this be heard.'

SALESMAN [*grinning*]: Say, this is rich! [*He calls encouragement.*] That's swell dope, young feller. Give us some more.

RICHARD [*ignoring him – goes on more rhetorically*]:

> 'Some do it with a bitter look,
> Some with a flattering word,
> The coward does it with a kiss,
> The brave man with a sword!'

[*He stares at* BELLE *gloomily and mutters tragically.*] I did it with a kiss! I'm a coward.

SALESMAN: That's the old stuff, Kid. You've got something on the ball, all right, all right! Give us another – right over the old pan, now!

BELLE [*with a laugh*]: Get the hook!

RICHARD [*glowering at her – tragically*]:

> '"Oho," they cried, "the world is wide,
> But fettered limbs go lame!
> And once, or twice, to throw the dice
> Is a gentlemanly game,
> But he does not win who plays with Sin
> In the secret House of Shame!"'

BELLE [*angrily*]: Aw, can it! Give us a rest from that bunk!

SALESMAN [*mockingly*]: This gal of yours don't appreciate poetry. She's a lowbrow. But I'm the kid that eats it up. My middle name is Kelly and Sheets! Give us some more of the same! Do you know 'The Lobster and the Wise Guy'? [*Turns to* BELLE *seriously.*] No kidding, that's a peacherino. I heard a guy recite it at Poli's. Maybe this nut knows it. Do you, Kid? [*But* RICHARD *only glowers at him gloomily without answering.*]

BELLE [*surveying* RICHARD *contemptuously*]: He's copped a fine skinful – and gee, he's hardly had anything.

RICHARD [*suddenly – with a dire emphasis*]: 'And then – at ten o'clock – Eilert Lovberg will come – with vine leaves in his hair!'

BELLE: And bats in his belfry, if he's you!

RICHARD [*regards her bitterly – then starts to his feet bellicosely – to the* SALESMAN]: I don't believe you ever knew her in New Haven at all! You just picked her up now! You leave her alone, you hear! You won't do anything to her – not while I'm here to protect her!

BELLE [*laughing*]: Oh, my God! Listen to it!

SALESMAN: Ssshh! This is a scream! Wait! [*He addresses* RICHARD *in tones of exaggerated melodrama.*] Curse you, Jack Dalton, if I won't unhand her, what then?

RICHARD [*threateningly*]: I'll give you a good punch in the snoot, that's what! [*He moves toward their table.*]

SALESMAN [*with mock terror – screams in falsetto*]: Help! Help!

[*The* BARTENDER *comes in irritably.*]

BARTENDER: Hey. Cut out the noise. What the hell's up with you?

RICHARD [*tipsily*]: He's too – damn fresh!

SALESMAN [*with a wink*]: He's going to murder me! [*Then gets a bright idea for eliminating* RICHARD *– seriously to the* BARTENDER.] It's none of my business, Brother, but if I were in your boots I'd give this young souse the gate. He's under age; any fool can see that.

BARTENDER [*guiltily*]: He told me he was over eighteen.

SALESMAN: Yes, and I tell you I'm the Pope – but you don't have to believe me. If you're not looking for trouble, I'd advise you to get him started for some other gin mill and let them do the lying, if anything comes up.

BARTENDER: Hmm. [*He turns to* RICHARD *angrily and gives him a push.*] Come on, now. On your way! You'll start no trouble in here! Beat it now!

RICHARD: I will not beat it!

BARTENDER: Oho, won't you? [*He gives him another push that almost sends him sprawling.*]

BELLE [*callously*]: Give him the bum's rush! I'm sick of his bull!

[RICHARD *turns furiously and tries to punch the* BARTENDER.]

BARTENDER [*avoids the punch*]: Oho, you would, would you! [*He grabs* RICHARD *by the back of the neck and the seat of the pants and marches him ignominiously toward the swinging door.*]

RICHARD: Leggo of me, you dirty coward!

BARTENDER: Quiet now – or I'll pin a Mary Ann on your jaw that'll quiet you! [*He rushes him through the screen door and a moment later the outer doors are heard swinging back and forth.*]

SALESMAN [*with a chuckle*]: Hand it to me, Kid. How was that for a slick way of getting rid of him?

BELLE [*suddenly sentimental*]: Poor kid. I hope he makes home all right. I liked him – before he got soused.

SALESMAN: Who is he?

BELLE: The boy who's upstairs with my friend told me, but I didn't pay much attention. Name's Miller. His old man runs a paper in this one-horse burg, I think he said.

SALESMAN [*with a whistle*]: Phew! He must be Nat Miller's kid, then.

BARTENDER [*coming back from the bar*]: Well, he's on his way – with a good boot in the tail to help him!

SALESMAN [*with a malicious chuckle*]: Yes? Well maybe that boot will cost you a job, Brother. Know Nat Miller who runs the *Globe*? That's his kid.

BARTENDER [*his face falling*]: The hell he is! Who said so?

SALESMAN: This baby doll. [*Getting up*] Say, I'll go keep cases on him – see he gets on the trolley all right, anyway. Nat Miller's a good scout. [*He hurries out.*]

BARTENDER [*viciously*]: God damn the luck! If he ever finds out I served his kid, he'll run me out of town. [*He turns on* BELLE *furiously.*] Why didn't you put me wise, you lousy tramp, you!

BELLE: Hey! I don't stand for that kind of talk – not from no hick beer-squirter like you, see!

BARTENDER [*furiously*]: You don't, don't you! Who was it but you told me to hand him dynamite in that fizz? [*He gives her chair a push that almost throws her to the floor.*] Beat it, you – and beat it quick – or I'll call Sullivan from the corner and have you run in for street-walking! [*He gives her a push that lands her against the family-entrance door.*] Get the hell out of here – and no long waits!

BELLE [*opens the door and goes out – turns and calls back viciously*]: I'll fix you for this, you thick Mick, if I have to go to jail for it. [*She goes out and slams the door.*]

BARTENDER [*looks after her worriedly for a second – then shrugs his shoulders*]: That's only her bull. [*Then with a sigh as he returns to the bar*] Them lousy tramps is always getting this dump in Dutch!

CURTAIN

SCENE 2

Same as Act One – Sitting-room of the Millers' home – about eleven o'clock the same night.

[MILLER *is sitting in his favourite rocking-chair at left of table, front. He has discarded collar and tie, coat, and shoes, and wears an old, worn, brown dressing-gown and disreputable-looking carpet slippers. He has his reading specs on and is running over items in a newspaper. But his mind is plainly preoccupied and worried, and he is not paying much attention to what he reads.*

MRS MILLER *sits by the table at right, front. She also has on her specs. A sewing-basket is on her lap and she is trying hard to keep her attention fixed on the doily she is doing. But, as in the case of her husband, but much more apparently, her mind is preoccupied, and she is obviously on tenterhooks of nervous uneasiness.*

LILY *is sitting in the armchair by the table at rear, facing right.*

She is pretending to read a novel, but her attention wanders, too, and her expression is sad, although now it has lost all its bitterness and become submissive and resigned again.

MILDRED *sits at the desk at right, front, writing two words over and over again, stopping each time to survey the result critically, biting her tongue, intensely concentrated on her work.*

TOMMY *sits on the sofa at left, front. He has had a hard day and is terribly sleepy but will not acknowledge it. His eyes blink shut on him, his head begins to nod, but he isn't giving up, and every time he senses any of the family glancing in his direction, he goads himself into a bright-eyed wakefulness.*]

MILDRED [*finally surveys the words she has been writing and is satisfied with them*]: There. [*She takes the paper over to her mother.*] Look, Ma. I've been practising a new way of writing my name. Don't look at the others, only the last one. Don't you think it's the real goods?

MRS MILLER [*pulled out of her preoccupation*]: Don't talk that horrible slang. It's bad enough for boys, but for a young girl supposed to have manners – my goodness, when I was your age, if my mother'd ever heard me –

MILDRED: Well, don't you think it's nice, then?

MRS MILLER [*sinks back into preoccupation – scanning the paper – vaguely*]: Yes, very nice, Mildred – very nice, indeed. [*Hands the paper back mechanically.*]

MILDRED [*is a little piqued, but smiles*]: Absent-minded! I don't believe you even saw it.

[*She passes around the table to show her* AUNT LILY. MILLER *gives an uneasy glance at his wife and then, as if afraid of meeting her eye, looks quickly back at his paper again.*]

MRS MILLER [*staring before her – sighs worriedly*]: Oh, I do wish Richard would come home!

MILLER: There now, Essie. He'll be in any minute now. Don't worry about him.

MRS MILLER: But I do worry about him!

LILY [*surveying* MILDRED'S *handiwork – smiling*]: This is fine, Mildred. Your penmanship is improving wonderfully. But don't you think that maybe you've got a little too many flourishes?

MILDRED [*disappointedly*]: But, Aunt Lily, that's just what I was practising hardest on.

MRS MILLER [*with another sigh*]: What time is it now, Nat?

MILLER [*adopting a joking tone*]: I'm going to buy a clock for in here. You have me reaching for my watch every couple of minutes. [*He has pulled his watch out of his vest pocket – with forced carelessness.*] Only a little past ten.

MRS MILLER: Why, you said it was that an hour ago! Nat Miller, you're telling me a fib, so's not to worry me. You let me see that watch!

MILLER [*guiltily*]: Well, it's quarter to eleven – but that's not so late – when you remember it's Fourth of July.

MRS MILLER: If you don't stop talking Fourth of July – ! To hear you go on, you'd think that was an excuse for anything from murder to picking pockets!

MILDRED [*has brought her paper around to her father and now shoves it under his nose*]: Look, Pa.

MILLER [*seizes on this interruption with relief*]: Let's see. Hmm. Seems to me you've been inventing a new signature every week lately. What are you in training for – writing cheques? You must be planning to catch a rich husband.

MILDRED [*with an arch toss of her head*]: No wedding bells for me! But how do you like it, Pa?

MILLER: It's overpowering – no other word for it, overpowering! You could put it on the Declaration of Independence and not feel ashamed.

MRS MILLER [*desolately, almost on the verge of tears*]: It's all right for you to laugh and joke with Mildred! I'm the only one in this house seems to care – [*Her lips tremble.*]

MILDRED [*a bit disgustedly*]: Ah, Ma, Dick only sneaked off to the fireworks at the beach, you wait and see.

MRS MILLER: Those fireworks were over long ago. If he had, he'd be home.

LILY [*soothingly*]: He probably couldn't get a seat, the trolleys are so jammed, and he had to walk home.

MILLER [*seizing on this with relief*]: Yes, I never thought of that, but I'll bet that's it.

MILDRED: Ah, don't let him worry you, Ma. He just wants to show off he's heart-broken about that silly Muriel – and get everyone fussing over him and wondering if he hasn't drowned himself or something.

MRS MILLER [*snappily*]: You be quiet! The way you talk at times, I really believe you're that hard-hearted you haven't got a heart in you! [*With an accusing glance at her husband*] One thing I know, you don't get that from me!

[*He meets her eye and avoids it guiltily. She sniffs and looks away from him around the room.* TOMMY, *who is nodding and blinking, is afraid her eye is on him. He straightens alertly and speaks in a voice that, in spite of his effort, is dripping with drowsiness.*]

TOMMY: Let me see what you wrote, Mid.

MILDRED [*cruelly mocking*]: You? You're so sleepy you couldn't see it!

TOMMY [*valiantly*]: I am not sleepy!

MRS MILLER [*has her eye fixed on him*]: My gracious, I was forgetting you were still up! You run up to bed this minute! It's hours past your bedtime!

TOMMY: But it's the Fourth of July. Ain't it, Pa?

MRS MILLER [*gives her husband an accusing stare*]: There! You see what you've done? You might know he'd copy your excuses! [*Then sharply to* TOMMY] You heard what I said, Young Man!

TOMMY: Aw, Ma, can't I stay up a *little* longer?

MRS MILLER: I said, no! You obey me and no more arguing about it!

TOMMY [*drags himself to his feet*]: Aw! I should think I could stay up till Dick –

MILLER [*kindly but firmly*]: You heard your ma say no more arguing. When she says git, you better git.

[TOMMY *accepts his fate resignedly and starts around kissing them all good night.*]

TOMMY [*kissing her*]: Good night, Aunt Lily.

LILY: Good night, dear. Sleep well.

TOMMY [*pecking at Mildred*]: Good night, you.

MILDRED: Good night, you.

TOMMY [*kissing him*]: Good night, Pa.

MILLER: Good night, Son. Sleep tight.

TOMMY [*kissing her*]: Good night, Ma.

MRS MILLER: Good night. Here! You look feverish. Let me feel of your head. No, you're all right. Hurry up, now. And don't forget your prayers.

[TOMMY *goes slowly to the doorway – then turns suddenly, the discovery of another excuse lighting up his face.*]

TOMMY: Here's another thing, Ma. When I was up to the water-closet last –

MRS MILLER [*sharply*]: When you were *where*?

TOMMY: The bathroom.

MRS MILLER: That's better.

TOMMY: Uncle Sid was snoring like a fog-horn – and he's right next to my room. How can I ever get to sleep while he's – [*He is overcome by a jaw-cracking yawn.*]

MRS MILLER: I guess you'd get to sleep all right if you were inside a fog-horn. You run along now.

[TOMMY *gives up, grins sleepily, and moves off to bed. As soon as he is off her mind, all her former uneasiness comes back on* MRS MILLER *tenfold. She sighs, moves restlessly, then finally asks:*]

What time is it now, Nat?

MILLER: Now, Essie, I just told you a minute ago.

MRS MILLER [*resentfully*]: I don't see how you can take it so calm! Here it's midnight, you might say, and our Richard still out, and we don't even know where he is.

MILDRED: I hear someone on the piazza. Bet that's him now, Ma.

MRS MILLER [*her anxiety immediately turning to relieved anger*]: You give him a good piece of your mind, Nat, you hear me! You're too easy with him, that's the whole trouble! The idea of him daring to stay out like this!

[*The front door is heard being opened and shut, and someone whistling* '*Waltz Me Around Again, Willie*'.]

MILDRED: No, that isn't Dick. It's Art.

MRS MILLER [*her face falling*]: Oh.

[*A moment later* ARTHUR *enters through the front parlour, whistling softly, half under his breath, looking complacently pleased with himself.*]

MILLER [*surveys him over his glasses, not with enthusiasm – shortly*]: So you're back, eh? We thought it was Richard.

ARTHUR: Is he still out? Where'd he go to?

MILLER: That's just what we'd like to know. You didn't run into him anywhere, did you?

ARTHUR: No. I've been at the Rands' ever since dinner. [*He sits down in the armchair at left of table, rear.*] I suppose he sneaked off to the beach to watch the fireworks.

MILLER [*pretending an assurance he is far from feeling*]: Of course. That's what we've been trying to tell your mother, but she insists on worrying her head off.

MRS MILLER: But if he was going to the fireworks, why wouldn't he say so? He knew we'd let him.

ARTHUR [*with calm wisdom*]: That's easy, Ma. [*He grins superiorly.*] Didn't you hear him this morning showing off bawling out the Fourth like an anarchist? He wouldn't want to reneg on that to you – but he'd want to see the old fireworks just the same. [*He adds complacently.*] I know. He's at the foolish age.

MILLER [*stares at* ARTHUR *with ill-concealed astonishment, then grins*]: Well, Arthur, by gosh, you make me feel as if I owed you an apology when you talk horse sense like that. [*He turns to his wife, greatly relieved.*] Arthur's hit the nail right on the head, I think, Essie. That was what I couldn't figure out – why he – but now it's clear as day.

MRS MILLER [*with a sigh*]: Well, I hope you're right. But I wish he was home.

ARTHUR [*takes out his pipe and fills and lights it with solemn gravity*]: He oughtn't to be allowed out this late at his age. I wasn't, Fourth or no Fourth – if I remember.

MILLER [*a twinkle in his eyes*]: Don't tax your memory trying to recall those ancient days of your youth.

[MILDRED *laughs and* ARTHUR *looks sheepish. But he soon regains his aplomb.*]

ARTHUR [*importantly*]: We had a corking dinner at the Rands'. We had sweetbreads on toast.

MRS MILLER [*arising momentarily from her depression*]: Just like the Rands to put on airs before you! I never could see anything to sweetbreads. Always taste like soap to me. And no real nourishment to them. I wouldn't have the pesky things on my table!

[ARTHUR *again feels sat upon.*]

MILDRED [*teasingly*]: Did you kiss Elsie good night?

ARTHUR: Stop trying to be so darn funny all the time! You give me a pain in the ear!

MILDRED: And that's where she gives me a pain, the stuck-up thing! – thinks she's the whole cheese!

MILLER [*irritably*]: And it's where your everlasting wrangling gives me a pain, you two! Give us a rest!

[*There is silence for a moment.*]

MRS MILLER [*sighs worriedly again*]: I do wish that boy would get home!

MILLER [*glances at her uneasily, peeks surreptitiously at his watch – then has an inspiration and turns to* ARTHUR]: Arthur, what's this I hear about your having such a good singing voice?

Rand was telling me he liked nothing better than to hear you sing – said you did every night you were up there. Why don't you ever give us folks at home here a treat?

ARTHUR [*pleased, but still nursing wounded dignity*]: I thought you'd only sit on me.

MRS MILLER [*perking up – proudly*]: Arthur has a real nice voice. He practises when you're not at home. I didn't know you cared for singing, Nat.

MILLER: Well, I do – nothing better – and when I was a boy I had a fine voice myself and folks used to say I'd ought – [*Then abruptly, mindful of his painful experience with reminiscence at dinner, looking about him guiltily*] Hmm. But don't hide your light under a bushel, Arthur. Why not give us a song or two now? You can play for him, can't you, Mildred?

MILDRED [*with a toss of her head*]: I can play as well as Elsie Rand, at least!

ARTHUR [*ignoring her – clearing his throat importantly*]: I've been singing a lot tonight. I don't know if my voice –

MILDRED [*forgetting her grudge, grabs her brother's hand and tugs at it*]: Come on. Don't play modest. You know you're just dying to show off.

[*This puts* ARTHUR *off at once. He snatches his hand away from her angrily.*]

ARTHUR: Let go of me, you! [*Then with surly dignity*] I don't feel like singing tonight, Pa. I will some other time.

MILLER: You let him alone, Mildred!

[*He winks at* ARTHUR, *indicating with his eyes and a nod of his head* MRS MILLER, *who has again sunk into worried brooding. He makes it plain by this pantomime that he wants him to sing to distract his mother's mind.*]

ARTHUR [*puts aside his pipe and gets up promptly*]: Oh – sure, I'll do the best I can. [*He follows* MILDRED *into the front parlour, where he switches on the lights.*]

MILLER [*to his wife*]: It won't keep Tommy awake. Nothing

could. And Sid, he'd sleep through an earthquake. [*Then suddenly, looking through the front parlour – grumpily*] Darn it, speak of the devil, here he comes. Well, he's had a good sleep and he'd ought to be sobered up. [LILY *gets up from her chair and looks around her huntedly, as if for a place to hide.* MILLER *says soothingly:*] Lily, you just sit down and read your book and don't pay any attention to him.

[*She sits down again and bends over her book tensely. From the front parlour comes the tinkling of a piano as* MILDRED *runs over the scales. In the midst of this,* SID *enters through the front parlour. All the effervescence of his jag has worn off and he is now suffering from a bad case of hangover – nervous, sick, a prey to gloomy remorse and bitter feelings of self-loathing and self-pity. His eyes are bloodshot and puffed, his face bloated, the fringe of hair around his baldness tousled and tufty. He sidles into the room guiltily, his eyes shifting about, avoiding looking at anyone.*]

SID [*forcing a sickly, twitching smile*]: Hello.

MILLER [*considerately casual*]: Hello, Sid. Had a good nap?

[*Then, as* SID *swallows hard and is about to break into further speech,* MILDRED'S *voice comes from the front parlour,* 'I haven't played that in ever so long, but I'll try,' *and she starts an accompaniment.* MILLER *motions* SID *to be quiet.*]

Ssshh! Arthur's going to sing for us.

[SID *flattens himself against the edge of the bookcase at centre, rear, miserably selfconscious and ill at ease there but nervously afraid to move anywhere else.* ARTHUR *begins to sing. He has a fairly decent voice but his method is untrained sentimentality to a dripping degree. He sings that old sentimental favourite, 'Then You'll Remember Me'. The effect on his audience is instant.* MILLER *gazes before him with a ruminating melancholy, his face seeming to become gently sorrowful and old.* MRS MILLER *stares before her, her expression becoming more and more doleful.* LILY *forgets to pretend to read her book but looks over it, her face growing tragically sad. As for* SID, *he is moved to his remorseful, guilt-stricken depths. His mouth pulls down at the corners and he seems about to cry. The song comes to an end.* MILLER *starts, then claps his hands enthusiastically and calls:*]

Well done, Arthur – well done! Why, you've got a splendid voice! Give us some more! You liked that, didn't you, Essie?

MRS MILLER [*dolefully*]: Yes – but it's sad – terrible sad.

SID [*after swallowing hard, suddenly blurts out*]: Nat and Essie – and Lily – I – I want to apologize – for coming home – the way I did – there's no excuse – but I didn't mean –

MILLER [*sympathetically*]: Of course, Sid. It's all forgotten.

MRS MILLER [*rousing herself – affectionately pitying*]: Don't be a goose, Sid. We know how it is with picnics. You forget it.

[*His face lights up a bit but his gaze shifts to* LILY *with a mute appeal, hoping for a word from her which is not forthcoming. Her eyes are fixed on her book, her body tense and rigid.*]

SID [*finally blurts out desperately*]: Lily – I'm sorry – about the fireworks. Can you – forgive me?

[*But* LILY *remains implacably silent. A stricken look comes over* SID'S *face. In the front parlour* MILDRED *is heard saying* 'But I only know the chorus' – *and she starts another accompaniment.*]

MILLER [*comes to Sid's rescue*]: Ssshh! We're going to have another song. Sit down, Sid.

[SID, *hanging his head, flees to the farthest corner, left, front, and sits at the end of the sofa, facing front, hunched up, elbows on knees, face in hands, his round eyes childishly wounded and woebegone.* ARTHUR *sings the popular 'Dearie', playing up its sentimental values for all he is worth. The effect on his audience is that of the previous song, intensified – especially upon* SID. *As he finishes,* MILLER *again starts and applauds.*]

Mighty fine, Arthur! You sang that darned well! Didn't he, Essie?

MRS MILLER [*dolefully*]: Yes – but I wish he wouldn't sing such sad songs. [*Then, her lips trembling*] Richard's always whistling that.

MILLER [*hastily – calls*]: Give us something cheery, next one, Arthur. You know, just for variety's sake.

SID [*suddenly turns toward* LILY *– his voice choked with tears – in a passion of self-denunciation*]: You're right, Lily! – right not to forgive me! – I'm no good and never will be! – I'm a no-good drunken bum! – you shouldn't even wipe your feet on me! – I'm a dirty, rotten drunk! – no good to myself or anybody else! – if I had any guts I'd kill myself, and good riddance! – but I haven't! – I'm yellow, too! – a yellow, drunken bum!

[*He hides his face in his hands and begins to sob like a sick little boy. This is too much for* LILY. *All her bitter hurt and steely resolve to ignore and punish him vanish in a flash, swamped by a pitying love for him. She runs and puts her arm around him – even kisses him tenderly and impulsively on his bald head, and soothes him as if he were a little boy.* MRS MILLER, *almost equally moved, has half risen to go to her brother, too, but* MILLER *winks and shakes his head vigorously and motions her to sit down.*]

LILY: There! Don't cry, Sid! I can't bear it! Of course, I forgive you! Haven't I always forgiven you? I know you're not to blame – So don't, Sid!

SID [*lifts a tearful, humbly grateful, pathetic face to her – but a face that the dawn of a cleansed conscience is already beginning to restore to its natural Puckish expression*]: Do you really forgive me – I know I don't deserve it – can you really – ?

LILY [*gently*]: I told you I did, Sid – and I do.

SID [*kisses her hand humbly, like a big puppy licking it*]: Thanks, Lily. I can't tell you –

[*In the front parlour,* ARTHUR *begins to sing rollickingly 'Waiting at the Church', and after the first line or two* MILDRED *joins in.* SID'*s face lights up with appreciation and, automatically, he begins to tap one foot in time, still holding fast to* LILY'S *hand. When they come to 'sent around a note, this is what she wrote', he can no longer resist, but joins in a shaky bawl.*]

'Can't get away to marry you today, My wife won't let me!'

[*As the song finishes, the two in the other room laugh.* MILLER *and* SID *laugh.* LILY *smiles at* SID'S *laughter. Only,* MRS MILLER *remains dolefully preoccupied, as if she hadn't heard.*]

MILLER: That's fine, Arthur and Mildred. That's darned good.

SID [*turning to* LILY *enthusiastically*]: You ought to hear Vesta Victoria sing that! Gosh, she's great! I heard her at Hammerstein's Victoria – you remember, that trip I made to New York.

LILY [*her face suddenly tired and sad again – for her memory of certain aspects of that trip is the opposite from what he would like her to recall at this moment – gently disengaging her hand from his – with a hopeless sigh*]: Yes, I remember, Sid.

[*He is overcome momentarily by guilty confusion. She goes quietly and sits down in her chair again. In the front parlour, from now on,* MILDRED *keeps starting to run over popular tunes but always gets stuck and turns to another.*]

MRS MILLER [*suddenly*]: What time is it now, Nat? [*Then without giving him a chance to answer*] Oh, I'm getting worried something dreadful, Nat. You don't know what might have happened to Richard! You read in the papers every day about boys getting run over by automobiles.

LILY: Oh, don't say that, Essie!

MILLER [*sharply, to conceal his own reawakened apprehension*]: Don't get to imagining things, now!

MRS MILLER: Well, why couldn't it happen, with everyone that owns one out tonight, and lots of those driving, drunk? Or he might have gone down to the beach dock and fallen overboard! [*On the verge of hysteria*] Oh, I know something dreadful's happened! And you can sit there listening to songs and laughing as if – Why don't you do something? Why don't you go out and find him? [*She bursts into tears.*]

LILY [*comes to her quickly and puts her arm around her*]: Essie, you mustn't worry so! You'll make yourself sick! Richard's all right. I've got a feeling in my bones he's all right.

MILDRED [*comes hurrying in from the front parlour*]: What's the trouble? [ARTHUR *appears in the doorway beside her. She goes to her mother and also puts an arm around her.*] Ah, don't cry, Ma! Dick'll turn up in a minute or two, wait and see!

ARTHUR: Sure, he will!

MILLER [*has gotten to his feet, frowning – soberly*]: I was going out to look – if he wasn't back by twelve sharp. That'd be the time it'd take him to walk from the beach if he left after the last car. But I'll go now, if it'll ease your mind. I'll take the auto and drive out the beach road – and likely pick him up on the way. [*He has taken his collar and tie from where they hang from one corner of the bookcase at rear, centre, and is starting to put them on.*] You better come with me, Arthur.

ARTHUR: Sure thing, Pa. [*Suddenly he listens and says:*] Ssshh! There's someone on the piazza now – coming around to this door, too. That must be him. No one else would –

MRS MILLER: Oh, thank God, thank God!

MILLER [*with a sheepish smile*]: Darn him! I've a notion to give him hell for worrying us all like this.

[*The screen door is pushed violently open and* RICHARD *lurches in and stands swaying a little, blinking his eyes in the light. His face is a pasty pallor, shining with perspiration, and his eyes are glassy. The knees of his trousers are dirty, one of them torn from the sprawl on the sidewalk he had taken, following the* BARTENDER'S *kick. They all gape at him, too paralysed for a moment to say anything.*]

MRS MILLER: Oh, God, what's happened to him! He's gone crazy! Richard!

SID [*the first to regain presence of mind – with a grin*]: Crazy, nothing. He's only soused!

ARTHUR: He's drunk, that's what! [*Then shocked and condemning*] You've got your nerve! You fresh kid! We'll take that out of you when we get you down to Yale!

RICHARD [*with a wild gesture of defiance – maudlinly dramatic*]:

'Yesterday this Day's Madness did prepare
Tomorrow's Silence, Triumph, or Despair.
Drink! for –'

MILLER [*his face grown stern and angry, takes a threatening step toward him*]: Richard! How dare – !

MRS MILLER [*hysterically*]: Don't you strike him, Nat! Don't you – !

SID [*grabbing his arm*]: Steady Nat! Keep your temper! No good bawling him out now! He don't know what he's doing!

MILLER [*controlling himself and looking a bit ashamed*]: All right – you're right, Sid.

RICHARD [*drunkenly glorying in the sensation he is creating – recites with dramatic emphasis*]: 'And then – I will come – with vine leaves in my hair!' [*He laughs with a double-dyed sardonicism.*]

MRS MILLER [*staring at him as if she couldn't believe her eyes*]: Richard! You're intoxicated! – you bad, wicked boy, you!

RICHARD [*forces a wicked leer to his lips and quotes with ponderous mockery*]: 'Fancy that, Hedda!' [*Then suddenly his whole expression changes, his pallor takes on a greenish, seasick tinge, his eyes seem to be turned inward uneasily – and, all pose gone, he calls to his mother appealingly, like a sick little boy.*] Ma! I feel – rotten!

[MRS MILLER *gives a cry and starts to go to him, but* SID *steps in her way.*]

SID: You let me take care of him, Essie. I know this game backwards.

MILLER [*putting his arm around his wife*]: Yes, you leave him to Sid.

SID [*his arm around* RICHARD *– leading him off through the front parlour*]: Come on, Old Sport! Upstairs we go! Your old Uncle Sid'll fix you up. He's the kid that wrote the book!

MRS MILLER [*staring after them – still aghast*]: Oh, it's too terrible! Imagine our Richard! And did you hear him talking about some Hedda? Oh, I know he's been with one of those bad women, I know he has – my Richard! [*She hides her face on* MILLER'S *shoulder and sobs heart-brokenly.*]

MILLER [*a tired, harassed, deeply worried look on his face – soothing her*]: Now, now, you mustn't get to imagining such things! You mustn't, Essie! [LILY *and* MILDRED *and* ARTHUR *are standing about awkwardly with awed, shocked faces.*]

CURTAIN

ACT FOUR

SCENE 1

The same – sitting-room of the Miller house – about one o'clock in the afternoon of the following day.

[*As the curtain rises, the family, with the exception of* RICHARD, *are discovered coming in through the back parlour from dinner in the dining-room.* MILLER *and his wife come first. His face is set in an expression of frowning severity.* MRS MILLER'S *face is drawn and worried. She has evidently had no rest yet from a sleepless, tearful night.* SID *is himself again, his expression as innocent as if nothing had occurred the previous day that remotely concerned him. And, outside of eyes that are bloodshot and nerves that are shaky, he shows no after-effects except that he is terribly sleepy.* LILY *is gently sad and depressed.* ARTHUR *is self-consciously a virtuous young man against whom nothing can be said.* MILDRED *and* TOMMY *are subdued, covertly watching their father.*
They file into the sitting-room in silence and then stand around uncertainly, as if each were afraid to be the first to sit down. The atmosphere is as stiltedly grave as if they were attending a funeral service. Their eyes keep fixed on the head of the house, who has gone to the window at right and is staring out frowningly, savagely chewing a toothpick.]

MILLER [*finally – irritably*]: Damn it, I'd ought to be back at the office putting in some good licks! I've a whole pile of things that have got to be done today!

MRS MILLER [*accusingly*]: You don't mean to tell me you're going back without seeing him? It's your duty – !

MILLER [*exasperatedly*]: 'Course I'm not! I wish you'd stop jumping to conclusions! What else did I come home for,

I'd like to know? Do I usually come way back here for dinner on a busy day? I was only wishing this hadn't come up – just at this particular time.

[*He ends up very lamely and is irritably conscious of the fact.*]

TOMMY [*who has been fidgeting restlessly – unable to bear the suspense a moment longer*]: What is it Dick done? Why is everyone scared to tell me?

MILLER [*seizes this as an escape valve – turns and fixes his youngest son with a stern, forbidding eye*]: Young man, I've never spanked you yet, but that don't mean I never will! Seems to me that you've been just itching for it lately! You keep your mouth shut till you're spoken to – or I warn you something's going to happen!

MRS MILLER: Yes, Tommy, you keep still and don't bother your pa. [*Then warningly to her husband*] Careful what you say, Nat. Little pitchers have big ears.

MILLER [*peremptorily*]: You kids skedaddle – all of you. Why are you always hanging around the house? Go out and play in the yard, or take a walk, and get some fresh air.

[MILDRED *takes* TOMMY's *hand and leads him out through the front parlour.* ARTHUR *hangs back, as if the designation 'kids' couldn't possibly apply to him. His father notices this – impatiently.*]

You, too, Arthur.

[ARTHUR *goes out with a stiff, wounded dignity.*]

LILY [*tactfully*]: I think I'll go for a walk, too.

[*She goes out through the front parlour.* SID *makes a movement as if to follow her.*]

MILLER: I'd like you to stay, Sid – for a while, anyway.

SID: Sure. [*He sits down in the rocking-chair at right, rear, of table, and immediately yawns.*] Gosh, I'm dead. Don't know what's the matter with me today. Can't seem to keep awake.

MILLER [*with caustic sarcasm*]: Maybe that demon chowder you drank at the picnic poisoned you!

[SID *looks sheepish and forces a grin. Then* MILLER *turns to his wife with the air of one who determinedly faces the unpleasant.*]

Where is Richard?

MRS MILLER [*flusteredly*]: He's still in bed. I made him stay in bed to punish him – and I thought he ought to, anyway, after being so sick. But he says he feels all right.

SID [*with another yawn*]: 'Course he does. When you're young you can stand anything without it feazing you. Why, I remember when I could come down on the morning after, fresh as a daisy, and eat a breakfast of pork chops and fried onions and – [*He stops guiltily.*]

MILLER [*bitingly*]: I suppose that was before eating lobster shells had ruined your iron constitution!

MRS MILLER [*regards her brother severely*]: If I was in your shoes, I'd keep still! [*Then turning to her husband*] Richard must be feeling better. He ate all the dinner I sent up, Norah says.

MILLER: I thought you weren't going to give him any dinner – to punish him.

MRS MILLER [*guiltily*]: Well – in his weakened condition – I thought it best – [*Then defensively*] But you needn't think I haven't punished him. I've given him pieces of my mind he won't forget in a hurry. And I've kept reminding him his real punishment was still to come – that you were coming home to dinner on purpose – and then he'd learn that you could be terrible stern when he did such awful things.

MILLER [*stirs uncomfortably*]: Hmm!

MRS MILLER: And that's just what it's your duty to do – punish him good and hard! The idea of him daring – [*Then hastily*] But you be careful how you go about it, Nat. Remember he's like you inside – too sensitive for his own good. And he never would have done it, I know, if it hadn't been for that darned little dunce, Muriel, and her numbskull father – and then all of us teasing him and hurting his feelings all day – and then you lost your temper and were so sharp with him right after dinner before he went out.

MILLER [*resentfully*]: I see this is going to work round to where it's all my fault!

MRS MILLER: Now, I didn't say that, did I? Don't go losing your temper again. And here's another thing. You know as well as I, Richard would never have done such a thing alone. Why, he wouldn't know how! He must have been influenced and led by someone.

MILLER: Yes, I believe that. Did you worm out of him who it was? [*Then angrily*] By God, I'll make whoever it was regret it!

MRS MILLER: No, he wouldn't admit there was anyone. [*Then triumphantly*] But there is one thing I did worm out of him – and I can tell you it relieved my mind more'n anything. You know, I was afraid he'd been with one of those bad women. Well, turns out there wasn't any Hedda. She was just out of those books he's been reading. He swears he's never known a Hedda in his life. And I believe him. Why, he seemed disgusted with me for having such a notion. [*Then lamely*] So somehow – I can't kind of feel it's all as bad as I thought it was. [*Then quickly and indignantly*] But it's bad enough, goodness knows – and you punish him good just the same. The idea of a boy of his age – ! Shall I go up now and tell him to get dressed, you want to see him?

MILLER [*helplessly – and irritably*]: Yes! I can't waste all day listening to you!

MRS MILLER [*worriedly*]: Now you keep your temper, Nat, remember!

[*She goes out through the front parlour.*]

MILLER: Darn women, anyway! They always get you mixed up. Their minds simply don't know what logic is! [*Then he notices that* SID *is dozing – sharply*] Sid!

SID [*blinking – mechanically*]: I'll take the same. [*Then hurriedly*] What'd you say, Nat?

MILLER [*caustically*]: What I didn't say was what'll you have. [*Irritably*] Do you want to be of some help, or don't you? Then keep awake and try and use your brains! This is a damned sight more serious than Essie has any idea! She thinks there weren't any girls mixed up with Richard's spree last night – but I happen to know there were! [*He takes a letter from his pocket.*] Here's a note a woman left with one of the boys downstairs at the office this morning – didn't ask to see me, just said give me this. He'd never seen her before – said she looked like a tart. [*He has opened the letter and reads:*] 'Your son got the booze he drank last night at the Pleasant Beach House. The bartender there knew he was under age but served him just the same. He thought it was a good joke to get him soused. If you have any guts you will run that bastard out of town.' Well, what do you think of that? It's a woman's handwriting – not signed, of course.

SID: She's one of the babies, all right – judging from her elegant language.

MILLER: See if you recognize the handwriting.

SID [*with a reproachful look*]: Nat, I resent the implication that I correspond with all the tramps around this town. [*Looking at the letter*] No, I don't know who this one could be. [*Handing the letter back*] But I deduce that the lady had a run-in with the barkeep and wants revenge.

MILLER [*grimly*]: And I deduce that before that she must have picked up Richard – or how would she know who he was? – and took him to this dive.

SID: Maybe. The Pleasant Beach House is nothing but a bed house – [*Quickly*] At least, so I've been told.

MILLER: That's just the sort of damned fool thing he might do to spite Muriel, in the state of mind he was in – pick up some tart. And she'd try to get him drunk so –

SID: Yes, it might have happened like that – and it might not. How're we ever going to prove it? Everyone at the Pleasant Beach will lie their heads off.

MILLER [*simply and proudly*]: Richard won't lie.

SID: Well, don't blame him if he don't remember everything that happened last night. [*Then sincerely concerned*] I hope you're wrong, Nat. That kind of baby is dangerous for a kid like Dick – in more ways than one. You know what I mean.

MILLER [*frowningly*]: Yep – and that's just what's got me worried. Damn it, I've got to have a straight talk with him – about women and all those things. I ought to have long ago.

SID: Yes. You ought.

MILLER: I've tried to a couple of times. I did it all right with Wilbur and Lawrence and Arthur, when it came time – but, hell, with Richard I always get sort of ashamed of myself and can't get started right. You feel, in spite of all his bold talk out of books, that he's so darned innocent inside.

SID: I know. I wouldn't like the job. [*Then after a pause – curiously*] How were you figuring to punish him for his sins?

MILLER [*frowning*]: To be honest with you, Sid, I'm damned if I know. All depends on what I feel about what he feels when I first size him up – and then it'll be like shooting in the dark.

SID: If I didn't know you so well, I'd say don't be too hard on him. [*He smiles a little bitterly.*] If you remember, I was always getting punished – and see what a lot of good it did me!

MILLER [*kindly*]: Oh, there's lots worse than you around, so don't take to boasting. [*Then, at a sound from the front parlour – with a sigh*] Well, here comes the Bad Man, I guess.

SID [*getting up*]: I'll beat it.

[*But it is* MRS MILLER *who appears in the doorway, looking guilty and defensive.* SID *sits down again.*]

MRS MILLER: I'm sorry, Nat – but he was sound asleep and I didn't have the heart to wake him. I waited for him to wake up but he didn't.

MILLER [*concealing a relief of which he is ashamed – exasperatedly*]: Well, I'll be double damned! If you're not the –

MRS MILLER [*defensively aggressive*]: Now don't lose your temper at me, Nat Miller! You know as well as I do he needs all the sleep he can get today – after last night's ructions! Do you want him to be taken down sick? And what difference does it make to you, anyway? You can see him when you come home for supper, can't you? My goodness, I never saw you so savage-tempered! You'd think you couldn't bear waiting to punish him?

MILLER [*outraged*]: Well, I'll be eternally – [*Then he suddenly laughs.*] No use talking, you certainly take the cake! But you know darned well I told you I'm not coming home to supper tonight. I've got a date with Jack Lawson that may mean a lot of new advertising and it's important.

MRS MILLER: Then you can see him when you do come home.

MILLER [*covering his evident relief at this respite with a fuming manner*]: All right! All right! I give up! I'm going back to the office. [*He starts for the front parlour.*] Bring a man all the way back here on a busy day and then you – No consideration –

[*He disappears, and a moment later the front door is heard shutting behind him.*]

MRS MILLER: Well, I never saw Nat so bad-tempered.

SID [*with a chuckle*]: Bad temper, nothing. He's so tickled to get out of it for a while he can't see straight!

MRS MILLER [*with a sniff*]: I hope I know him better than you. [*Then fussing about the room, setting this and that in place, while* SID *yawns drowsily and blinks his eyes*] Sleeping like a baby – so innocent-looking. You'd think butter wouldn't melt in his mouth. It all goes to show you never can tell by appearances – not even when it's your own child. The idea!

SID [*drowsily*]: Oh, Dick's all right, Essie. Stop worrying.

MRS MILLER [*with a sniff*]: Of course, you'd say that. I suppose you'll have him out with you painting the town red the next thing!

[*As she is talking,* RICHARD *appears in the doorway from the sitting-room. He shows no ill-effects from his experience the night before. In fact, he looks surprisingly healthy. He is dressed in old clothes that look as if they had been hurriedly flung on. His expression is one of hang-dog guilt mingled with a defensive defiance.*]

RICHARD [*with self-conscious unconcern, ignoring his mother*]: Hello, Sid.

MRS MILLER [*whirls on him*]: What are you doing here, Young Man? I thought you were asleep! Seems to me you woke up pretty quick – just after your Pa left the house!

RICHARD [*sulkily*]: I wasn't asleep. I heard you in the room.

MRS MILLER [*outraged*]: Do you mean to say you were deliberately deceiving –

RICHARD: I wasn't deceiving. You didn't ask if I was asleep.

MRS MILLER: It amounts to the same thing and you know it! It isn't enough your wickedness last night, but now you have to take to lying!

RICHARD: I wasn't lying, Ma. If you'd asked if I was asleep I'd have said no.

MRS MILLER: I've a good mind to send you straight back to bed and make you stay there!

RICHARD: Ah, what for, Ma? It was only giving me a headache, lying there.

MRS MILLER: If you've got a headache, I guess you know it doesn't come from that! And imagine me standing there, and feeling sorry for you, like a fool – even having a run-in with your Pa because – But you wait till he comes back tonight! If you don't catch it!

RICHARD [*sulkily*]: I don't care.

MRS MILLER: You don't care? You talk as if you weren't sorry for what you did last night!

RICHARD [*defiantly*]: I'm not sorry.

MRS MILLER: Richard! You ought to be ashamed! I'm beginning to think you're hardened in wickedness, that's what!

RICHARD [*with bitter despondency*]: I'm not sorry because I don't care a darn what I did, or what's done to me, or anything about anything! I won't do it again –

MRS MILLER [*seizing on this to relent a bit*]: Well, I'm glad to hear you say that, anyway!

RICHARD: But that's not because I think it was wicked or any such old-fogy moral notion, but because it wasn't any fun. It didn't make me happy and funny like it does Uncle Sid –

SID [*drowsily*]: What's that? Who's funny?

RICHARD [*ignoring him*]: It only made me sadder – and sick – so I don't see any sense in it.

MRS MILLER: Now you're talking sense! That's a good boy.

RICHARD: But I'm not sorry I tried it once – curing the soul by means of the senses, as Oscar Wilde says. [*Then with despairing pessimism*] But what does it matter what I do or don't do? Life is all a stupid farce! I'm through with it! [*With a sinister smile*] It's lucky there aren't any of General Gabler's pistols around – or you'd see if I'd stand it much longer!

MRS MILLER [*worriedly impressed by this threat – but pretending scorn*]: I don't know anything about General Gabler – I suppose that's more of those darned books – but you're a silly gabbler yourself when you talk that way!

RICHARD [*darkly*]: That's how little you know about me.

MRS MILLER [*giving in to her worry*]: I wish you wouldn't say those terrible things – about life and pistols! You don't want to worry me to death, do you?

RICHARD [*reassuringly stoical now*]: You needn't worry, Ma. It was only my despair talking. But I'm not a coward. I'll face – my fate.

MRS MILLER [*stands looking at him puzzledly – then gives it up with a sigh*]: Well, all I can say is you're the queerest boy I ever did hear of! [*Then solicitously, putting her hand on his forehead*] How's your headache? Do you want me to get you some Bromo Seltzer?

RICHARD [*taken down – disgustedly*]: No, I don't! Aw, Ma, you don't understand anything!

MRS MILLER: Well, I understand this much: It's your liver, that's what! You'll take a good dose of salts tomorrow morning, and no nonsense about it! [*Then suddenly*] My goodness, I wonder what time it's getting to be. I've got to go upstreet. [*She goes to the front-parlour doorway – then turns.*] You stay here, Richard, you hear? Remember you're not allowed out today – for a punishment.

[*She hurries away.* RICHARD *sits in tragic gloom.* SID, *without opening his eyes, speaks to him drowsily.*]

SID: Well, how's my fellow Rum Pot, as good old Dowie calls us? Got a head?

RICHARD [*startled – sheepishly*]: Aw, don't go dragging that up, Uncle Sid. I'm never going to be such a fool again, I tell you.

SID [*with drowsy cynicism – not unmixed with bitterness at the end*]: Seems to me I've heard someone say that before. Who could it have been, I wonder? Why, if it wasn't Sid Davis! Yes, sir, I've heard him say that very thing a thousand times, must be. But then he's always fooling; you can't take a word he says seriously; he's a card, that Sid is!

RICHARD [*darkly*]: I was desperate, Uncle – even if she wasn't worth it. I was wounded to the heart.

SID: I like to the quick better myself – more stylish. [*Then sadly*] But you're right. Love is hell on a poor sucker. Don't I know it?

[RICHARD *is disgusted and disdains to reply.* SID'S *chin sinks on his chest and he begins to breathe noisily, fast asleep.* RICHARD *glances at him with aversion. There is a sound of someone on the porch and the screen door is opened and* MILDRED *enters. She smiles on seeing her uncle, then gives a start on seeing* RICHARD.]

MILDRED: Hello! Are you allowed up?

RICHARD: Of course, I'm allowed up.

MILDRED [*comes and sits in her father's chair at right, front, of table*]: How did Pa punish you?

RICHARD: He didn't. He went back to the office without seeing me.

MILDRED: Well, you'll catch it later. [*Then rebukingly*] And you ought to. If you'd ever seen how awful you looked last night!

RICHARD: Ah, forget it, can't you?

MILDRED: Well, are you ever going to do it again, that's what I want to know.

RICHARD: What's that to you?

MILDRED [*with suppressed excitement*]: Well, if you don't solemnly swear you won't – then I won't give you something I've got for you.

RICHARD: Don't try to kid me. You haven't got anything.

MILDRED: I have, too.

RICHARD: What?

MILDRED: Wouldn't you like to know! I'll give you three guesses.

RICHARD [*with disdainful dignity*]: Don't bother me. I'm in no mood to play riddles with kids!

MILDRED: Oh, well, if you're going to get snippy! Anyway, you haven't promised yet.

RICHARD [*a prey to keen curiosity now*]: I promise. What is it?

MILDRED: What would you like best in the world?

RICHARD: I don't know. What?

MILDRED: And you pretend to be in love! If I told Muriel that!

RICHARD [*breathlessly*]: Is it – from her?

MILDRED [*laughing*]: Well, I guess it's a shame to keep you guessing. Yes. It is from her. I was walking past her place just now when I saw her waving from their parlour window, and I went up and she said give this to Dick, and she didn't have a chance to say anything else because her mother called her and said she wasn't allowed to have company. So I took it – and here it is. [*She gives him a letter folded many times into a tiny square.* RICHARD *opens it with a trembling eagerness and reads.* MILDRED *watches him curiously – then sighs affectedly.*] Gee, it must be nice to be in love like you are – all with one person.

RICHARD [*his eyes shining*]: Gee, Mid, do you know what she says – that she didn't mean a word in that other letter. Her old man made her write it. And she loves me and only me and always will, no matter how they punish her!

MILDRED: My! I'd never think she had that much spunk.

RICHARD: Huh! You don't know her! Think I could fall in love with a girl that was afraid to say her soul's her own? I should say not! [*Then more gleefully still*] And she's going to try and sneak out and meet me tonight. She says she thinks she can do it. [*Then suddenly feeling this enthusiasm before* MILDRED *is entirely the wrong note for a cynical pessimist – with an affected bitter laugh*] Ha! I knew darned well she couldn't hold out – that she'd ask to see me again. [*He misquotes cynically.*] 'Women never know when the curtain has fallen. They always want another act.'

MILDRED: Is that so, Smarty?

RICHARD [*as if he were weighing the matter*]: I don't know whether I'll consent to keep this date or not.

MILDRED: Well, I know! You're not allowed out, you silly! So you can't!

RICHARD [*dropping all pretence – defiantly*]: Can't I, though! You wait and see if I can't! I'll see her tonight if it's the last thing I ever do! I don't care how I'm punished after!

MILDRED [*admiringly*]: Goodness! I never thought you had such nerve!

RICHARD: You promise to keep your face shut, Mid – until after I've left – then you can tell Pa and Ma where I've gone – I mean, if they're worrying I'm off like last night.

MILDRED: All right. Only you've got to do something for me when I ask.

RICHARD: 'Course I will. [*Then excitedly*] And say, Mid! Right now's the best chance for me to get away – while everyone's out! Ma'll be coming back soon and she'll keep watching me like a cat – [*He starts for the back parlour.*] I'm going. I'll sneak out the back.

MILDRED [*excitedly*]: But what'll you do till night-time? It's ages to wait.

RICHARD: What do I care how long I wait! [*Intensely sincere now*] I'll think of her – and dream! I'd wait a million years and never mind it – for her! [*He gives his sister a superior scornful glance.*] The trouble with you is, you don't understand what love means!

[*He disappears through the back parlour.* MILDRED *looks after him admiringly.* SID *puffs and begins to snore peacefully.*]

CURTAIN

SCENE 2

A strip of beach along the harbour. At left, a bank of dark earth, running half-diagonally back along the beach, marking the line where the sand of the beach ends and fertile land begins. The top of the bank is grassy and the trailing boughs of willow trees extend out over it and over a part of the beach. At left, front, is a path leading up the bank, between the willows. On the beach, at centre, front, a white, flat-bottomed rowboat is drawn up, its bow about touching the bank, the painter trailing up the bank, evidently made fast to the trunk of a willow. Halfway down the sky, at rear, left, the crescent of the new moon casts a soft, mysterious, caressing light over everything. The sand of the beach shimmers palely. The forward half (left of centre) of the rowboat is in the deep shadows cast by the willow, the stern section is in moonlight. In the distance, the orchestra of a summer hotel can be heard very faintly at intervals.

[RICHARD *is discovered sitting sideways on the gunwhale of the rowboat near the stern. He is facing left, watching the path. He is in a great state of anxious expectancy, squirming about uncomfortably on the narrow gunwhale, kicking at the sand restlessly, twirling his straw hat, with a bright-coloured band in stripes, around on his finger.*]

RICHARD [*thinking aloud*]: Must be nearly nine. . . . I can hear the Town Hall clock strike, it's so still tonight . . . Gee, I'll bet Ma had a fit when she found out I'd sneaked out . . . I'll catch hell when I get back, but it'll be worth it . . . if only Muriel turns up . . . she didn't say for certain she could . . . gosh, I wish she'd come! . . . am I sure she wrote nine? . . . [*He puts the straw hat on the seat amidships and pulls the folded letter out of his pocket and peers at it in the moonlight.*] Yes, it's nine, all right. [*He starts to put the note back in his pocket, then stops and kisses it – then shoves it away hastily, sheepish, looking around him shamefacedly, as if afraid he were being observed.*] Aw, that's silly . . . no, it isn't either . . . not when you're really in love. . . . [*He jumps to his feet restlessly.*] Darn it, I wish she'd show up! . . . think of something else . . . that'll make the time pass quicker . . . where was I this time last night? . . . waiting outside the Pleasant Beach House . . . Belle . . . ah, forget her! . . . now, when Muriel's coming . . . that's a fine time to think of – ! . . . but you hugged and kissed her . . . not until I was drunk, I didn't . . . and then it was all showing off . . . darned fool! . . . and I didn't go upstairs with her . . . even if she was pretty . . . aw, she wasn't pretty . . . she was all painted up . . . she was just a whore . . . she was everything dirty . . . Muriel's a million times prettier anyway . . . Muriel and I will go upstairs . . . when we're married . . . but that will be beautiful . . . but I oughtn't even to think of that yet . . . it's not right . . . I'd never – now . . . and she'd never . . . she's a decent girl . . . I couldn't love her if she wasn't . . . but after we're married. . . . [*He gives a little shiver of passionate longing – then resolutely turns his mind away from these improper, almost desecrating thoughts.*] That damned barkeep kicking me . . . I'll bet you if I hadn't been drunk I'd have given him one good punch in the nose, even if he could have licked me after! . . . [*Then with a shiver of shamefaced revulsion and self-disgust*] Aw, you deserved a kick in the pants . . . making such a darned slob of yourself . . . reciting the Ballad of Reading Gaol to those lowbrows! . . . you must have been a fine sight when you got home! . . . having to be put to bed and getting sick! . . . Phaw! . . . [*He squirms disgustedly.*] Think of something else, can't you? . . . recite something . . . see if you remember . . .

'Nay, let us walk from fire unto fire,
From passionate pain to deadlier delight –
I am too young to live without desire,
Too young art thou to waste this summer night –'

. . . gee, that's a peach! . . . I'll have to memorize the rest and recite it to Muriel the next time. . . . I wish I could write poetry . . . about her and me. . . . [*He sighs and stares around him at the night.*] Gee, it's beautiful tonight . . . as if it was a special night . . . for me and Muriel. . . . Gee, I love tonight. . . . I love the sand, and the trees, and the grass, and the water, and the sky, and the moon . . . it's all in me and I'm in it . . . God, it's so beautiful! [*He stands staring at the moon with a rapt face. From the distance the Town Hall clock begins to strike. This brings him back to earth with a start.*] There's nine now. . . . [*He peers at the path apprehensively.*] I don't see her . . . she must have got caught. . . . [*Almost tearfully*] Gee, I hate to go home and catch hell . . . without having seen her! . . . [*Then calling a manly cynicism to his aid*] Aw, who ever heard of a woman ever being on time. . . . I ought to know enough about life by this time not to expect... [*Then with sudden excitement*] There she comes now. ... Gosh! [*He heaves a huge sigh of relief – then recites dramatically to himself, his eyes on the approaching figure.*]

'And lo my love, mine own soul's heart, more dear
Than mine own soul, more beautiful than God,
Who hath my being between the hands of her –'

[*Then hastily*] Mustn't let her know I'm so tickled. ... I ought to be about that first letter, anyway ... if women are too sure of you, they treat you like slaves ... let her suffer, for a change. ... [*He starts to stroll around with exaggerated carelessness, turning his back on the path, hands in pockets whistling with insouciance* '*Waiting at the Church*'.

[MURIEL MCCOMBER *enters from down the path, left, front. She is fifteen, going on sixteen. She is a pretty girl with a plump, graceful little figure, fluffy, light-brown hair, big naïve wondering dark eyes, a round, dimpled face, a melting drawly voice. Just now she is in a great thrilled state of timid adventurousness. She hesitates in the shadow at the foot of the path, waiting for* RICHARD *to see her; but he resolutely goes on whistling with back turned, and she has to call him.*]

MURIEL: Oh, Dick!

RICHARD [*turns around with an elaborate simulation of being disturbed in the midst of profound meditation*]: Oh, hello. Is it nine already? Gosh, time passes – when you're thinking.

MURIEL [*coming toward him as far as the edge of the shadow – disappointedly*]: I thought you'd be waiting right here at the end of the path. I'll bet you'd forgotten I was even coming.

RICHARD [*strolling a little toward her but not too far – carelessly*]: No, I hadn't forgotten, honest. But I got to thinking about life.

MURIEL: You might think of me for a change, after all the risk I've run to see you! [*Hesitating timidly on the edge of the shadows*] Dick! You come here to me. I'm afraid to go out in that bright moonlight where anyone might see me.

RICHARD [*coming toward her – scornfully*]: Aw, there you go again – always scared of life!

MURIEL [*indignantly*]: Dick Miller, I do think you've got an awful nerve to say that after all the risks I've run making this date and then sneaking out! You didn't take the trouble to sneak any letter to me, I notice!

RICHARD: No, because after your first letter, I thought everything was dead and past between us.

MURIEL: And I'll bet you didn't care one little bit! [*On the verge of humiliated tears*] Oh, I was a fool ever to come here! I've got a good notion to go right home and never speak to you again! [*She half turns back toward the path.*]

RICHARD [*frightened – immediately becomes terribly sincere – grabbing her hand*]: Aw, don't go, Muriel! Please! I didn't mean anything like that, honest I didn't! Gee, if you knew how broken-hearted I was by that first letter, and how darned happy your second letter made me – !

MURIEL [*happily relieved – but appreciates she has the upper hand now and doesn't relent at once*]: I don't believe you.

RICHARD: You ask Mid how happy I was. She can prove it.

MURIEL: She'd say anything you told her to. I don't care anything about what she'd say. It's you. You've got to swear to me –

RICHARD: I swear!

MURIEL [*demurely*]: Well then, all right, I'll believe you.

RICHARD [*his eyes on her face lovingly – genuine adoration in his voice*]: Gosh, you're pretty tonight, Muriel! It seems ages since we've been together! If you knew how I've suffered – !

MURIEL: I did, too.

RICHARD [*unable to resist falling into his tragic literary pose for a moment*]: The despair in my soul – [*He recites dramatically:*] 'Something was dead in each of us, And what was dead was Hope!' That was me! My hope of happiness was dead! [*Then with sincere boyish fervour*] Gosh, Muriel, it sure is wonderful to be with you again! [*He puts a timid arm around her awkwardly.*]

MURIEL [*shyly*]: I'm glad – it makes you happy. I'm happy, too.

RICHARD: Can't I – won't you let me kiss you – now? Please! [*He bends his face toward hers.*]

MURIEL [*ducking her head away – timidly*]: No. You mustn't. Don't –

RICHARD: Aw, why can't I?

MURIEL: Because – I'm afraid.

RICHARD [*discomfited – taking his arm from around her – a bit sulky and impatient with her*]: Aw, that's what you always say! You're always so afraid! Aren't you ever going to let me?

MURIEL: I will – sometime.

RICHARD: When?

MURIEL: Soon, maybe.

RICHARD: Tonight, will you?

MURIEL [*coyly*]: I'll see.

RICHARD: Promise?

MURIEL: I promise – maybe.

RICHARD: All right. You remember you've promised. [*Then coaxingly*] Aw, don't let's stand here. Come on out and we can sit down in the boat.

MURIEL [*hesitantly*]: It's so bright out there.

RICHARD: No one'll see. You know there's never anyone around here at night.

MURIEL [*illogically*]: I know there isn't. That's why I thought it would be the best place. But there might be someone.

RICHARD [*taking her hand and tugging at it gently*]: There isn't a soul. [MURIEL *steps out a little and looks up and down fearfully.* RICHARD *goes on insistently.*] Aw, what's the use of a moon if you can't see it!

MURIEL: But it's only a new moon. That's not much to look at.

RICHARD: But I want to see you. I can't here in the shadow. I want to – drink in – all your beauty.

MURIEL [*can't resist this*]: Well, all right – only I can't stay only a few minutes. [*She lets him lead her toward the stern of the boat.*]

RICHARD [*pleadingly*]: Aw, you can stay a little while, can't you? Please! [*He helps her in and she settles herself in the stern seat of the boat, facing diagonally left front.*]

MURIEL: A little while. [*He sits beside her.*] But I've got to be home in bed again pretending to be asleep by ten o'clock. That's the time Pa and Ma come up to bed, as regular as clockwork, and Ma always looks into my room.

RICHARD: But you'll have oodles of time to do that.

MURIEL [*excitedly*]: Dick, you have no idea what I went through to get here tonight! My, but it was exciting! You know Pa's punishing me by sending me to bed at eight sharp, and I had to get all undressed and into bed 'cause at half past he sends Ma up to make sure I've obeyed, and she came up, and I pretended to be asleep, and she went down again, and I got up and dressed in such a hurry – I must look a sight, don't I?

RICHARD: You do not! You look wonderful!

MURIEL: And then I sneaked down the back stairs. And the pesky old stairs squeaked, and my heart was in my mouth, I was so scared, and then I sneaked out through the back yard, keeping in the dark under the trees, and – My, but it was exciting! Dick, you don't realize how I've been punished for your sake. Pa's been so mean and nasty, I've almost hated him!

RICHARD: And you don't realize what I've been through for you – and what I'm in for – for sneaking out – [*Then darkly*] And for what I did last night – what your letter made me do!

MURIEL [*made terribly curious by his ominous tone*]: What did my letter make you do?

RICHARD [*beginning to glory in this*]: It's too long a story – and let the dead past bury its dead. [*Then with real feeling*] Only it isn't past, I can tell you! What I'll catch when Pa gets hold of me!

MURIEL: Tell me, Dick! Begin at the beginning and tell me!

RICHARD [*tragically*]: Well, after your old – your father left our place I caught holy hell from Pa.

MURIEL: Dick! You mustn't swear!

RICHARD [*sombrely*]: Hell is the only word that can describe it. And on top of that, to torture me more, he gave me your letter. After I'd read that I didn't want to live any more. Life seemed like a tragic farce.

MURIEL: I'm so awful sorry, Dick – honest I am! But you might have known I'd never write that unless –

RICHARD: I thought your love for me was dead. I thought you'd never loved me, that you'd only been cruelly mocking me – to torture me!

MURIEL: Dick! I'd never! You know I'd never!

RICHARD: I wanted to die. I sat and brooded about death. Finally I made up my mind I'd kill myself.

MURIEL [*excitedly*]: Dick! You didn't!

RICHARD: I did, too! If there'd been one of Hedda Gabler's pistols around, you'd have seen if I wouldn't have done it beautifully! I thought, when I'm dead, she'll be sorry she ruined my life!

MURIEL [*cuddling up a little to him*]: If you ever had! I'd have died, too! Honest, I would!

RICHARD: But suicide is the act of a coward. That's what stopped me. [*Then with a bitter change of tone*] And anyway, I thought to myself, she isn't worth it.

MURIEL [*huffily*]: That's a nice thing to say!

RICHARD: Well, if you meant what was in that letter, you wouldn't have been worth it, would you?

MURIEL: But I've told you Pa –

RICHARD: So I said to myself, I'm through with women; they're all alike!

MURIEL: I'm not

RICHARD: And I thought, what difference does it make what I do now? I might as well forget her and lead the pace that kills, and drown my sorrows! You know I had eleven dollars saved up to buy you something for your birthday, but I thought, she's dead to me now and why shouldn't I throw it away? [*Then hastily*] I've still got almost five left, Muriel, and I can get you something nice with that.

MURIEL [*excitedly*]: What do I care about your old presents? You tell me what you did!

RICHARD [*darkly again*]: After it was dark, I sneaked out and went to a low dive I know about.

MURIEL: Dick Miller, I don't believe you ever!

RICHARD: You ask them at the Pleasant Beach House if I didn't! They won't forget me in a hurry!

MURIEL [*impressed and horrified*]: You went there? Why, that's a terrible place! Pa says it ought to be closed by the police!

RICHARD [*darkly*]: I said it was a dive, didn't I? It's a 'secret house of shame'. And they let me into a secret room behind the bar-room. There wasn't anyone there but a Princeton Senior I know – he belongs to Tiger Inn and he's full-back on the football team – and he had two chorus girls from New York with him, and they were all drinking champagne.

MURIEL [*disturbed by the entrance of the chorus girls*]: Dick Miller! I hope you didn't notice –

RICHARD [*carelessly*]: I had a highball by myself and then I noticed one of the girls – the one that wasn't with the full-back – looking at me. She had strange-looking eyes. And then she asked me if I wouldn't drink champagne with them and come and sit with her.

MURIEL: She must have been a nice thing! [*Then a bit falteringly*] And did – you?

RICHARD [*with tragic bitterness*]: Why shouldn't I, when you'd told me in that letter you'd never see me again?

MURIEL [*almost tearfully*]: But you ought to have known Pa made me –

RICHARD: I didn't know that then. [*Then rubbing it in*] Her name was Belle. She had yellow hair – the kind that burns and stings you!

MURIEL: I'll bet it was dyed!

RICHARD: She kept smoking one cigarette after another – but that's nothing for a chorus girl.

MURIEL [*indignantly*]: She was low and bad, that's what she was or she couldn't be a chorus girl, and her smoking cigarettes proves it! [*Then falteringly again*] And then what happened?

RICHARD [*carelessly*]: Oh, we just kept drinking champagne – I bought a round – and then I had a fight with the barkeep and knocked him down because he'd insulted her. He was a great big thug but –

MURIEL [*huffily*]: I don't see how he could – insult that kind! And why did you fight for her? Why didn't the Princeton full-back who'd brought them there? He must have been bigger than you.

RICHARD [*stopped for a moment – then quickly*]: He was too drunk by that time.

MURIEL: And were you drunk?

RICHARD: Only a little then. I was worse later. [*Proudly*] You ought to have seen me when I got home! I was on the verge of delirium tremens!

MURIEL: I'm glad I didn't see you. You must have been awful. I hate people who get drunk. I'd have hated you!

RICHARD: Well, it was all your fault, wasn't it? If you hadn't written that letter –

MURIEL: But I've told you I didn't mean – [*Then faltering but fascinated*] But what happened with that Belle – after – before you went home?

RICHARD: Oh, we kept drinking champagne and she said she'd fallen in love with me at first sight and she came and sat on my lap and kissed me.

MURIEL [*stiffening*]: Oh!

RICHARD [*quickly, afraid he has gone too far*]: But it was only all in fun, and then we just kept on drinking champagne, and finally I said good night and came home.

MURIEL: And did you kiss her?

RICHARD: No, I didn't.

MURIEL [*distractedly*]: You did, too! You're lying and you know it. You did, too! [*Then tearfully*] And there I was right at that time lying in bed not able to sleep, wondering how I was ever going to see you again and crying my eyes out, while you – ! [*She suddenly jumps to her feet in a tearful fury.*] I hate you! I wish you were dead! I'm going home this minute! I never want to lay eyes on you again! And this time I mean it!

[*She tries to jump out of the boat, but he holds her back. All the pose has dropped from him now and he is in a frightened state of contrition.*]

RICHARD [*imploringly*]: Muriel! Wait! Listen!

MURIEL: I don't want to listen! Let me go! If you don't I'll bite your hand!

RICHARD: I won't let you go! You've got to let me explain! I never – ! Ouch!

[*For* MURIEL *has bitten his hand and it hurts, and, stung by the pain, he lets go instinctively, and she jumps quickly out of the boat and starts running toward the path.* RICHARD *calls after her with bitter despair and hurt.*]

All right! Go if you want to – if you haven't the decency to let me explain! I hate you, too! I'll go and see Belle!

MURIEL [*seeing he isn't following her, stops at the foot of the path – defiantly*]: Well, go and see her – if that's the kind of girl you like! What do I care? [*Then as he only stares before him broodingly, sitting dejectedly in the stern of the boat, a pathetic figure of injured grief*] You can't explain! What can you explain? You owned up you kissed her!

RICHARD: I did not. I said she kissed me.

MURIEL [*scornfully, but drifting back a step in his direction*]: And I suppose you just sat and let yourself be kissed! Tell that to the Marines!

RICHARD [*injuredly*]: All right! If you're going to call me a liar every word I say –

MURIEL [*drifting back another step*]: I didn't call you a liar. I only meant – it sounds fishy. Don't you know it does?

RICHARD: I don't know anything. I only know I wish I was dead!

MURIEL [*gently reproving*]: You oughtn't to say that. It's wicked. [*Then after a pause*] And I suppose you'll tell me you didn't fall in love with her?

RICHARD [*scornfully*]: I should say not! Fall in love with that kind of girl! What do you take me for?

MURIEL [*practically*]: How do you know what you did if you drank so much champagne?

RICHARD: I kept my head – with her. I'm not a sucker, no matter what you think!

MURIEL [*drifting nearer*]: Then you didn't – love her?

RICHARD: I hated her! She wasn't even pretty! And I had a fight with her before I left, she got so fresh. I told her I loved you and never could love anyone else, and for her to leave me alone.

MURIEL: But you said just now you were going to see her –

RICHARD: That was only bluff. I wouldn't – unless you left me. Then I wouldn't care what I did – any more than I did last night. [*Then suddenly defiant*] And what if I did kiss her once or twice? I only did it to get back at you!

MURIEL: Dick!

RICHARD: You're a fine one to blame me – when it was all your fault! Why can't you be fair? Didn't I think you were out of my life for ever? Hadn't you written me you were? Answer me that!

MURIEL: But I've told you a million times that Pa –

RICHARD: Why didn't you have more sense than to let him make you write it? Was it my fault you didn't?

MURIEL: It was your fault for being so stupid! You ought to have known he stood right over me and told me each word to write. If I'd refused, it would only have made everything worse. I had to pretend, so I'd get a chance to see you. Don't you see, Silly? And I had sand enough to sneak out to meet you tonight, didn't I? [*He doesn't answer. She moves nearer.*] Still I can see how you felt the way you did – and maybe I am to blame for that. So I'll forgive and forget, Dick – if you'll swear to me you didn't even think of loving that –

RICHARD [*eagerly*]: I didn't! I swear, Muriel. I couldn't. I love you!

MURIEL: Well, then – I still love you.

RICHARD: Then come back here, why don't you?

MURIEL [*coyly*]: It's getting late.

RICHARD: It's not near half past yet.

MURIEL [*comes back and sits down by him shyly*]: All right – only I'll have to go soon, Dick. [*He puts his arm around her. She cuddles up close to him.*] I'm sorry – I hurt your hand.

RICHARD: That was nothing. It felt wonderful – even to have you bite!

MURIEL [*impulsively takes his hand and kisses it*]: There! That'll cure it. [*She is overcome by confusion at her boldness.*]

RICHARD: You shouldn't – waste that – on my hand. [*Then tremblingly*] You said – you'd let me –

MURIEL: I said, maybe.

RICHARD: Please, Muriel. You know – I want it so!

MURIEL: Will it wash off – her kisses – make you forget you ever – for always?

RICHARD: I should say so! I'd never remember – anything but it – never want anything but it – ever again.

MURIEL [*shyly lifting her lips*]: Then – all right – Dick. [*He kisses her tremblingly and for a moment their lips remain together.*

Then she lets her head sink on his shoulder and sighs softly.] The moon *is* beautiful, isn't it?

RICHARD [*kissing her hair*]: Not as beautiful as you! Nothing is! [*Then after a pause*] Won't it be wonderful when we're married?

MURIEL: Yes – but it's so long to wait.

RICHARD: Perhaps I needn't go to Yale. Perhaps Pa will give me a job. Then I'd soon be making enough to –

MURIEL: You better do what your Pa thinks best – and I'd like you to be at Yale. [*Then patting his face*] Poor you! Do you think he'll punish you awful?

RICHARD [*intensely*]: I don't know and I don't care! Nothing would have kept me from seeing you tonight – not if I'd had to crawl over red-hot coals! [*Then falling back on Swinburne – but with passionate sincerity*] You have my being between the hands of you! You are 'my love, mine own soul's heart, more dear than mine own soul, more beautiful than God!'

MURIEL [*shocked and delighted*]: Ssshh! It's wrong to say that.

RICHARD [*adoringly*]: Gosh, but I love you! Gosh, I love you – Darling!

MURIEL: I love you, too – Sweetheart!

[*They kiss. Then she lets her head sink on his shoulder again and they both sit in a rapt trance, staring at the moon.*]

[*After a pause* – [Where'll we go on our honeymoon, Dick? To Niagara Falls?

RICHARD [*scornfully*]: That dump where all the silly fools go? I should say not! [*With passionate romanticism*] No, we'll go to some far-off wonderful place! [*He calls on Kipling to help him.*] Somewhere out on the Long Trail – the trail that is always new – on the road to Mandalay! We'll watch the dawn come up like thunder out of China!

MURIEL [*hazily but happily*]: That'll be wonderful, won't it?

CURTAIN

SCENE 3

The sitting-room of the Miller house again – about ten o'clock the same night.

[MILLER *is sitting in his rocker at left, front, of table, his wife in the rocker at right, front, of table. Moonlight shines through the screen door at right, rear. Only the green-shaded reading lamp is lit and by its light* MILLER, *his specs on, is reading a book while his wife, sewing basket in lap, is working industriously on a doily.* MRS MILLER'S *face wears an expression of unworried content.* MILLER'S *face has also lost its look of harassed preoccupation, although he still is a prey to certain misgivings, when he allows himself to think of them. Several books are piled on the table by his elbow, the books that have been confiscated from* RICHARD.]

MILLER [*chuckles at something he reads – then closes the book and puts it on the table.* MRS MILLER *looks up from her sewing*]: This Shaw's a comical cuss – even if his ideas are so crazy they oughtn't to allow them to be printed. And that Swinburne's got a fine swing to his poetry – if he'd only choose some other subjects besides loose women.

MRS MILLER [*smiling teasingly*]: I can see where you're becoming corrupted by those books, too – pretending to read them out of duty to Richard, when your nose has been glued to the page!

MILLER: No, no – but I've got to be honest. There's something to them. That Rubaiyat of Omar Khayyám, now. I read that over again and liked it even better than I had before – parts of it that is, where it isn't all about boozing.

MRS MILLER [*has been busy with her own thoughts during this last – with a deep sigh of relief*]: My, but I'm glad Mildred told me where Richard went off to. I'd have worried my heart out if she hadn't. But now, it's all right.

MILLER [*frowning a little*]: I'd hardly go so far as to say that.

Just because we know he's all right tonight doesn't mean last night is wiped out. He's still got to be punished for that.

MRS MILLER [*defensively*]: Well, if you ask me, I think after the way I punished him all day, and the way I know he's punished himself, he's had about all he deserves. I've told you how sorry he was, and how he said he'd never touch liquor again. It didn't make him feel happy like Sid, but only sad and sick, so he didn't see anything in it for him.

MILLER: Well, if he's really got that view of it driven into his skull, I don't know but I'm glad it all happened. That'll protect him more than a thousand lectures – just horse sense about himself. [*Then frowning again*] Still, I can't let him do such things and go scot-free. And then; besides, there's another side to it – [*He stops abruptly.*]

MRS MILLER [*uneasily*]: What do you mean, another side?

MILLER [*hastily*]: I mean, discipline. There's got to be some discipline in a family. I don't want him to get the idea he's got a stuffed shirt at the head of the table. No, he's got to be punished, if only to make the lesson stick in his mind, and I'm going to tell him he can't go to Yale, seeing he's so undependable.

MRS MILLER [*up in arms at once*]: Not go to Yale! I guess he can go to Yale! Every man of your means in town is sending his boys to college! What would folks think of you? You let Wilbur go, and you'd have let Lawrence, only he didn't want to, and you're letting Arthur! If our other children can get the benefit of a college education, you're not going to pick on Richard –

MILLER: Hush up, for God's sake! If you'd let me finish what I started to say! I said I'd *tell* him that now – bluff – then later on I'll change my mind, if he behaves himself.

MRS MILLER: Oh well, if that's all – [*Then defensively again*] But it's your duty to give him every benefit. He's got an exceptional brain, that boy has! He's proved it by the way he likes to read all those deep plays and books and poetry.

MILLER: But I thought you – [*He stops, grinning helplessly.*]

MRS MILLER: You, thought I what?

MILLER: Never mind.

MRS MILLER [*sniffs, but thinks it better to let this pass*]: You mark my words, that boy's going to turn out to be a great lawyer, or a great doctor, or a great writer, or –

MILLER [*grinning*]: You agree he's going to be great, anyway.

MRS MILLER: Yes, I most certainly have a lot of faith in Richard.

MILLER: Well, so have I, as far as that goes.

MRS MILLER [*after a pause – judicially*]: And as for his being in love with Muriel, I don't see but what it might work out real well. Richard could do worse.

MILLER: But I thought you had no use for her, thought she was stupid.

MRS MILLER: Well, so I did, but if she's good for Richard and he wants her – [*Then inconsequentially*] Ma used to say you weren't overbright, but she changed her mind when she saw I didn't care if you were or not.

MILLER [*not exactly pleased by this*]: Well, I've been bright enough to –

MRS MILLER [*going on as if he had not spoken*]: And Muriel's real cute-looking, I have to admit that. Takes after her mother. Alice Briggs was the prettiest girl before she married.

MILLER: Yes, and Muriel will get as big as a house after she's married, the same as her mother did. That's the trouble. A man never can tell what's he's letting himself in for – [*He stops, feeling his wife's eyes fixed on him with indignant suspicion.*]

MRS MILLER [*sharply*]: I'm not too fat and don't you say it!

MILLER: Who was talking about you?

MRS MILLER: And I'd rather have some flesh on my bones than be built like a string bean and bore a hole in a chair every time I sat down – like some people!

MILLER [*ignoring the insult – flatteringly*]: Why, no one'd ever call you fat, Essie. You're only plump, like a good figure ought to be.

MRS MILLER [*childishly pleased – gratefully giving tit for tat*]: Well, you're not skinny, either – only slender – and I think you've been putting on weight lately, too.

[*Having thus squared matters she takes up her sewing again. A pause. Then* MILLER *asks incredulously.*]

MILLER: You don't mean to tell me you're actually taking this Muriel crush of Richard's seriously, do you? I know it's a good thing to encourage right now but – pshaw, why, Richard'll probably forget all about her before he's away six months, and she'll have forgotten him.

MRS MILLER: Don't be so cynical. [*Then, after a pause, thoughtfully*] Well, anyway, he'll always have it to remember – no matter what happens after – and that's something.

MILLER: You bet that's something. [*Then with a grin*] You surprise me at times with your deep wisdom.

MRS MILLER: You don't give me credit for ever having common sense, that's why. [*She goes back to her sewing.*]

MILLER [*after a pause*]: Where'd you say Sid and Lily had gone off to?

MRS MILLER: To the beach to listen to the band. [*She sighs sympathetically.*] Poor Lily! Sid'll never change, and she'll never marry him. But she seems to get some queer satisfaction out of fussing over him like a hen that's hatched a duck – though Lord knows I wouldn't in her shoes!

MILLER: Arthur's up with Elsie Rand, I suppose?

MRS MILLER: Of course.

MILLER: Where's Mildred?

MRS MILLER: Out walking with her latest. I've forgot who it is. I can't keep track of them. [*She smiles.*]

MILLER [*smiling*]: Then, from all reports, we seem to be completely surrounded by love!

MRS MILLER: Well, we've had our share, haven't we? We don't have to begrudge it to our children. [*Then has a sudden thought*] But I've done all this talking about Muriel and Richard and clean forgot how wild old McComber was against it. But he'll get over that, I suppose.

MILLER [*with a chuckle*]: He has already. I ran into him upstreet this afternoon and he was meek as pie. He backed water and said he guessed I was right. Richard had just copied stuff out of books, and kids would be kids, and so on. So I came off my high horse a bit – but not too far – and I guess all that won't bother anyone any more. [*Then rubbing his hands together – with a boyish grin of pleasure*] And I told you about getting that business from Lawson, didn't I? It's been a good day, Essie – a darned good day!

[*From the hall beyond the front parlour the sound of the front door being opened and shut is heard.* MRS MILLER *leans forward to look, pushing her specs up.*]

MRS MILLER [*in a whisper*]: It's Richard.

MILLER [*immediately assuming an expression of becoming gravity*]: Hmm.

[*He takes off his spectacles and puts them back in their case and straightens himself in his chair.* RICHARD *comes slowly in from the front parlour. He walks like one in a trance, his eyes shining with a dreamy happiness, his spirit still too exalted to be conscious of his surroundings, or to remember the threatened punishment. He carries his straw hat dangling in his hand, quite unaware of its existence.*]

RICHARD [*dreamily, like a ghost addressing fellow shades*]: Hello.

MRS MILLER [*staring at him worriedly*]: Hello, Richard.

MILLER [*sizing him up shrewdly*]: Hello, Son.

[RICHARD *moves past his mother and comes to the far corner, left front, where the light is dimmest, and sits down on the sofa, and stares before him, his hat dangling in his hand.*]

MRS MILLER [*with frightened suspicion now*]: Goodness, he acts queer! Nat, you don't suppose he's been –

MILLER [*with a reassuring smile*]: No. It's love, not liquor, this time.

MRS MILLER [*only partly reassured – sharply*]: Richard! What's the matter with you? [*He comes to himself with a start. She goes on scoldingly.*] How many times have I told you to hang up your hat in the hall when you come in! [*He looks at his hat as if he were surprised at its existence. She gets up fussily and goes to him.*] Here. Give it to me. I'll hang it up for you this once. And what are you sitting over here in the dark for? Don't forget your father's been waiting to talk to you!

[*She comes back to the table and he follows her, still half in a dream, and stands by his father's chair.* MRS MILLER *starts for the hall with his hat.*]

MILLER [*quietly but firmly now*]: You better leave Richard and me alone for a while, Essie.

MRS MILLER [*turns to stare at him apprehensively*]: Well – all right. I'll go sit on the piazza. Call me if you want me. [*Then a bit pleadingly*] But you'll remember all I've said, Nat, won't you?

[MILLER *nods reassuringly. She disappears through the front parlour.* RICHARD, *keenly conscious of himself as the about-to-be-sentenced criminal by this time, looks guilty and a bit defiant, searches his father's expressionless face with uneasy side glances, and steels himself for what is coming.*]

MILLER [*casually, indicating Mrs Miller's rocker*]: Sit down Richard.

[RICHARD *slumps awkwardly into the chair and sits in a selfconscious, unnatural position.* MILLER *sizes him up keenly – then suddenly smiles and asks with quiet mockery.*]

Well, how are the vine leaves in your hair this evening?

RICHARD [*totally unprepared for this approach – shamefacedly mutters*]: I don't know, Pa.

MILLER: Turned out to be poison ivy, didn't they? [*Then kindly*] But you needn't look so alarmed. I'm not going to read you any temperance lecture. That'd bore me more than it would you. And, in spite of your damn foolishness last night, I'm still giving you credit for having brains.

So I'm pretty sure anything I could say to you you've already said to yourself.

RICHARD [*his head down – humbly*]: I know I was a darned fool.

MILLER [*thinking it well to rub in this aspect – disgustedly*]: You sure were – not only a fool but a downright, stupid, disgusting fool!

[RICHARD *squirms, his head still lower.*]

It was bad enough for you to let me and Arthur see you, but to appear like that before your mother and Mildred – ! And I wonder if Muriel would think you were so fine if she ever saw you as you looked and acted then. I think she'd give you your walking papers for keeps. And you couldn't blame her. No nice girl wants to give her love to a stupid drunk!

RICHARD [*writhing*]: I know, Pa.

MILLER [*after a pause – quietly*]: All right. Then that settles – the booze end of it. [*He sizes* RICHARD *up searchingly – then suddenly speaks sharply.*] But there is another thing that's more serious. How about that tart you went to bed with at the Pleasant Beach House?

RICHARD [*flabbergasted – stammers*]: You know – ? But I didn't! If they've told you about her down there, they must have told you I didn't! She wanted me to – but I wouldn't. I gave her the five dollars just so she'd let me out of it. Honest Pa, I didn't! She made everything seem rotten and dirty – and – I didn't want to do a thing like that to Muriel – no matter how bad I thought she'd treated me – even after I felt drunk, I didn't. Honest!

MILLER: How'd you happen to meet this lady, anyway?

RICHARD: I can't tell that, Pa. I'd have to snitch on someone – and you wouldn't want me to do that.

MILLER [*a bit taken aback*]: No. I suppose I wouldn't. Hmm. Well, I believe you – and I guess that settles that. [*Then, after a quick, furtive glance at* RICHARD, *he nerves himself for the ordeal and begins with a shamefaced, selfconscious solemnity.*] But listen here, Richard, it's about time you and I had a serious talk about – hmm – certain matters pertaining to – and now that the subject's come up of its own accord, it's good time – I mean, there's no use in procrastinating further – so, here goes.

[*But it doesn't go smoothly and as he goes on he becomes more and more guiltily embarrassed and selfconscious and his expressions more stilted.* RICHARD *sedulously avoids even glancing at him, his own embarrassment made tenfold more painful by his father's.*]

Richard, you have now come to the age when – Well, you're a fully developed man, in a way, and it's only natural for you to have certain desires of the flesh, to put it that way – I mean, pertaining to the opposite sex – certain natural feelings and temptations – that'll want to be gratified – and you'll want to gratify them. Hmm – well, human society being organized as it is, there's only one outlet for – unless you're a scoundrel and go around ruining decent girls – which you're not, of course. Well, there are a certain class of women – always have been and always will be as long as human nature is what it is – It's wrong, maybe, but what can you do about it? I mean, girls like that one you – girls there's something doing with – and lots of 'em are pretty, and it's human nature if you – But that doesn't mean to ever get mixed up with them seriously! You just have what you want and pay 'em and forget it. I know that sounds hard and unfeeling, but we're talking facts and – But don't think I'm encouraging you to – If you can stay away from 'em, all the better – but if – why – hmm – Here's what I'm driving at, Richard. They're apt to be whited sepulchres – I mean, your whole life might be ruined if – so, darn it, you've got to know how to – I mean, there are ways and means – [*Suddenly he can go no farther and winds up helplessly.*] But, hell, I suppose you boys talk all this over among yourselves and you know more about it than I do. I'll admit I'm no authority. I never had anything to do with such women, and it'll be a hell of a lot better for you if you never do!

RICHARD [*without looking at him*]: I'm never going to, Pa. [*Then shocked indignation coming into his voice*] I don't see how you could think I could – now – when you know I love Muriel and am going to marry her. I'd die before I'd – !

MILLER [*immensely relieved – enthusiastically*]: That's the talk! By God, I'm proud of you when you talk like that! [*Then hastily*] And now that's all of that. There's nothing more to say and we'll forget it, eh?

RICHARD [*after a pause*]: How are you going to punish me, Pa?

MILLER: I *was* sort of forgetting that, wasn't I? Well, I'd thought of telling you you couldn't go to Yale –

RICHARD [*eagerly*]: Don't I have to go? Gee, that's great! Muriel thought you'd want me to. I was telling her I'd rather you gave me a job on the paper because then she and I could get married sooner. [*Then with a boyish grin*] Gee, Pa, you picked a lemon. That isn't any punishment. You'll have to do something besides that.

MILLER [*grimly – but only half concealing an answering grin*]: Then you'll go to Yale and you'll stay there till you graduate, that's the answer to that! Muriel's got good sense and you haven't! [RICHARD *accepts this philosophically.*] And now we're finished, you better call your mother.

[RICHARD *opens the screen door and calls* 'Ma', *and a moment later she comes in. She glances quickly from son to husband and immediately knows that all is well and tactfully refrains from all questions.*]

MRS MILLER: My, it's a beautiful night. The moon's way down low – almost setting.

[*She sits in her chair contentedly.* RICHARD *remains standing by the door, staring out at the moon, his face pale in the moonlight.*]

MILLER [*with a nod at* RICHARD, *winking at his wife*]: Yes, I don't believe I've hardly ever seen such a beautiful night – with such a wonderful moon. Have you, Richard?

RICHARD [*turning to them – enthusiastically*]: No! It was wonderful – down at the beach – [*He stops abruptly, smiling shyly.*]

MILLER [*watching his son – after a pause – quietly*]: I can only remember a few nights that were as beautiful as this – and they were long ago, when your mother and I were young and planning to get married.

RICHARD [*stares at him wonderingly for a moment, then quickly from his father to his mother and back again, strangely, as if he'd never seen them before – then he looks almost disgusted and swallows as if an acrid taste had come into his mouth – but then suddenly his face is transfigured by a smile of shy understanding and sympathy. He speaks shyly*]: Yes, I'll bet those must have been wonderful nights, too. You sort of forget the moon was the same way back then – and everything.

MILLER [*huskily*]: You're all right, Richard. [*He gets up and blows his nose.*]

MRS MILLER [*fondly*]: You're a good boy, Richard.

[RICHARD *looks dreadfully shy and embarrassed at this. His father comes to his rescue.*]

MILLER: Better get to bed early tonight, Son, hadn't you?

RICHARD: I couldn't sleep. Can't I go out on the piazza and sit for a while – until the moon sets?

MILLER: All right. Then you better say good night now. I don't know about your mother, but I'm going to bed right away. I'm dead tired.

MRS MILLER: So am I.

RICHARD [*goes to her and kisses her*]: Good night, Ma.

MRS MILLER: Good night. Don't you stay up till all hours now.

RICHARD [*comes to his father and stands awkwardly before him*]: Good night, Pa.

MILLER [*puts his arm around him and gives him a hug*]: Good-night, Richard.

[RICHARD *turns impulsively and kisses him – then hurries out the screen door.* MILLER *stares after him – then says huskily.*]

First time he's done that in years. I don't believe in kissing between fathers and sons after a certain age – seems mushy and silly – but that meant something! And I don't think we'll ever have to worry about his being safe – from himself – again. And I guess no matter what life will do to him, he can take care of it now. [*He sighs with satisfaction and, sitting down in his chair, begins to unlace his shoes.*] My darned feet are giving me fits.

MRS MILLER [*laughing*]: Why do you bother unlacing your shoes now, you big goose – when we're going right up to bed?

MILLER [*as if he hadn't thought of that before, stops*]: Guess you're right. [*Then getting to his feet – with a grin*] Mind if I don't say my prayers tonight, Essie? I'm certain God knows I'm too darned tired.

MRS MILLER: Don't talk that way. It's real sinful. [*She gets up – then laughing fondly.*] If that isn't you all over! Always looking for an excuse to – You're worse than Tommy! But all right. I suppose tonight you needn't. You've had a hard day. [*She puts her hand on the reading lamp switch.*] I'm going to turn out the light. All ready?

MILLER: Yep. Let her go, Gallagher. [*She turns out the lamp. In the ensuing darkness the faint moonlight shines full in through the screen door. Walking together toward the front parlour they stand full in it for a moment, looking out.* MILLER *puts his arm around her. He says in a low voice.*] There he is – like a statue of Love's Young Dream. [*Then he sighs and speaks with a gentle nostalgic melancholy.*] What's it that Rubaiyat says:

'Yet Ah, that Spring should vanish with the Rose!

That Youth's sweet-scented manuscript should close!'

[*Then throwing off his melancholy, with a loving smile at her*]

Well, spring isn't everything, is it, Essie? There's a lot to be said for autumn. That's got beauty, too. And winter – if you're together.

MRS MILLER [*simply*]: Yes, Nat.

[*She kisses him and they move quietly out of the moonlight, back into the darkness of the front parlour.*]

CURTAIN

THE HAIRY APE

A Comedy of Ancient and Modern Life

CHARACTERS

Robert Smith, 'Yank'
Paddy
Long
Mildred Douglas
Her Aunt
Second Engineer
A Guard
A Secretary of an Organization
Stokers, Ladies, Gentlemen, etc.

Time – The Modern

SCENE ONE

The firemen's forecastle of a transatlantic liner an hour after sailing from New York for the voyage across. Tiers of narrow, steel bunks, three deep, on all sides. An entrance in rear. Benches on the floor before the bunks. The room is crowded with men, shouting, cursing, laughing, singing – a confused, inchoate uproar swelling into a sort of unity, a meaning – the bewildered, furious, baffled defiance of a beast in a cage. Nearly all the men are drunk. Many bottles are passed from hand to hand. All are dressed in dungaree trousers and heavy ugly shoes. Some wear vests, but the majority are stripped to the waist.

The treatment of this scene, or of any other scene in the play, should by no means be naturalistic. The effect sought after is a cramped space in the bowels of a ship, imprisoned by white steel. The lines of bunks, the uprights supporting them, cross each other like the steel framework of a cage. The ceiling crushes down upon the men's heads. They cannot stand upright. This accentuates the natural stooping posture which shovelling coal and the resultant over-development of back and shoulders muscles have given them. The men themselves should resemble those pictures in which the appearance of Neanderthal Man is guessed at. All are hairy-chested, with long arms of tremendous power, and low, receding brows above their small, fierce, resentful eyes. All the civilized white races are represented, but except for the slight differentiation in colour of hair, skin, eyes, all these men are alike.

[*The curtain rises on a tumult of sound.* YANK *is seated in the foreground. He seems broader, fiercer, more truculent, more powerful, more sure of himself than the rest. They respect his superior strength – the grudging respect of fear. Then, too, he represents to them a self-expression, the very last word in what they are, their most highly developed individual.*]

VOICES: Gif me trink dere, you!
'Ave a wet!
Salute!
Gesundheit!
Skoal!
Drunk as a lord, God stiffen you!
Here's how!
Luck!
Pass back that bottle, damn you!
Pourin' it down his neck!
Ho, Froggy! Where the devil have you been?
La Touraine.
I hit him smash in yaw, py Gott!
Jenkins – the First – he's a rotten swine –
And the coppers nabbed him – and I run –
I like peer better. It don't pig head gif you.
A slut, I'm sayin'! She robbed me aslape –
To hell with 'em all!
You're a bloody liar!
Say dot again! [*Commotion. Two men about to fight are pulled apart.*]
No scrappin' now!
Tonight –
See who's the best man!
Bloody Dutchman!
Tonight on the for'ard square.
I'll bet on Dutchy.
He packa da wallop, I tella you!
Shut up, Wop!
No fightin', maties. We're all chums, ain't we?

[*A voice starts bawling a song.*]

'Beer, beer, glorious beer!
Fill yourselves right up to here.'

YANK [*for the first time seeming to take notice of the uproar about him, turns around threateningly – in a tone of contemptuous authority*]: Choke off dat noise! Where d'yuh get dat beer stuff? Beer, hell! Beer's for goils – and Dutchmen. Me for somep'n wit a kick to it! Gimme a drink, one of youse guys. [*Several bottles are eagerly offered. He takes a tremendous gulp at one of them; then, keeping the bottle in his hand, glares belligerently at the owner, who hastens to acquiesce in this robbery by saying:*] All right-o, Yank. Keep it and have another. [YANK *contemptuously turns his back on the crowd again. For a second there is an embarrassed silence. Then –*]

VOICES: We must be passing the Hook.
She's beginning to roll to it.
Six days in hell – and then Southampton.
Py Yesus, I vish somepody take my first vatch for me!
Gittin' seasick, Square-head?
Drink up and forget it!
What's in your bottle?
Gin.
Dot's nigger trink.
Absinthe? It's doped. You'll go off your chump, Froggy!
Cochon!
Whisky, that's the ticket!
Where's Paddy?
Going asleep.
Sing us that whisky song, Paddy.

[*They all turn to an old, wizened Irishman who is dozing, very drunk, on the benches forward. His face is extremely monkey-like with all the sad, patient pathos of that animal in his small eyes.*]

Singa da song, Caruso Pat!
He's gettin' old. The drink is too much for him.
He's too drunk.

PADDY [*blinking about him, starts to his feet resentfully, swaying, holding on to the edge of a bunk*]: I'm never too drunk to sing.

'Tis only when I'm dead to the world I'd be wishful to sing at all. [*With a sort of sad contempt*] 'Whisky, Johnny', ye want? A chanty, ye want? Now, that's a queer wish from the ugly like of you, God help you. But no matther. [*He starts to sing in a thin, nasal, doleful tone:*]

Oh, whisky is the life of man!
  Whisky! O Johnny! [*They all join in on this.*]
Oh, whisky is the life of man!
  Whisky for my Johnny! [*Again chorus.*]
Oh, whisky drove my old man mad!
  Whisky! O Johnny!
Oh, whisky drove my old man mad!
  Whisky for my Johnny!

YANK [*again turning around scornfully*]: Aw hell! Nix on dat old sailing-ship stuff! All dat bull's dead, see? And you're dead, too, yuh damned old Harp, on'y yuh don't know it. Take it easy, see. Give us a rest. Nix on de loud noise. [*With a cynical grin*] Can't youse see I'm tryin' to tink?

ALL [*repeating the word after him as one with the same cynical amused mockery*]: Think! [*The chorused word has a brazen, metallic quality, as if their throats were phonograph horns. It is followed by a general uproar of hard, barking laughter.*]

VOICES: Don't be cracking your head wid ut, Yank.
You gat headache, py yingo!
One thing about it – it rhymes with drink!
Ha, ha, ha!
Drink, don't think!
Drink, don't think!
Drink, don't think!

[*A whole chorus of voices has taken up this refrain, stamping on the floor, pounding on the benches with fists.*]

YANK [*taking a gulp from his bottle – good-naturedly*]: Aw right. Can de noise. I got yuh de foist time. [*The uproar subsides. A very drunken sentimental tenor begins to sing:*]

'Far away in Canada,
Far across the sea,
There's a lass who fondly waits
Making a home for me – '

YANK [*fiercely contemptuous*]: Shut up, yuh lousey boob! Where d'yuh get dat tripe? Home? Home, hell! I'll make a home for yuh! I'll knock yuh dead. Home! T'hell wit home! Where d'yuh get dat tripe? Dis is home, see? What d'yuh want wit home? [*Proudly*] I runned away from mine when I was a kid. On'y too glad to beat it, dat was me. Home was lickings for me, dat's all. But yuh can bet your shoit no one ain't never licked me since! Wanter try it, any of youse? Huh! I guess not. [*In a more placated but still contemptuous tone*] Goils waitin' for yuh, huh? Aw, hell! Dat's all tripe. Dey don't wait for no one. Dey'd double-cross yuh for a nickel. Dey're all tarts, get me? Treat 'em rough, dat's me. To hell wit 'em. Tarts, dat's what, de whole bunch of 'em.

LONG [*very drunk, jumps on a bench excitedly, gesticulating with a bottle in his hand*]: Listen 'ere, Comrades! Yank 'ere is right. 'E says this 'ere stinkin' ship is our 'ome. And 'e says as 'ome is 'ell. And 'e's right! This is 'ell. We lives in 'ell, Comrades – and right enough we'll die in it. [*Raging*] And who's ter blame, I arsks yer? We ain't. We wasn't born this rotten way. All men is born free and ekal. That's in the bleedin' Bible, maties. But what d'they care for the Bible – them lazy, bloated swine what travels first cabin? Them's the ones. They dragged us down till we're on'y wage slaves in the bowels of a bloody ship, sweatin', burnin' up, eatin' coal-dust! Hit's them's ter blame – the damned capitalist clarss! [*There had been a gradual murmur of contemptuous resentment rising among the men until now he is interrupted by a storm of catcalls, hisses, boos, hard laughter.*]

VOICES: Turn it off!
Shut up!

Sit down!
Closa da face!
Tamn fool! [*Etc.*]

YANK [*standing up and glaring at* LONG]: Sit down before I knock yuh down! [LONG *makes haste to efface himself.* YANK *goes on contemptuously.*] De Bible, huh? De Cap'tlist class, huh? Aw nix on dat Salvation Army-Socialist bull. Git a soap-box! Hire a hall! Come and be saved, huh? Jerk us to Jesus, huh? Aw g'wan! I've listened to lots of guys like you, see. Yuh're all wrong. Wanter know what I tink? Yuh ain't no good for no one. Yuh're de bunk. Yuh ain't got no noive, get me? Yuh're yellow, dat's what. Yellow, dat's you. Say! What's dem slobs in de foist cabin got to do wit us? We're better men dan dey are, ain't we? Sure! One of us guys could clean up de whole mob wit one mit. Put one of 'em down here for one watch in de stokehole, what'd happen? Dey'd carry him off on a stretcher. Dem boids don't amount to nothin'. Dey're just baggage. Who makes dis old tub run? Ain't it us guys? Well den, we belong, don't we? We belong and dey don't. Dat's all. [*A loud chorus of approval.* YANK *goes on*] As for dis bein' hell – aw, nuts! Yuh lost your noive, dat's what. Dis is a man's job, get me? It belongs. It runs dis tub. No stiffs need apply. But yuh're a stiff, see? Yuh're yellow, dat's you.

VOICES [*with a great hard pride in them*]:

Right-o!
A man's job!
Talk is cheap, Long.
He never could hold up his end.
Divil take him!
Yank's right. We make it go.
Py Gott, Yank say right ting!
We don't need no one cryin' over us.
Makin' speeches.
Throw him out!

Yellow!
Chuck him overboard!
I'll break his jaw for him!

[*They crowd around* LONG *threateningly.*]

YANK [*half good-natured again – contemptuously*]: Aw, take it easy. Leave him alone. He ain't woith a punch. Drink up. Here's how, whoever owns dis. [*He takes a long swallow from his bottle. All drink with him. In a flash all is hilarious amiability again, back-slapping, loud talk, etc.*]

PADDY [*who has been sitting in a blinking, melancholy daze – suddenly cries out in a voice full of old sorrow*]: We belong to this, you're saying? We make the ship to go, you're saying? Yerra then, that Almighty God have pity on us! [*His voice runs into the wail of a keen, he rocks back and forth on his bench. The men stare at him, startled and impressed in spite of themselves.*] Oh, to be back in the fine days of my youth, ochone! Oh, there was fine beautiful ships them days – clippers wid tall masts touching the sky – fine strong men in them – men that was sons of the sea as if 'twas the mother that bore them. Oh, the clean skins of them, and the clear eyes, the straight backs and full chests of them! Brave men they was, and bold men surely! We'd be sailing out, bound down round the Horn maybe. We'd be making sail in the dawn, with a fair breeze, singing a chanty song wid no care to it. And astern the land would be sinking low and dying out, but we'd give it no heed but a laugh, and never a look behind. For the day that was, was enough, for we was free men – and I'm thinking 'tis only slaves do be giving heed to the day that's gone or the day to come – until they're old like me. [*With a sort of religious exaltation*] Oh, to be scudding south again wid the power of the Trade Wind driving her on steady through the nights and the days! Full sail on her! Nights and days! Nights when the foam of the wake would be flaming wid fire, when the sky'd be blazing and winking wid stars. Or the full of the moon maybe. Then you'd see her driving through the grey night, her sails stretching aloft all silver and white, not a sound on the deck, the lot of us dreaming dreams, till you'd believe 'twas no real ship at all you was on but a ghost ship like the Flying Dutchman they say does be roaming the seas for evermore widout touching a port. And there was the days, too. A warm sun on the clean decks. Sun warming the blood of you, and wind over the miles of shiny green ocean like strong drink to your lungs. Work – aye, hard work – but who'd mind that at all? Sure, you worked under the sky, and 'twas work wid skill and daring to it. And wid the day done, in the dog-watch, smoking me pipe at ease, the look out would be raising land, maybe, and we'd see the mountains of South Americy wid the red fire of the setting sun painting their white tops and the clouds floating by them! [*His tone of exaltation ceases. He goes on mournfully.*] Yerra, what's the use of talking? 'Tis a dead man's whisper. [*To* YANK *resentfully*] 'Twas them days men belonged to ships, not now. 'Twas them days a ship was part of the sea, and a man was part of a ship, and the sea joined all together and made it one. [*Scornfully*] Is it one wid this you'd be, Yank – black smoke from the funnels smudging the sea, smudging the decks – the bloody engines pounding and throbbing and shaking – wid divil a sight of sun or a breath of clean air – choking our lungs wid coal-dust – breaking our backs and hearts in the hell of the stokehole – feeding the bloody furnace – feeding our lives along wid the coal, I'm thinking – caged in by steel from a sight of the sky like bloody apes in the Zoo! [*With a harsh laugh*] Ho-ho, divil mend you! Is it to belong to that you're wishing? Is it a flesh and blood wheel of the engines you'd be?

YANK [*who has been listening with a contemptuous sneer, barks out the answer*]: Sure ting! Dat's me! What about it?

PADDY [*as if to himself – with great sorrow*]: Me time is past due. That a great wave wid sun in the heart of it may sweep me over the side sometime I'd be dreaming of the days that's gone!

YANK: Aw, yuh crazy Mick! [*He springs to his feet and advances on* PADDY *threateningly – then stops, fighting some queer struggle within himself – lets his hands fall to his sides – contemptuously*.] Aw, take it easy. Yuh're aw right at dat. Yuh're bugs, dat's all – nutty as a cuckoo. All dat tripe yuh been pullin' – Aw, dat's all right. On'y it's dead, get me? Yuh don't belong no more, see. Yuh don't get de stuff. Yuh're too old. [*Disgustedly*] But aw say, come up for air onct in a while, can't yuh? See what's happened since yuh croaked. [*He suddenly bursts forth vehemently, growing more and more excited*.] Say! Sure! Sure I meant it! What de hell – Say, lemme talk! Hey! Hey, you old Harp! Hey, youse guys! Say, listen to me – wait a moment – I gotter talk, see. I belong and he don't. He's dead but I'm livin'. Listen to me! Sure I'm part of de engines! Why de hell not! Dey move, don't dey? Dey're speed, ain't dey? Dey smash trou, don't dey? Twenty-five knots a' hour! Dat's going some! Dat's new stuff! Dat belongs! But him, he's too old. He gets dizzy. Say, listen. All dat crazy tripe about nights and days; all dat crazy tripe about stars and moons; all dat crazy tripe about suns and winds, fresh air and de rest of it – aw hell, dat's all a dope dream! Hittin' de pipe of de past, dat's what he's doin'. He's old and don't belong no more. But me, I'm young! I'm in de pink! I move wit it! It, get me! I mean de ting dat's de guts of all dis. It ploughs trou all de tripe he's been sayin'. It blows dat up! It knocks dat dead! It slams dat offen de face of de oith! It, get me! De engines and de coal and de smoke and all de rest of it! He can't breathe and swallow coal-dust, but I kin, see? Dat's fresh air for me! Dat's food for me! I'm new, get me? Hell in de stokehole? Sure! It takes a man to work in hell. Hell, sure, dat's my fav'rite climate. I eat it up! I git fat on it! It's me makes it hot! It's me makes it roar! It's me makes it move! Sure, on'y for me everyting stops. It all goes dead, get me? De noise and smoke and all de engines movin' de woild, dey stop. Dere ain't nothin' no more! Dat's what I'm sayin'. Everyting else dat makes de woild move, somep'n makes it move. I can't move witout somep'n else, see? Den yuh get down to me. I'm at de bottom, get me! Dere ain't nothin' foither. I'm de end! I'm de start! I start somep'n and de woild moves! It – dat's me! – de new dat's moiderin' de old! I'm de ting in coal dat makes it boin; I'm steam and oil for de engines; I'm de ting dat makes yuh hear it; I'm smoke and express trains and steamers and factory whistles; I'm de ting in gold dat makes it money! And I'm what makes iron into steel! Steel, dat stands for de whole ting! And I'm steel – steel – steel! I'm de muscles in steel, de punch behind it! [*As he says this he pounds with his fist against the steel bunks. All the men, roused to a pitch of frenzied self-glorification by his speech, do likewise. There is a deafening metallic roar, through which* YANK'S *voice can be heard bellowing.*] Slaves, hell! We run de whole woiks. All de rich guys dat tink dey're somep'n, dey ain't nothin'! Dey don't belong. But us guys, we're in de move, we're at de bottom, de whole ting is us! [PADDY *from the start of* YANK'S *speech has been taking one gulp after another from his bottle, at first frightenedly, as if he were afraid to listen, then desperately, as if to drown his senses, but finally has achieved complete indifferent, even amused, drunkenness.* YANK *sees his lips moving. He quells the uproar with a shout.*] Hey, youse guys, take it easy! Wait a moment! De nutty Harp is sayin' somep'n.

PADDY [*is heard now – throws his head back with a mocking burst of laughter*]: Ho-ho-ho-ho-ho –

YANK [*drawing back his fist, with a snarl*]: Aw! Look out who yuh're givin' the bark!

PADDY [*begins to sing the 'Miller of Dee' with enormous good nature*]:

'I care for nobody, no, not I,
And nobody cares for me.'

YANK [*good natured himself in a flash, interrupts* PADDY *with a slap on the bare back like a report*]: Dat's de stuff! Now yuh're getting' wise to somep'n. Care for nobody, dat's de dope! To hell wit 'em all! And nix on nobody else carin'. I kin care for myself, get me! [*Eight bells sound, muffled, vibrating through the steel walls as if some enormous brazen gong were embedded in the heart of the ship. All the men jump up mechanically, file through the door silently close upon each other's heels in what is very like a prisoners' lockstep.* YANK *slaps* PADDY *on the back.*] Our watch, yuh old Harp! [*Mockingly*] Come on down in hell. Eat up de coal-dust. Drink in de heat. It's it, see! Act like yuh liked it, yuh better – or croak yuhself.

PADDY [*with jovial defiance*]: To the divil wid it! I'll not report this watch. Let thim log me and be damned. I'm no slave the like of you. I'll be sittin' here at me ease, and drinking, and thinking, and dreaming dreams.

YANK [*contemptuously*]: T'inkin' and dreamin', what'll that get yuh? What's t'inkin' got to do wit it? We move, don't we? Speed, ain't it? Fog, dat's all you stand for. But we drive trou dat, don't we? We split dat up and smash trou – twenty-five knots a' hour! [*Turns his back on* PADDY *scornfully.*] Aw, yuh make me sick! Yuh don't belong! [*He strides out the door in rear.* PADDY *hums to himself, blinking drowsily.*]

CURTAIN

SCENE TWO

Two days out. A section of the promenade deck.

[MILDRED DOUGLAS *and her* AUNT *are discovered reclining in deck chairs. The former is a girl of twenty, slender, delicate, with a pale, pretty face marred by a self-conscious expression of disdainful superiority. She looks fretful, nervous, and discontented, bored by her own anaemia. Her* AUNT *is a pompous and proud – and fat – old lady. She is a type even to the point of a double chin and lorgnettes. She is dressed pretentiously, as if afraid her face alone would never indicate her position in life.* MILDRED *is dressed all in white.*

The impression to be conveyed by this scene is one of the beautiful, vivid life of the sea all about – sunshine on the deck in a great flood, the fresh sea wind blowing across it. In the midst of this, these two, incongruous, artificial figures, inert and disharmonious, the elder like a grey lump of dough touched up with rouge, the younger looking as if the vitality of her stock had been sapped before she was conceived, so that she is the expression not of its life energy but merely of the artificialities that energy had won for itself in the spending.]

MILDRED [*looking up with affected dreaminess*]: How the black smoke swirls back against the sky! Is it not beautiful?

AUNT [*without looking up*]: I dislike smoke of any kind.

MILDRED: My great-grandmother smoked a pipe – a clay pipe.

AUNT [*ruffling*]: Vulgar!

MILDRED: She was too distant a relative to be vulgar. Time mellows pipes.

AUNT [*pretending boredom but irritated*]: Did the sociology you took up at college teach you that – to play the ghoul on every possible occasion, excavating old bones? Why not let your great-grandmother rest in her grave?

MILDRED [*dreamily*]: With her pipe beside her – puffing in Paradise.

AUNT [*with spite*]: Yes, you are a natural born ghoul. You are even getting to look like one, my dear.

MILDRED [*in a passionless tone*]: I detest you, aunt. [*Looking at her critically*] Do you know what you remind me of? Of a cold pork pudding against a background of linoleum table-cloth in the kitchen of a – but the possibilities are wearisome. [*She closes her eyes.*]

AUNT [*with a bitter laugh*]: Merci for your candour. But since I am and must be your chaperon – in appearance, at least – let us patch up some sort of armed truce. For my part you are quite free to indulge any pose of eccentricity that beguiles you – as long as you observe the amenities –

MILDRED [*drawling*]: The inanities?

AUNT [*going on as if she hadn't heard*]: After exhausting the morbid thrills of social service work on New York's East Side – how they must have hated you, by the way, the poor that you made so much poorer in their own eyes! – you are now bent on making your slumming international. Well, I hope Whitechapel will provide the needed nerve tonic. Do not ask me to chaperon you there, however. I told your father I would not. I loathe deformity. We will hire an army of detectives and you may investigate everything – they allow you to see.

MILDRED [*protesting with a trace of genuine earnestness*]: Please do not mock at my attempts to discover how the other half lives. Give me credit for some sort of groping sincerity in that at least. I would like to help them. I would like to be some use in the world. Is it my fault I don't know how? I would like to be sincere, to touch life somewhere. [*With weary bitterness*] But I'm afraid I have neither the vitality nor integrity. All that was burnt out in our stock before I was born. Grandfather's blast furnaces, flaming to the sky, melting steel, making millions – then father keeping those home fires burning, making more millions – and little me at the tail end of it all. I'm a waste product in the Bessemer process – like the millions. Or rather, I inherit the acquired trait of the by-product, wealth, but none of the energy, none of the strength of the steel that made it. I am sired by gold and dammed by it, as they say at the race track – damned in more ways than one. [*She laughs mirthlessly.*]

AUNT [*unimpressed – superciliously*]: You seem to be going in for sincerity today. It isn't becoming to you, really – except as an obvious pose. Be as artificial as you are, I advise. There's a sort of sincerity in that, you know. And, after all, you must confess you like that better.

MILDRED [*again affected and bored*]: Yes, I suppose I do. Pardon me for my outburst. When a leopard complains of its spots, it must sound rather grotesque. [*In a mocking tone*] Purr, little leopard. Purr, scratch, tear, kill, gorge yourself, and be happy – only stay in the jungle where your spots are camouflage. In a cage they make you conspicuous.

AUNT: I don't know what you are talking about.

MILDRED: It would be rude to talk about anything to you. Let's just talk. [*She looks at her wrist watch.*] Well, thank goodness, it's about time for them to come for me. That ought to give me a new thrill, aunt.

AUNT [*affectedly troubled*]: You don't mean to say you're really going? The dirt – the heat must be frightful –

MILDRED: Grandfather started as a puddler. I should have inherited an immunity to heat that would make a salamander shiver. It will be fun to put it to the test.

AUNT: But don't you have to have the captain's – or some one's – permission to visit the stokehole?

MILDRED [*with a triumphant smile*]: I have it – both his and the chief engineer's. Oh, they didn't want to at first, in spite of my social service credentials. They didn't seem a bit anxious that I should investigate how the other half lives and works on a ship. So I had to tell them that my father, the president of Nazareth Steel, chairman of the board of directors of this line, had told me it would be all right.

AUNT: He didn't.

MILDRED: How naïve age makes one! But I said he did, aunt. I even said he had given me a letter to them – which I had lost. And they were afraid to take the chance that I might be lying. [*Excitedly*] So it's ho! for the stokehole. The second engineer is to escort me. [*Looking at her watch again*] It's time. And here he comes, I think.

[*The* SECOND ENGINEER *enters. He is a fine-looking man of thirty-five or so. He stops before the two and tips his cap, visibly embarrassed and ill at ease.*]

SECOND ENGINEER: Miss Douglas?

MILDRED: Yes. [*Throwing off her rugs and getting to her feet*] Are we all ready to start?

SECOND ENGINEER: In just a second, ma'am. I'm waiting for the Fourth. He's coming along.

MILDRED [*with a scornful smile*]: You don't care to shoulder this responsibility alone, is that it?

SECOND ENGINEER [*forcing a smile*]: Two are better than one. [*Disturbed by her eyes, glances out to sea – blurts out*] A fine day we're having.

MILDRED: Is it?

SECOND ENGINEER: A nice warm breeze –

MILDRED: It feels cold to me.

SECOND ENGINEER: But it's hot enough in the sun –

MILDRED: Not hot enough for me. I don't like Nature. I was never athletic.

SECOND ENGINEER [*forcing a smile*]: Well, you'll find it hot enough where you're going.

MILDRED: Do you mean hell?

SECOND ENGINEER [*flabbergasted, decides to laugh*]: Ho-ho! No, I mean the stokehole.

MILDRED: My grandfather was a puddler. He played with boiling steel.

SECOND ENGINEER [*all at sea – uneasily*]: Is that so? Hum, you'll excuse me, ma'am, but are you intending to wear that dress?

MILDRED: Why not?

SECOND ENGINEER: You'll likely rub against oil and dirt. It can't be helped.

MILDRED: It doesn't matter. I have lots of white dresses.

SECOND ENGINEER: I have an old coat you might throw over –

MILDRED: I have fifty dresses like this. I will throw this one into the sea when I come back. That ought to wash it clean, don't you think?

SECOND ENGINEER [*doggedly*]: There's ladders to climb down that are none too clean – and dark alley-ways –

MILDRED: I will wear this very dress and none other.

SECOND ENGINEER: No offence meant. It's none of my business. I was only warning you –

MILDRED: Warning? That sounds thrilling.

SECOND ENGINEER [*looking down the deck – with a sigh of relief*]: There's the Fourth now. He's waiting for us. If you'll come –

MILDRED: Go on. I'll follow you. [*He goes. Mildred turns a mocking smile on her aunt.*] An oaf – but a handsome, virile oaf.

AUNT [*scornfully*]: Poser!

MILDRED: Take care. He said there were dark alley-ways –

AUNT [*in the same tone*]: Poser!

MILDRED [*biting her lips angrily*]: You are right. But would that my millions were not so anaemically chaste!

AUNT: Yes, for a fresh pose I have no doubt you would drag the name of Douglas in the gutter!

MILDRED: From which it sprang. Good-bye, aunt. Don't pray too hard that I may fall into the fiery furnace.

AUNT: Poser!

MILDRED [*viciously*]: Old hag! [*She slaps her* AUNT *insultingly across the face and walks off, laughing gaily.*]

AUNT [*screams after her*]: I said poser!

CURTAIN

SCENE THREE

The stokehole. In the rear, the dimly-outlined bulks of the furnaces and boilers. High overhead one hanging electric bulb sheds just enough light through the murky air laden with coal-dust to pile up masses of shadows everywhere. A line of men, stripped to the waist, is before the furnace doors. They bend over, looking neither to right nor left, handling their shovels as if they were part of their bodies, with a strange, awkward, swinging rhythm. They use the shovels to throw open the furnace doors. Then from these fiery round holes in the black a flood of terrific light and heat pours full upon the men who are outlined in silhouette in the crouching, inhuman attitudes of chained gorillas. The men shovel with a rhythmic motion, swinging as on a pivot from the coal which lies in heaps on the floor behind to hurl it into the flaming mouths before them. There is a tumult of noise – the brazen clang of the furnace doors as they are flung open or slammed shut, the grating, teeth-gritting grind of steel against steel, of crunching coal. This clash of sounds stuns one's ears with its rending dissonance. But there is order in it, rhythm, a mechanical, regulated recurrence, a tempo. And rising above all, making the air hum with the quiver of liberated energy, the roar of leaping flames in the furnaces, the monotonous throbbing beat of the engines.

[*As the curtain rises, the furnace doors are shut. The men are taking a breathing spell. One or two are arranging the coal behind them, pulling it into more accessible heaps. The others can be dimly made out leaning on their shovels in relaxed attitudes of exhaustion.*]

PADDY [*from somewhere in the line – plaintively*]: Yerra, will this divil's own watch nivir end? Me back is broke. I'm destroyed entirely.

YANK [*from the centre of the line – with exuberant scorn*]: Aw, yuh make me sick! Lie down and croak, why don't yuh? Always beefin', dat's you! Say, dis is a cinch! Dis was made for me! It's my meat, get me! [*A whistle is blown – a thin, shrill note from somewhere overhead in the darkness.* YANK *curses without resentment.*] Dere's de damn engineer crackin' de whip. He tinks we're loafin'.

PADDY [*vindictively*]: God stiffen him!

YANK [*in an exultant tone of command*]: Come on, youse guys! Git into de game! She's gittin' hungry! Pile some grub in her! Trow it into her belly! Come on now, all of youse! Open her up! [*At this last all the men, who have followed his movements of getting into position, throw open their furnace doors with a deafening clang. The fiery light floods over their shoulders as they bend round for the coal. Rivulets of sooty sweat have traced maps on their backs. The enlarged muscles form bunches of high light and shadow.*]

YANK [*chanting a count as he shovels without seeming effort*]: One – two – three – [*His voice rising exultantly in the joy of battle*] Dat's de stuff! Let her have it! All togedder now! Sling it into her! Let her ride! Shoot de piece now! Call de toin on her. Drive her into it! Feel her move! Watch her smoke! Speed, dat's her middle name! Give her coal, youse guys! Coal, dat's her booze! Drink it up, baby! Let's see yuh sprint! Dig in and gain a lap! Dere she go-o-es. [*This last in the chanting formula of the gallery gods at the six-day bike race. He slams his furnace door shut. The others do likewise with as much unison as their wearied bodies will permit. The effect is of one fiery eye after another being blotted out with a series of accompanying bangs.*]

PADDY [*groaning*]: Me back is broke. I'm bate out – bate – [*There is a pause. Then the inexorable whistle sounds again from the dim regions above the electric light. There is a growl of cursing rage from all sides.*]

YANK [*shaking his fist upward – contemptuously*]: Take it easy dere, you! Who d'yuh tink's runnin' dis game, me or you?

When I git ready, we move. Not before! When I git ready, get me!

VOICES [*approvingly*]:

That's the stuff!
Yank tal him, py golly!
Yank ain't affeerd.
Goot poy, Yank!
Give him hell!
Tell 'im 'e's a bloody swine!
Bloody slave-driver!

YANK [*contemptuously*]: He ain't got no noive. He's yellow, get me? All de engineers is yellow. Dey got streaks a mile wide. Aw, to hell wit him! Let's move, youse guys. We had a rest. Come on, she needs it! Give her pep! It ain't for him. Him and his whistle, dey don't belong. But we belong, see! We gotter feed de baby! Come on!

[*He turns and flings his furnace door open. They all follow his lead. At this instant the* SECOND *and* FOURTH ENGINEERS *enter from the darkness on the left with* MILDRED *between them. She starts, turns paler, her pose is crumbling, she shivers with fright in spite of the blazing heat, but forces herself to leave the engineers and take a few steps nearer the men. She is right behind* YANK. *All this happens quickly while the men have their backs turned.*]

Come on, youse guys! [*He is turning to get coal when the whistle sounds again in a peremptory, irritating note. This drives* YANK *into a sudden fury. While the other men have turned full around and stopped dumbfounded by the spectacle of* MILDRED *standing there in her white dress,* YANK *does not turn far enough to see her. Besides, his head is thrown back, he blinks upward through the murk trying to find the owner of the whistle, he brandishes his shovel murderously over his head in one hand, pounding on his chest, gorilla-like, with the other, shouting:*] Toin off dat whistle! Come down outa dere, yuh yellow, brass-buttoned, Belfast scut, yuh! Come down and I'll knock yer brains out! Yuh lousey, stinkin', yellow mut of a Catholic-moiderin' bastard! Come down and I'll moider yuh! Pullin' dat whistle on me, huh? I'll show yuh! I'll crash yer skull in! I'll drive yer teet' down yer troat! I'll slam yer nose trou de back of yer head! I'll cut yer guts out for a nickel, yuh lousey boob, yuh dirty, crummy, muck-eatin' son of a – [*Suddenly he becomes conscious of all the other men staring at something directly behind his back. He whirls defensively with a snarling, murderous growl, crouching to spring, his lips drawn back over his teeth, his small eyes gleaming ferociously. He sees* MILDRED, *like a white apparition in the full light from the open furnace doors. He glares into her eyes, turned to stone. As for her, during his speech she has listened, paralysed with horror, terror, her whole personality crushed, beaten in, collapsed, by the terrific impact of this unknown, abysmal brutality, naked and shameless. As she looks at his gorilla face, as his eyes bore into hers, she utters a low, choking cry and shrinks away from him, putting both hands up before her eyes to shut out the sight of his face, to protect her own. This startles* YANK *to a reaction. His mouth falls open, his eyes grow bewildered.*]

MILDRED [*about to faint – to the* ENGINEERS, *who now have her one by each arm – whimperingly*]: Take me away! Oh, the filthy beast! [*She faints. They carry her quickly back, disappearing in the darkness at the left, rear. An iron door clangs shut. Rage and bewildered fury rush back on* YANK. *He feels himself insulted in some unknown fashion in the very heart of his pride. He roars:* God damn yuh! *And hurls his shovel after them at the door which has just closed. It hits the steel bulkhead with a clang and falls clattering on the steel floor. From overhead the whistle sounds again in a long, angry, insistent command.*]

CURTAIN

SCENE FOUR

The fireman's forecastle.

[YANK'S *watch has just come off duty and had dinner. Their faces and bodies shine from a soap and water scrubbing, but around their eyes, where a hasty dousing does not touch, the coal-dust sticks like black make-up, giving them a queer, sinister expression.* YANK *has not washed either face or body. He stands out in contrast to them, a blackened, brooding figure. He is seated forward on a bench in the exact attitude of Rodin's 'The Thinker'. The others, most of them smoking pipes, are staring at* YANK *half apprehensively, as if fearing an outburst; half amusedly, as if they saw a joke somewhere that tickled them.*]

VOICES: He aint ate nothin'.
Py golly, a fallar gat gat grub in him.
Divil a lie.
Yank feeds da fire, no feeda da face.
Ha-ha.
He ain't even washed hisself.
He's forgot.
Hey, Yank, you forgot to wash.

YANK [*sullenly*]: Forgot nothin'! To hell wit washin'.

VOICES: It'll stick to you.
It'll get under your skin.
Give yer the bleedin' itch, that's wot.
It makes spots on you – like a leopard.
Like a piebald nigger, you mean.
Better wash up, Yank.
You sleep better.
Wash up, Yank.
Wash up! Wash up!

YANK [*resentfully*]: Aw, say, youse guys. Lemme alone. Can't youse see I'm tryin' to tink?

ALL [*repeating the word after him as one with cynical mockery*]: Think! [*The word has a brazen metallic quality as if their throats were phonograph horns. It is followed by a chorus of hard, barking laughter.*]

YANK [*springing to his feet and glaring at them belligerently*]: Yes, tink! Tink, dat's what I said! What about it! [*They are silent, puzzled by his sudden resentment at what used to be one of his jokes.* YANK *sits down again in the same attitude of* '*The Thinker*'.]

VOICES: Leave him alone.
He's got a grouch on.
Why wouldn't he?

PADDY [*with a wink at the others*]: Sure I know what's the matther. 'Tis aisy to see. He's fallen in love, I'm telling you.

ALL [*repeating the word after him as one with cynical mockery*]: Love! [*The word has a brazen, metallic quality as if their throats were phonograph horns. It is followed by a chorus of hard barking laughter.*]

YANK [*with a contemptuous snort*]: Love, hell! Hate, dat's what. I've fallen in hate, get me?

PADDY [*philosophically*]: 'Twould take a wise man to tell one from the other. [*With a bitter, ironical scorn, increasing as he goes on*] But I'm telling you it's love that's in it. Sure what else but love for us poor bastes in the stokehole would be bringing a fine lady, dressed like a white quane, down a mile of ladders and steps to be havin' a look at us? [*A growl of anger goes up from all sides.*]

LONG [*jumping on a bench – hecticly*]: Hinsultin' us! Hinsultin' us, the bloody cow! And them bloody engineers! What right 'as they got to be exhibitin' us 's if we was bleedin' monkeys in a menagerie? Did we sign for hinsults to our dignity as 'onest workers? Is that in the ship's articles? You kin bloody well bet it ain't! But I knows why they done it.

I arsked a deck steward 'o she was and 'e told me. 'Er old man's a bleedin' millionaire, a bloody Capitalist! 'E's got enuf bloody gold to sink this bleedin' ship! 'E makes arf the bloody steel in the world! 'E owns this bloody boat! And you and me, comrades, we're 'is slaves! And the skipper and mates and engineers, they're 'is slaves! And she's 'is bloody daughter and we're all 'er slaves, too! And she gives 'er orders as 'ow she wants to see the bloody animals below decks and down they takes 'er! [*There is a roar of rage from all sides.*]

YANK [*blinking at him, bewildered*]: Say! Wait a moment! Is all dat straight goods?

LONG: Straight as string! The bleedin' steward as waits on 'em, 'e told me about 'er. And what're we goin' ter do, I arsks yer? 'Ave we got ter swaller 'er hinsults like dogs? It ain't in the ship's articles. I tell yer we got a case. We kin go ter law –

YANK [*with abysmal contempt*]: Hell! Law!

ALL [*repeating the word after him as one with cynical mockery*]: Law! [*The word has a brazen, metallic quality as if their throats were phonograph horns. It is followed by a chorus of hard, barking laughter.*]

LONG [*feeling the ground slipping from under his feet – desperately*] As voters and citizens we kin force the bloody Governments –

YANK [*with abysmal contempt*]: Hell! Governments!

ALL [*repeating the word after him as one with cynical mockery*] Governments! [*The word has a brazen metallic quality as if their throats were phonograph horns. It is followed by a chorus of hard, barking laughter.*]

LONG [*hysterically*]: We're free and equal in the sight of God –

YANK [*with abysmal contempt*]: Hell! God!

ALL [*repeating the word after him as one with cynical mockery*]: God! [*The word has a brazen, metallic quality as if their throats were phonograph horns. It is followed by a chorus of hard, barking laughter.*]

YANK [*witheringly*]: Aw, join de Salvation Army!

ALL: Sit down! Shut up! Damn fool! Sea-lawyer! [LONG *slinks back out of sight.*]

PADDY [*continuing the trend of his thoughts as if he had never been interrupted – bitterly*]: And there she was standing behind us, and the Second pointing at us like a man you'd hear in a circus would be saying: In this cage is a queerer kind of baboon than ever you'd find in darkest Africy. We roast them in their own sweat – and be damned if you won't hear some of thim saying they like it! [*He glances scornfully at* YANK.]

YANK [*with a bewildered, uncertain growl*]: Aw!

PADDY: And there was Yank roarin' curses and turning round wid his shovel to brain her – and she looked at him, and him at her –

YANK [*slowly*]: She was all white. I tought she was a ghost. Sure.

PADDY [*with heavy, biting sarcasm*]: 'Twas love at first sight, divil a doubt of it! If you'd seen the endearin' look on her pale mug when she shrivelled away with her hands over her eyes to shut out the sight of him! Sure, 'twas as if she'd seen a great hairy ape escaped from the Zoo!

YANK [*stung – with a growl of rage*]: Aw!

PADDY: And the loving way Yank heaved his shovel at the skull of her, only she was out the door! [*A grin breaking over his face.*] 'Twas touching, I'm telling you! It put the touch of home, swate home in the stokehole. [*There is a roar of laughter from all.*]

YANK [*glaring at Paddy menacingly*]: Aw, choke dat off, see!

PADDY [*not heeding him – to the others*]: And her grabbin' at the Second's arm for protection. [*With a grotesque imitation of a woman's voice*] Kiss me, Engineer dear, for it's dark down here and me old man's in Wall Street making money! Hug me tight, darlin', for I'm afeerd in the dark and me mother's on deck makin' eyes at the skipper! [*Another roar of laughter.*]

YANK [*threateningly*]: Say! What yuh tryin' to do, kid me, yuh old Harp?

PADDY: Divil a bit! Ain't I wishin' myself you'd brained her?

YANK [*fiercely*]: I'll brain her! I'll brain her yet, wait'n see! [*Coming over to* PADDY *– slowly*] Say, is dat what she called me – a hairy ape?

PADDY: She looked it at you if she didn't say the word itself.

YANK [*grinning horribly*]: Hairy ape, huh? Sure! Dat's de way she looked at me, aw right. Hairy ape! So dat's me, huh? [*Bursting into rage – as if she were still in front of him*] Yuh skinny tart! Yuh white-faced slut, yuh! I'll show yuh who's a ape! [*Turning to the others, bewilderment seizing him again*] Say, youse guys. I was bawlin' him out for pullin' de whistle on us. You heard me. And den I seen youse lookin' at somep'n and I tought he'd sneaked down to come up in back of me, and I hopped round to knock him dead wit de shovel. And dere she was wit de light on her! Christ, yuh could a-pushed me over with a finger! I was scared, get me? Sure! I tought she was a ghost, see? She was all in white like dey wrap around stiffs. You seen her. Kin yuh blame me? She didn't belong, dat's what. And den when I come to and seen it was a real skoit and seen de way she was lookin' at me – like Paddy said – Christ, I was sore, get me? I don't stand for dat stuff from nobody. And I flung de shovel – on'y she'd beat it. [*Furiously*] I wished it'd banged her! I wished it'd knocked her block off!

LONG: And be 'anged for murder or 'lectrocuted? She ain't bleedin' well worth it.

YANK: I don't give a damn what! I'd be square wit her, wouldn't I? Tink I wanter let her put somep'n over on me? Tink I'm going to let her git away wit dat stuff? Yuh don't know me! No one ain't never put nothin' over on me and got away wit it, see! – not dat kind of stuff – no guy and no skoit neither! I'll fix her! Maybe she'll come down again –

VOICE: No chance, Yank. You scared her out of a year's growth.

YANK: I scared her? Why de hell should I scare her? Who de hell is she? Ain't she de same as me? Hairy ape, huh? [*With his old confident bravado*] I'll show her I'm better'n her, if she on'y knew it. I belong and she don't, see! I move and she's dead! Twenty-five knots a hour, dat's me! Dat carries her, but I make dat. She's on'y baggage. Sure! [*Again bewildered*] But, Christ, she was funny lookin'! Did yuh pipe her hands? White and skinny. Yuh could see de bones trough 'em. And her mush, dat was dead white, too. And her eyes, dey was like dey'd seen a ghost. Me, dat was! Sure! Hairy ape! Ghost, huh? Look at dat arm! [*He extends his right arm, swelling out the great muscles.*] I could a-took her wit dat, wit' just my little finger even, and broke her in two. [*Again, bewildered*] Say, who is dat skoit, huh? What is she? What's she come from? Who made her? Who give her de noive to look at me like dat? Dis ting's got my goat right. I don't get her. She's new to me. What does a skoit like her mean, huh? She don't belong, get me! I can't see her. [*With growing anger*] But one ting I'm wise to, aw right, aw right! Youse all kin bet your shoits I'll get even wit her. I'll show her if she tinks she – She grinds de organ and I'm on de string, huh? I'll fix her! Let her come down again and I'll fling her in de furnace! She'll move den! She won't shiver at nothin', den! Speed, dat'll be her! She'll belong den! [*He grins horribly.*]

PADDY: She'll never come. She's had her belly-full, I'm telling you. She'll be in bed now, I'm thinking, wid ten doctors and nurses feedin' her salts to clean the fear out of her.

YANK [*enraged*]: Yuh tink I made her sick, too, do yuh? Just lookin' at me, huh? Hairy ape, huh? [*In a frenzy of rage*] I'll fix her! I'll tell her where to git off! She'll git down on her knees and take it back or I'll bust de face offen her! [*Shaking one fist upward and beating on his chest with the other*] I'll find yuh! I'm comin', d'you hear? I'll fix yuh, God damn yuh! [*He makes a rush for the door.*]

VOICES: Stop him!
He'll get shot!
He'll murder her!
Trip him up!
Hold him!
He's gone crazy!
Gott, he's strong!
Hold him down!
Look out for a kick!
Pin his arms!

[*They have all piled on him and, after a fierce struggle, by sheer weight of numbers have borne him to the floor just inside the door.*]

PADDY [*who has remained detached*]: Kape him down till he's cooled off. [*Scornfully*] Yerra, Yank, you're a great fool. Is it paying attention at all you are to the like of that skinny sow widout one drop of rale blood in her?

YANK [*frenziedly, from the bottom of the heap*]: She done me doit! She done me doit, didn't she? I'll git square wit her! I'll get her some way! Git offen me, youse guys! Lemme up! I'll show her who's a ape!

CURTAIN

SCENE FIVE

Three weeks later. A corner of Fifth Avenue on a fine Sunday morning. A general atmosphere of clean, well-tidied, wide street; a flood of mellow, tempered sunshine; gentle, genteel breezes. In the rear, the show windows of two shops, a jewellery establishment on the corner, a furrier's next to it. Here the adornments of extreme wealth are tantalizingly displayed. The jeweller's window is gaudy with glittering diamonds, emeralds, rubies, pearls, etc., fashioned in ornate tiaras, crowns, necklaces, collars, etc. From each piece hangs an enormous tag from which a dollar sign and numerals in intermittent electric lights wink out the incredible prices. The same in the furrier's. Rich furs of all varieties hang there bathed in a downpour of artificial light. The general effect is of a background of magnificence cheapened and made grotesque by commercialism, a background in tawdry disharmony with the clear light and sunshine on the street itself.

[*Up the side street* YANK *and* LONG *come swaggering.* LONG *is dressed in shore clothes, wears a black tie and cloth cap.* YANK *is in his dirty dungarees. A fireman's cap with black peak is cocked defiantly on the side of his head. He has not shaved for days, and around his fierce, resentful eyes – as around those of* LONG *to a lesser degree – the black smudge of coal-dust still sticks like make-up. They hesitate and stand together at the corner, swaggering, looking about them with a forced, defiant contempt.*]

LONG [*indicating it all with an oratorical gesture*]: Well, 'ere we are. Fif' Avenoo. This 'ere's their bleedin' private lane, as yer might say. [*Bitterly*] We're trespassers 'ere. Proletarians keep orf the grass!

YANK [*dully*]: I don't see no grass, yuh boob. [*Staring at the pavement*] Clean, ain't it? Yuh could eat a fried egg offen it.

The white wings got some job sweepin' dis up. [*Looking up and down the avenue – surlily*] Where's all de white-collar stiffs yuh said was here – and de skoits – *her* kind?

LONG: In church, blarst 'em! Arskin' Jesus to give 'em more money.

YANK: Choich, huh? I useter go to choich onct – sure – when I was a kid. Me old man and woman, dey made me. Dey never went demselves dough. Always got too big a head on Sunday mornin', dat was dem. [*With a grin*] Dey was scrappers for fair, bot' of dem. On Satiday nights when dey bot' got a skinful dey could put up a bout oughter been staged at de Garden. When dey got trough dere wasn't a chair or table wit a leg under it. Or else dey bot' jumped on me for somep'n. Dat was where I loined to take punishment. [*With a grin and a swagger*] I'm a chip offen de old block, get me?

LONG: Did yer old man follow the sea?

YANK: Naw. Worked along shore. I runned away when me old lady croaked wit de tremens. I helped at truckin' and in de market. Den I shipped in de stokehole. Sure. Dat belongs. De rest was nothin'. [*Looking around him*] I ain't never seen dis before. De Brooklyn waterfront, dat was where I was dragged up. [*Taking a deep breath*] Dis ain't so bad at dat, huh?

LONG: Not bad? Well, we pays for it wiv our bloody sweat, if yer wants to know!

YANK [*with sudden angry disgust*]: Aw, hell! I don't see no one, see – like her. All dis gives me a pain. It don't belong. Say, ain't dere a back-room around dis dump? Let's go shoot a ball. All dis is too clean and quiet and dolled-up, get me! It gives me a pain.

LONG: Wait and yer'll bloody well see –

YANK: I don't wait for no one. I keep on de move. Say, what yuh drag me up here for, anyway? Tryin' to kid me, yuh simp, yuh?

LONG: Yer wants to get back at her, don't yer? That's what yer been sayin' every bloomin' 'our since she hinsulted yer.

YANK [*vehemently*]: Sure ting I do! Didn't I try to git even wit her in Southampton? Didn't I sneak on de dock and wait for her by de gangplank? I was goin' to spit in her pale mug, see! Sure, right in her pop-eyes! Dat would a-made me even, see? But no chanct. Dere was a whole army of plain clothes bulls around. Dey spotted me and gimme de rush. I never seen her. But I'll git square wit her yet, you watch! [*Furiously*] De lousy tart! She tinks she kin get away wit moider – but not wit me! I'll fix her! I'll tink of a way!

LONG [*as disgusted as he dares to be*]: Ain't that why I brought yer up 'ere – to show yer? Yer been lookin' at this 'ere 'ole affair wrong. Yer been actin' an' talkin's if it was all a bleedin' personal matter between yer and that bloody cow. I wants to convince yer she was on'y a representative of 'er clarss. I wants to awaken yer bloody clarss consciousness. Then yer'll see it's 'er clarss yer've got to fight, not 'er alone. There's a 'ole mob of 'em like 'er, Gawd blind 'em!

YANK [*spitting on his hands – belligerently*]: De more de merrier when I gits started. Bring on de gang!

LONG: Yer'll see 'em in arf a mo', when that church lets out. [*He turns and sees the window display in the two stores for the first time.*] Blimey! Look at that, will yer? [*They both walk back and stand looking in the jeweller's.* LONG *flies into a fury.*] Just look at this 'ere bloomin' mess! Just look at it! Look at the bleedin' prices on 'em – more'n our 'ole bloody stokehole makes in ten voyages sweatin' in 'ell! And they – her and her bloody clarss – buys 'em for toys to dangle on 'em! One of these 'ere would buy grub for a starvin' family for a year!

YANK: Aw, cut de sob stuff! T' hell wit de starvin' family! Yuh'll be passin' de hat to me next. [*With naïve admiration*] Say, dem tings is pretty, huh? Bet yuh dey'd hock for a piece of change aw right. [*Then turning away, bored*] But, aw hell, what good are dey? Let her have 'em. Dey don't belong no more'n she does. [*With a gesture of sweeping the jeweller's into oblivion*] All dat don't count, get me?

LONG [*who has moved to the furrier's – indignantly*]: And I s'pose this 'ere don't count neither – skins of poor, 'armless animals slaughtered so as 'er and 'ers can keep their bleedin' noses warm!

YANK [*who has been staring at something inside – with queer excitement*]: Take a slant at dat! Give it de once-over! Monkey fur – two t'ousand bucks! [*Bewildered*] Is dat straight goods – monkey fur? What de hell –

LONG [*bitterly*]: It's straight enuf. [*With grim humour*] They wouldn't bloody well pay that for a 'airy ape's skin – no, nor for the 'ole livin' ape with all 'is 'ead, and body, and soul thrown in!

YANK [*clenching his fists, his face growing pale with rage as if the skin in the window were a personal insult*]: Trowin' it up in my face! Christ! I'll fix her!

LONG [*excitedly*]: Church is out. 'Ere they come, the bleedin' swine. [*After a glance at Yank's lowering face – uneasily*] Easy goes, Comrade. Keep yer bloomin' temper. Remember force defeats itself. It ain't our weapon. We must impress our demands through peaceful means – the votes of the on-marching proletarians of the bloody world!

YANK [*with abysmal contempt*]: Votes, hell! Votes is a joke, see. Votes for women! Let dem do it!

LONG [*still more uneasily*]: Calm, now. Treat 'em wiv the proper contempt. Observe the bleedin' parasites, but 'old yer 'orses.

YANK [*angrily*]: Git away from me! Yuh're yellow, dat's what. Force, dat's me! De punch, dat's me every time, see!

[*The crowd from church enter from the right, sauntering slowly and affectedly, their heads held stiffly up, looking neither to right nor left, talking in toneless, simpering voices. The women are rouged, calcimined, dyed, overdressed to the nth degree. The men are in tail coats, tall hats, spats, canes, etc. A procession of gaudy marionettes, yet with something of the relentless horror of Frankensteins in their detached, mechanical unawareness.*]

VOICES: Dear Doctor Caiaphas! He is so sincere!
What was the sermon? I dozed off.
About the radicals, my dear – and the false doctrines that are being preached.
We must organize a hundred per cent American bazaar.
And let every one contribute one one-hundredth per cent of their income tax.
What an original idea!
We can devote the proceeds to rehabilitating the veil of the temple.
But that has been done so many times.

YANK [*glaring from one to the other of them – with an insulting snort of scorn*]: Huh! Huh!

[*Without seeming to see him, they make wide detours to avoid the spot where he stands in the middle of the pavement.*]

LONG [*frightened*]: Keep yer bloomin' mouth shut, I tells yer.

YANK [*viciously*]: G'wan! Tell it to Sweeney! [*He swaggers away and deliberately lurches into a top-hatted gentleman, then glares at him pugnaciously.*] Say, who d'yuh tink yuh're bumpin'? Tink yuh own de oith?

GENTLEMAN [*coldly and affectedly*]: I beg your pardon. [*He has not looked at* YANK *and passes on without a glance, leaving him bewildered.*]

LONG [*rushing up and grabbing Yank's arm*]: 'Ere! Come away! This wasn't what I meant. Yer'll 'ave the bloody coppers down on us.

YANK [*savagely – giving him a push that sends him sprawling*]: G'wan!

LONG [*picks himself up – hysterically*]: I'll pop orf then. This ain't what I meant. And whatever 'appens, yer can't blame me. [*He slinks off left.*]

YANK: T' hell wit youse! [*He approaches a lady – with a vicious grin and a smirking wink.*] Hallo, Kiddo. How's every little ting? Got anyting on for tonight? I know an old boiler down to de docks we kin crawl into. [*The lady stalks by without a look, without a change of pace.* YANK *turns to others – insultingly.*] Holy smokes, what a mug! Go hide yuh sel before de horses shy at yuh. Gee, pipe de heinie on dat one! Say, youse, yuh look like de stoin of a ferryboat. Paint and powder! All dolled up to kill! Yuh look like stiffs laid out for de boneyard! Aw, g'wan, de lot of youse! Yuh give me de eyeache. Yuh don't belong, get me! Look at me, why don't youse dare? I belong, dat's me! [*Pointing to a skyscraper across the street which is in process of construction – with bravado*] See dat building goin' up dere? See de steel work? Steel, dat's me! Youse guys live on it and tink yuh're somep'n. But I'm *in* it, see! I'm de hoistin' engine dat makes it go up! I'm it – de inside and bottom of it! Sure! I'm steel and steam and smoke and de rest of it! It moves – speed – twenty-five storeys up – and me at de top and bottom – movin'! Youse simps don't move. Yuh're on'y dolls I winds up to see'm spin. Yuh're de garbage, get me – de leavin's – de ashes we dump over de side! Now, what a-yuh got to say? [*But as they seem neither to see nor hear him, he flies into a fury.*] Pigs! Tarts! Bitches! [*He turns in a rage on the men, bumping viciously into them but not jarring them the least bit. Rather it is he who recoils after each collision. He keeps growling.*] Git off de oith! G'wan! Look where yuh're goin', can't yuh? Git out a-here! Fight, why don't yuh? Put up yer mits! Don't be a dog! Fight, or I'll knock yuh dead! [*But, without seeming to see him, they all answer with mechanical, affected politeness:* 'I beg your pardon.' *Then at a cry from one of the women, they all scurry to the furrier's window.*]

THE WOMAN [*ecstatically, with a gasp of delight*]: Monkey fur! [*The whole crowd of men and women chorus after her in the same tone of affected delight:*] Monkey fur!

YANK [*with a jerk of his head back on his shoulders, as if he had received a punch full in the face – raging*]: I see yuh, all in white! I see yuh, yuh white-faced tart, yuh! Hairy ape, huh? I'll hairy ape yuh!

[*He bends down and grips at the street kerbing as if to pluck it out and hurl it. Foiled in this, snarling with passion, he leaps to the lamp-post on the corner and tries to pull it up for a club. Just at that moment a bus is heard rumbling up. A fat, high-hatted, spatted gentleman runs out from the side street. He calls out plaintively:* 'Bus! Bus! Stop there!' *and runs full tilt into the bending, straining* YANK, *who is bowled off his balance.*]

YANK [*seeing a fight – with a roar of joy as he springs to his feet*]: At last! Bus, huh? I'll bust yuh!

[*He lets drive a terrific swing, his fist landing full on the fat gentleman's face. But the gentleman stands unmoved as if nothing had happened.*]

GENTLEMAN: I beg your pardon. [*Then irritably*] You have made me lose my bus. [*He claps his hands and begins to scream:*] Officer! Officer!

[*Many police whistles shrill out on the instant, and a whole platoon of policemen rush in on* YANK *from all sides. He tries to fight, but is clubbed to the pavement and fallen upon. The crowd at the window have not moved or noticed this disturbance. The clanging gong of the patrol wagon approaches with a clamouring din.*]

CURTAIN

SCENE SIX

Night of the following day. A row of cells in the prison on Blackwells Island. The cells extend back diagonally from right front to left rear. They do not stop, but disappear in the dark background as if they ran on, numberless, into infinity. One electric bulb from the low ceiling of the narrow corridor sheds its light through the heavy steel bars of the cell at the extreme front and reveals part of the interior.

[YANK *can be seen within, crouched on the edge of his cot in the attitude of Rodin's 'The Thinker'. His face is spotted with black and blue bruises. A blood-stained bandage is wrapped around his head.*]

YANK [*suddenly starting as if awakening from a dream, reaches out and shakes the bars – aloud to himself, wonderingly*]: Steel. Dis is de Zoo, huh? [*A burst of hard, barking laughter comes from the unseen occupants of the cells, runs back down the tier, and abruptly ceases.*]

VOICES [*mockingly*]:

The Zoo? That's a new name for this coop – a damn good name!

Steel, eh? You said a mouthful. This is the old iron house.

Who is that boob talkin'?

He's the bloke they brung in out of his head. The bulls had beat him up fierce.

YANK [*dully*]: I must a-been dreamin'. I tought I was in a cage at de Zoo – but de apes don't talk, do they?

VOICES [*with mocking laughter*]:

You're in a cage aw right.

A coop!

A pen!

A sty!
A kennel! [*Hard laughter – a pause.*]
Say, guy! Who are you? No, never mind lying. What are you?
Yes, tell us your sad story. What's your game?
What did they jug yuh for?

YANK [*dully*]: I was a fireman – stokin' on de liners. [*Then with sudden rage, rattling his cell bars*] I'm a hairy ape, get me? And I'll bust youse all in de jaw if yuh don't lay off kiddin' me.

VOICES: Huh! You're a hard-boiled duck, ain't you!
When you spit, it bounces! [*Laughter.*]
Aw, can it. He's a regular guy. Ain't you?
What did he say he was – a ape?

YANK [*defiantly*]: Sure ting! Ain't dat what youse all are – apes? [*A silence. Then a furious rattling of bars from down the corridor.*]

A VOICE [*thick with rage*]: I'll show yuh who's a ape, yuh mut!

VOICES: Ssshh! Nix!
Can de noise!
Piano!
You'll have the guard down on us!

YANK [*scornfully*]: De guard? Yuh mean de keeper, don't yuh? [*Angry exclamations from all the cells.*]

VOICE [*placatingly*]: Aw, don't pay no attention to him. He's off his nut from the beatin'-up he got. Say, you guy! We're waitin' to hear what they landed you for – or ain't yuh tellin'?

YANK: Sure, I'll tell youse. Sure! Why de hell not? On'y – youse won't get me. Nobody gets me but me, see? I started to tell de Judge and all he says was: 'Toity days to tink it over.' Tink it over! Christ, dat's all I been doin' for weeks! [*After a pause*] I was tryin' to git even wit some one, see? – some one dat done me doit.

VOICES [*cynically*]:

De old stuff, I bet. Your goil, huh?
Give yuh the double-cross, huh?
That's them every time!
Did yuh beat up de odder guy?

YANK [*disgustedly*]: Aw, yuh're all wrong! Sure, dere was a skoit in it – but not what youse mean, not dat old tripe. Dis was a new kind of skoit. She was dolled up all in white – in de stokehole. I tought she was a ghost. Sure. [*A pause.*]

VOICES [*whispering*]:

Gee, he's still nutty.
Let him rave. It's fun listenin'.

YANK [*unheeding – groping in his thoughts*]: Her hands – dey was skinny and white like dey wasn't real but painted on somep'n. Dere was a million miles from me to her – twenty-five knots a hour. She was like some dead ting de cat brung in. Sure, dat's what. She didn't belong. She belonged in de window of a toy store, or on de top of a garbage can, see! Sure! [*He breaks out angrily.*] But would yuh believe it, she had de noive to do me doit. She lamped me like she was seein' somep'n broke loose from de menagerie. Christ, yuh'd oughter seen her eyes! [*He rattles the bars of his cell furiously.*] But I'll get back at her yet, you watch! And if I can't find her I'll take it out on de gang she runs wit. I'm wise to where dey hangs out now. I'll show her who belongs! I'll show her who's in de move and who ain't. You watch my smoke!

VOICES [*serious and joking*]:

Dat's de talkin'!
Take her for all she's got!
What was this dame, anyway? Who was she, eh?

YANK: I dunno. First cabin stiff. Her old man's a millionaire, dey says – name of Douglas.

VOICES: Douglas? That's the President of the Steel Trust, I bet.

Sure. I seen his mug in de papers. He's filthy with dough.

VOICE: Hey, feller, take a tip from me. If you want to get back at that dame, you better join the Wobblies. You'll get some action then.

YANK: Wobblies? What de hell's dat?

VOICE: Ain't you ever heard of the I.W.W.?

YANK: Naw. What is it?

VOICE: A gang of blokes – a tough gang. I been readin' about 'em today in the paper. The guard give me the *Sunday Times.* There's a long spiel about 'em. It's from a speech made in the Senate by a guy named Senator Queen. [*He is in the cell next to Yank's. There is a rustling of paper.*] Wait'll I see if I got light enough and I'll read you. Listen. [*He reads:*] 'There is a menace existing in this country today which threatens the vitals of our fair Republic – as foul a menace against the very life-blood of the American Eagle as was the foul conspiracy of Cataline against the eagles of ancient Rome!'

VOICE [*disgustedly*]: Aw hell! Tell him to salt de tail of dat eagle!

VOICE [*reading*]: 'I refer to that devil's brew of rascals, jail-birds, murderers, and cut-throats who libel all honest working men by calling themselves the Industrial Workers of the World; but in the light of their nefarious plots, I call them the Industrious *Wreckers* of the World!'

YANK [*with vengeful satisfaction*]: Wreckers, dat's de right dope! Dat belongs! Me for dem!

VOICE: Ssshh! [*Reading*] 'This fiendish organization is a foul ulcer on the fair body of our Democracy –'

VOICE: Democracy, hell! Give him the boid, fellers – the raspberry! [*They do.*]

VOICE: Ssshh! [*Reading:*] 'Like Cato I say to this Senate, the I.W.W. must be destroyed! For they represent an ever-present dagger pointed at the heart of the greatest nation the world has ever known, where all men are born free and equal, with equal opportunities to all, where the Founding Fathers have guaranteed to each one happiness, where Truth, Honour, Liberty, Justice, and the Brotherhood of Man are a religion absorbed with one's mother's milk, taught at our father's knee, sealed, signed, and stamped upon in the glorious Constitution of these United States!' [*A perfect storm of hisses, catcalls, boos, and hard laughter.*]

VOICES [*scornfully*]:

Hurrah for de Fort' of July!
Pass de hat!
Liberty!
Justice!
Honour!
Opportunity!
Brotherhood!

ALL [*with abysmal scorn*]: Aw, hell!

VOICE: Give that Queen Senator guy the bark! All togedder now – one – two – tree – [*A terrific chorus of barking and yapping.*]

GUARD [*from a distance*]: Quiet, there, youse – or I'll git the hose. [*The noise subsides.*]

YANK [*with growling rage*]: I'd like to catch dat senator guy alone for a second. I'd loin him some trute!

VOICE: Ssshh! Here's where he gits down to cases on the Wobblies. [*Reads:*] 'They plot with fire in one hand and dynamite in the other. They stop not before murder to gain their ends, nor at the outraging of defenceless womanhood. They would tear down society, put the lowest scum in the seats of the mighty, turn Almighty God's revealed plan for the world topsy-turvy, and make of our sweet and lovely civilization a shambles, a desolation, where man, God's masterpiece, would soon degenerate back to the ape!'

VOICE [*to* YANK]: Hey, you guy. There's your ape stuff again.

YANK [*with a growl of fury*]: I got him. So dey blow up tings, do tey? Dey turn tings round, do dey? Hey, lend me dat paper, will yuh?

VOICE: Sure. Give it to him. On'y keep it to yourself, see. We don't wanter listen to no more of that slop.

VOICE: Here you are. Hide it under your mattress.

YANK [*reaching out*]: Tanks. I can't read much, but I kin manage. [*He sits, the paper in the hand at his side, in the attitude of Rodin's 'The Thinker'. A pause. Several snores from down the corridor. Suddenly* YANK *jumps to his feet with a furious groan as if some appalling thought had crashed on him.*] Sure – her old man – President of de Steel Trust – makes half de steel in de world – steel – where I tought I belonged – drivin' trou – movin' – in dat – to make *her* – and cage me in for her to spit on! Christ. [*He shakes the bars of his cell door till the whole tier trembles. Irritated, protesting exclamations from those awakened or trying to get to sleep.*] He made dis – dis cage! Steel! *It* don't belong, dat's what! Cages, cells, locks, bolts, bars – dat's what it means! – holdin' me down wit him at de top! But I'll drive trou! Fire, dat melts it! I'll be fire – under de heap – fire dat never goes out – hot as hell – breakin' out in de night –

[*While he has been saying this last he has shaken his cell door to a clanging accompaniment. As he comes to the 'breakin' out' he seizes one bar with both hands and, putting his two feet up against the others so that his position is parallel to the floor like a monkey's, he gives a great wrench backwards. The bar bends like a liquorice stick under his tremendous strength. Just at this moment the* PRISON GUARD *rushes in, dragging a hose behind him.*]

GUARD [*angrily*]: I'll loin youse to wake me up! [*Sees* YANK.] Hallo, it's you, huh? Got the D.T.s, hey? Well, I'll cure 'em. I'll drown your snakes for yuh! [*Noticing the bar*] Hell, look at dat bar bended! On'y a bug is strong enough for dat!

YANK [*glaring at him*]: Or a hairy ape, yuh big yellow scut! Look out! Here I come! [*He grabs another bar.*]

GUARD [*scared now – yelling off left*]: Toin de hose on, Ben! – full pressure! And call de others – and a strait-jacket! [*The curtain is falling. As it hides* YANK *from view, there is a splattering smash as the stream of water hits the steel of Yank's cell.*]

CURTAIN

SCENE SEVEN

Nearly a month later. An I.W.W. local near the waterfront, showing the interior of a front room on the ground-floor, and the street outside. Moonlight on the narrow street, buildings massed in black shadow. The interior of the room, which is general assembly room, office, and reading-room, resembles some dingy settlement boys' club. A desk and high stool are in one corner. A table with papers, stacks of pamphlets, chairs about it is at centre. The whole is decidedly cheap, banal, commonplace and unmysterious as a room could well be. The secretary is perched on the stool making entries in a large ledger. An eye-shade casts his face into shadows. Eight or ten men, longshoremen, iron workers, and the like, are grouped about the table. Two are playing checkers. One is writing a letter. Most of them are smoking pipes. A big signboard is on the wall at the rear, 'Industrial Workers of the World – Local No. 57'.

[YANK *comes down the street outside. He is dressed as in Scene V. He moves cautiously, mysteriously. He comes to a point opposite the door; tiptoes softly up to it, listens, is impressed by the silence within, knocks carefully, as if he were guessing at the password to some secret rite. Listens. No answer. Knocks again a bit louder. No answer. Knocks impatiently, much louder.*]

SECRETARY [*turning around on his stool*]: What the devil is that – some one knocking? [*Shouts:*] Come in, why don't you?

[*All the men in the room look up.* YANK *opens the door slowly, gingerly, as if afraid of an ambush. He looks around for secret doors, mystery, is taken aback by the commonplaceness of the room and the men in it, thinks he may have gotten in the wrong place, then sees the signboard on the wall and is reassured.*]

YANK [*blurts out*]: Hallo!

MEN [*reservedly*]: Hallo!

YANK [*more easily*]: I tought I'd bumped into de wrong dump.

SECRETARY [*scrutinizing him carefully*]: Maybe you have. Are you a member?

YANK: Naw, not yet. Dat's what I come for – to join.

SECRETARY: That's easy. What's your job – longshore?

YANK: Naw. Fireman – stoker on de liners.

SECRETARY [*with satisfaction*]: Welcome to our city. Glad to know you people are waking up at last. We haven't got many members in your line.

YANK: Naw. Dey're all dead to de woild.

SECRETARY: Well, you can help to wake 'em. What's your name? I'll make out your card.

YANK [*confused*]: Name? Lemme tink.

SECRETARY [*sharply*]: Don't you know your own name?

YANK: Sure; but I been just Yank for so long – Bob, dat's it – Bob Smith.

SECRETARY [*writing*]: Robert Smith. [*Fills out the rest of card.*] Here you are. Cost you half a dollar.

YANK: Is dat all – four bits? Dat's easy. [*Gives the* SECRETARY *the money.*]

SECRETARY [*throwing it in drawer*]: Thanks. Well, make yourself at home. No introductions needed. There's literature on the table. Take some of those pamphlets with you to distribute aboard ship. They may bring results. Sow the seed, only go about it right. Don't get caught and fired. We got plenty out of work. What we need is men who can hold their jobs – and work for us at the same time.

YANK: Sure. [*But he still stands, embarrassed and uneasy.*]

SECRETARY [*looking at him – curiously*]: What did you knock for? Think we had a coon in uniform to open doors?

YANK: Naw. I tought it was locked – and dat yuh'd wanter give me the once-over trou a peephole or somep'n to see if I was right.

SECRETARY [*alert and suspicious, but with an easy laugh*]: Think we were running a crap game? That door is never locked. What put that in your nut?

YANK [*with a knowing grin, convinced that this is all camouflage, a part of the secrecy*]: Dis burg is full of bulls, ain't it?

SECRETARY [*sharply*]: What have the cops got to do with us? We're breaking no laws.

YANK [*with a knowing wink*]: Sure. Youse wouldn't for woilds. Sure. I'm wise to dat.

SECRETARY: You seem to be wise to a lot of stuff none of us knows about.

YANK [*with another wink*]: Aw, dat's aw right, see. [*Then made a bit resentful by the suspicious glances from all sides.*] Aw, can it! Youse needn't put me trou de toid degree. Can't youse see I belong? Sure! I'm reg'lar. I'll stick, get me? I'll shoot de woiks for youse. Dat's why I wanted to join in.

SECRETARY [*breezily, feeling him out*]: That's the right spirit. Only are you sure you understand what you've joined? It's all plain and above board; still, some guys get a wrong slant on us. [*Sharply*] What's your notion of the purpose of the I.W.W.?

YANK: Aw, I know all about it.

SECRETARY [*sarcastically*]: Well, give us some of your valuable information.

YANK [*cunningly*]: I know enough not to speak out-a my toin. [*Then resentfully again*] Aw, say! I'm reg'lar. I'm wise to de game. I know yuh got to watch your step wit a stranger. For all youse know, I might be a plain-clothes dick, or somep'n, dat's what yuh're tinkin', huh? Aw, forget it! I belong, see? Ask any guy down to de docks if I don't.

SECRETARY: Who said you didn't?

YANK: After I'm 'nitiated, I'll show yuh.

SECRETARY [*astounded*]: Initiated? There's no initiation.

YANK [*disappointed*]: Ain't there no password – no grip nor nothin'?

SECRETARY: What'd you think this is – the Elks – or the Black Hand?

YANK: De Elks, hell! De Black Hand, dey're a lot of yellow backstickin' Ginees. Naw. Dis is a man's gang, ain't it?

SECRETARY: You said it! That's why we stand on our two feet in the open. We got no secrets.

YANK [*surprised but admiringly*]: Yuh mean to say yuh always run wide open – like dis?

SECRETARY: Exactly.

YANK: Den yuh sure got your noive wit youse!

SECRETARY [*sharply*]: Just what was it made you want to join us? Come out with that straight.

YANK: Yuh call me? Well, I got noive, too! Here's my hand. Yuh wanter blow tings up don't yuh? Well, dat's me! I belong!

SECRETARY [*with pretended carelessness*]: You mean, change the unequal conditions of society by legitimate direct action – or with dynamite?

YANK: Dynamite! Blow it offen de oith – steel – all de cages – all de factories, steamers, buildings, jails – de Steel Trust and all dat makes it go.

SECRETARY: So – that's your idea, eh? And did you have any special job in that line you wanted to propose to us?

[*He makes a sign to the men, who get up cautiously one by one and group behind* YANK.]

YANK [*boldly*]: Sure, I'll come out wit it. I'll show youse. I'm one of de gang. Dere's dat millionaire guy, Douglas –

SECRETARY: President of the Steel Trust, you mean? Do you want to assassinate him?

YANK: Naw, dat don't get yuh nothin'. I mean blow up de factory, de woiks, where he makes de steel. Dat's what I'm after – to blow up de steel, knock all de steel in de woild up to de moon. Dat'll fix tings! [*Eagerly, with a touch of bravado*] I'll do it by me lonesome! I'll show yuh! Tell me where his woiks is, how to git there, all de dope. Gimme de stuff, de old butter – and watch me do de rest! Watch de smoke and see it move! I don't give a damn if dey nab me – long as it's done! I'll soive life for it – and give 'em de laugh! [*Half to himself*] And I'll write her a letter and tell her de hairy ape done it. Dat'll square tings.

SECRETARY [*stepping away from* YANK]: Very interesting.

[*He gives a signal. The men, huskies all, throw themselves on* YANK, *and before he knows it they have his legs and arms pinioned. But he is too flabbergasted to make a struggle, anyway. They feel him over for weapons.*]

MAN: No gat, no knife. Shall we give him what's what and put the boots to him?

SECRETARY: No. He isn't worth the trouble we'd get into. He's too stupid. [*He comes closer and laughs mockingly in* YANK'S *face.*] Ho-ho! By God, this is the biggest joke they've put up on us yet. Hey, you Joke! Who sent you – Burns or Pinkerton? No, by God, you're such a bonehead I'll bet you're in the Secret Service! Well, you dirty spy, you rotten agent provocator, you can go back and tell whatever skunk is paying you blood-money for betraying your brothers that he's wasting his coin. You couldn't catch a cold. And tell him that all he'll ever get on us, or ever has got, is just his own sneaking plots that's he framed up to put us in jail. We are what our manifesto says we are, neither more or less – and we'll give him a copy of that any time he calls. And as for you – [*He glares scornfully at* YANK, *who is sunk in an oblivious stupor.*] Oh, hell, what's the use of talking? You're a brainless ape.

YANK [*aroused by the word to fierce but futile struggles*]: What's dat, yuh Sheeny, yuh!

SECRETARY: Throw him out, boys.

[*In spite of his struggles, this is done with gusto and éclat. Propelled by several parting kicks,* YANK *lands sprawling in the middle of the narrow cobbled street. With a growl he starts to get up and storm the closed door, but stops bewildered by the confusion in his brain, pathetically impotent. He sits there, brooding, in as near to the attitude of Rodin's 'Thinker' as he can get in his position.*]

YANK [*bitterly*]: So dem boids don't tink I belong, neider. Aw, to hell wit 'em! Dey're in de wrong pew – de same old bull – soapboxes and Salvation Army – no guts! Cut out an hour offen de job a day and make me happy! Gimme a dollar more a day and make me happy! Tree square a day, and cauliflowers in de front yard – ekal rights – a woman and kids – a lousy vote – and I'm all fixed for Jesus, huh? Aw, hell! What does dat get yuh? Dis ting's in your inside, but it ain't your belly. Feedin' your face – sinkers and coffee – dat don't touch it. It's way down – at de bottom. Yuh can't grab it, and yuh can't stop it. It moves, and everyting moves. It stops and de whole woild stops. Dat's me now – I don't tick, see? – I'm a busted Ingersoll, dat's what. Steel was me, and I owned de woild. Now I ain't steel, and de woild owns me. Aw, hell! I can't see – it's all dark, get me? It's all wrong! [*He turns a bitter, mocking face up like an ape gibbering at the moon.*] Say, youse up dere, Man in de Moon, yuh look so wise, gimme de answer, huh? Slip me de inside dope, de information right from de stable – where do I get off at, huh?

A POLICEMAN [*who has come up the street in time to hear this last – with grim humour*]: You'll get off at the station, you boob, if you don't get up out of that and keep movin'.

YANK [*looking up at him – with a hard, bitter laugh*]: Sure! Lock me up! Put me in a cage! Dat's de on'y answer yuh know. G'wan, lock me up!

POLICEMAN: What you been doin'?

YANK: Enuf to gimme life for! I was born, see? Sure, dat's de charge. Write it in de blotter. I was born, get me!

POLICEMAN [*jocosely*]: God pity your old woman! [*Then matter-of-fact*] But I've no time for kidding. You're soused. I'd run you in but it's too long a walk to the station. Come on now, get up, or I'll fan your ears with this club. Beat it now! [*He hauls* YANK *to his feet.*]

YANK [*in a vague, mocking tone*]: Say, where do I go from here?

POLICEMAN [*giving him a push – with a grin indifferently*]: Go to hell.

CURTAIN

SCENE EIGHT

[*Twilight of the next day. The monkey-house at the Zoo. One spot of clear, grey light falls on the front of one cage so that the interior can be seen. The other cages are vague, shrouded in shadow from which chatterings pitched in a conversational tone can be heard. On the one cage a sign from which the word 'gorilla' stands out. The gigantic animal himself is seen squatting on his haunches on a bench in much the same attitude as Rodin's 'Thinker'.* YANK *enters from the left. Immediately a chorus of angry chattering and screeching breaks out. The gorilla turns his eyes, but makes no sound or move.*]

YANK [*with a hard, bitter laugh*]: Welcome to your city, huh? Hail, hail, de gang's all here! [*At the sound of his voice the chattering dies away into an attentive silence.* YANK *walks up to the gorilla's cage and, leaning over the railing, stares in at its occupant, who stares back at him, silent and motionless. There is a pause of dead stillness. Then* YANK *begins to talk in a friendly, confidential tone, half-mockingly, but with a deep undercurrent of sympathy.*] Say, yuh're some hard-lookin' guy, ain't yuh? I seen lots of tough nuts dat de gang called gorillas, but yuh're de foist real one I ever seen. Some chest yuh got, and shoulders, and dem arms and mits! I bet yuh got a punch in eider fist dat'd knock 'em all silly! [*This with genuine admiration. The gorilla, as if he understood, stands upright, swelling out his chest and pounding on it with his fist.* YANK *grins sympathetically.*] Sure, I get yuh. Yuh challenge de whole woild, huh? Yuh got what I was sayin' even if yuh muffed de woids. [*Then bitterness creeping in*] And why wouldn't yuh get me? Ain't we both members of de same club – de Hairy Apes? [*They stare at each other – a pause – then* YANK *goes on slowly and bitterly.*] So yuh're what she seen when she looked at me, de white-faced tart! I was you to her, get me? On'y outa de cage – broke out – free to moider her, see? Sure! Dat's what she tought. She wasn't wise dat I was in a cage, too – worser'n yours – sure – a damn sight – 'cause you got some chanct to bust loose – but me – [*He grows confused.*] Aw, hell! It's all wrong, ain't it? [*A pause*] I s'pose yuh wanter know what I'm doin' here, huh? I been warmin' a bench down to de Battery – ever since last night. Sure. I seen de sun come up. Dat was pretty, too – all red and pink and green. I was lookin' at de sky-scrapers – steel – and all de ships comin' in, sailin' out, all over de oith – and dey was steel, too. De sun was warm, dey wasn't no clouds, and dere was a breeze blowin'. Sure, it was great stuff. I got it aw right – what Paddy said about dat bein' de right dope – on'y I couldn't get *in* it, see? I couldn't belong in dat. It was over my head. And I kept tinkin' – and den I beat it up here to see what youse was like. And I waited till dey was all gone to git yuh alone. Say, how d'yuh feel sittin' in dat pen all de time, havin' to stand for 'em comin' and starin' at yuh – de white-faced, skinny tarts and de boobs what marry 'em – makin' fun of yuh, laughin' at yuh, gittin' scared of yuh – damn 'em! [*He pounds on the rail with his fist. The gorilla rattles the bars of his cage and snarls. All the other monkeys set up an angry chattering in the darkness.* YANK *goes on excitedly.*] Sure! Dat's de way it hits me, too. On'y yuh're lucky, see? Yuh don't belong wit 'em and yuh know it. But me, I belong wit 'em – but I don't, see? Dey don't belong wit me, dat's what. Get me? Tinkin' is hard – [*He passes one hand across his forehead with a painful gesture. The gorilla growls impatiently.* YANK *goes on gropingly.*] It's dis way, what I'm drivin' at. Youse can sit and dope dream in de past, green woods, de jungle, and de rest of it. Den yuh belong and dey don't. Den yuh kin laugh at 'em, see? Yuh're de champ of de woild. But me – I ain't got no past to tink in, nor nothin' dat's comin' on'y what's now – and dat don't belong. Sure, you're de best off! Yuh can't tink, can yuh? Yuh can't talk neider. But I kin make a bluff at talkin' and tinkin' – a'most git away wit it – a'most! – and dat's where de joker comes in. [*He laughs.*] I ain't on oith and I ain't in Heaven, get me? I'm in de middle tryin' to separate 'em, takin' all de woist punches from bot' of 'em. Maybe dat's what dey call Hell, huh? But you, yuh're at de bottom. You belong! Sure! Yuh're de on'y one in de woild dat does, yuh lucky stiff! [*The gorilla growls proudly.*] And dat's why dey gotter put yuh in a cage, see? [*The gorilla roars angrily.*] Sure! Yuh get me. It beats it when you try to tink it or talk it – it's way down – deep – behind – you'n me we feel it. Sure! Bot' members of dis club! [*He laughs – then in a savage tone*] What de hell! T' hell wit it! A little action, dat's our meat! Dat belongs! Knock 'em down and keep bustin' 'em till dey croaks yuh wit a gat – wit steel! Sure! Are yuh game? Dey've looked at youse, ain't dey – in a cage? Wanter git even? Wanter wind up like a sport 'stead of croakin' slow in dere? [*The gorilla roars an emphatic affirmative.* YANK *goes on with a sort of furious exaltation*] Sure! Yuh're reg'lar! Yuh'll stick to de finish! Me'n you, huh? – bot' members of this club! We'll put up one last star bout dat'll knock 'em offen deir seats! Dey'll have to make de cages stronger after we're trou! [*The gorilla is straining at his bars, growling, hopping from one foot to the other.* YANK *takes a jimmy from under his coat and forces the lock on the cage door. He throws this open.*] Pardon from de governor! Step out and shake hands! I'll take yuh for a walk down Fif' Avenoo. We'll knock 'em offen de oith and croak wit de band playin'. Come on, Brother. [*The gorilla scrambles gingerly out of his cage. Goes to* YANK *and stands looking at him.* YANK *keeps his mocking tone – holds out his hand.*] Shake – de secret grip of our order. [*Something, the tone of mockery, perhaps, suddenly enrages the animal. With a spring he wraps his huge arms around* YANK *in a mur-*

derous hug. There is a crackling snap of crushed ribs – a gasping cry, still mocking, from YANK.] Hey, I didn't say kiss me. [*The gorilla lets the crushed body slip to the floor; stands over it uncertainly, considering; then picks it up, throws it in the cage, shuts the door, and shuffles off menacingly into the darkness at left. A great uproar of frightened chattering and whimpering comes from the other cages. Then* YANK *moves, groaning, opening his eyes, and there is silence. He mutters painfully.*] Say – dey oughter match him – wit Zybszko. He got me, aw right. I'm trou. Even him didn't tink I belonged. [*Then, with sudden, passionate despair*] Christ, where do I get off at? Where do I fit in? [*Checking himself as suddenly*] Aw, what de hell! No squakin', see! No quittin', get me! Croak wit your boots on! [*He grabs hold of the bars of the cage and hauls himself painfully to his feet – looks around him, bewildered – forces a mocking laugh.*] In de cage, huh? [*In the strident tones of a circus barker*] Ladies and gents, step forward and take a slant at de one and only – [*his voice weakening*] – one and original – Hairy Ape from de wilds of – [*He slips in a heap on the floor and dies. The monkeys set up a chattering, whimpering wail. And, perhaps, the Hairy Ape at last belongs.*]

CURTAIN

ALL GOD'S CHILLUN GOT WINGS

CHARACTERS

Jim Harris

Mrs Harris, his mother

Hattie, his sister

Ella Downey

Shorty

Joe

Mickey

Whites and Negroes

ACT ONE

SCENE 1

A corner in lower New York, at the edge of a coloured district. Three narrow streets converge. A triangular building in the rear, red brick, four-storeyed, its ground floor a grocery. Four-storey tenements stretch away down the skyline of the two streets. The fire escapes are crowded with people. In the street leading left, the faces are all white; in the street leading right, all black. It is hot spring.

[*On the sidewalk are eight children, four boys and four girls. Two of each sex are white, two black. They are playing marbles. One of the black boys is* JIM HARRIS. *The little blonde girl, her complexion rose and white, who sits behind his elbow and holds his marbles is* ELLA DOWNEY. *She is eight. They play the game with concentrated attention for a while. People pass, black and white, the Negroes frankly participants in the spirit of spring, the whites laughing constrainedly, awkward in natural emotion. Their words are lost. One only hears their laughter. It expresses the difference in race. There are street noises – the clattering roar of the Elevated, the puff of its locomotives, the ruminative lazy sound of a horse-car, the hoofs of its team clacking on the cobbles. From the street of the whites a high pitched, nasal tenor sings the chorus of 'Only a Bird in a Gilded Cage'. On the street of the blacks a Negro strikes up the chorus of 'I Guess I'll Have to Telegraph My Baby'. As this singing ends, there is laughter, distinctive in quality, from both streets. Then silence. The light in the street begins to grow brilliant with the glow of the setting sun. The game of marbles goes on.*

WHITE GIRL [*tugging at the elbow of her brother*]: Come on, Mickey!

HER BROTHER [*roughly*]: Aw, gwan, youse!

WHITE GIRL: Aw right, den. You kin git a lickin' if you wanter. [*Gets up to move off.*]

HER BROTHER: Aw, git off de eart'!

WHITE GIRL: De old woman'll be madder'n hell!

HER BROTHER [*worried now*]: I'm comin', ain't I! Hold your horses.

BLACK GIRL [*to a black boy*]: Come one, you Joe. We gwine git frailed too, you don't hurry.

JOE: Go along!

MICKEY: Bust up de game, huh? I gotta run! [*Jumps to his feet.*]

OTHER WHITE BOY: Me, too! [*Jumps up.*]

OTHER BLACK GIRL: Lawdy, it's late!

JOE: Me for grub!

MICKEY [*to* JIM HARRIS]: You's de winner, Jim Crow. Yeh gotta play tomorrer.

JIM [*readily*]: Sure t'ing, Mick. Come one, come all! [*He laughs.*]

OTHER WHITE BOY: Me too! I gotta git back at yuh.

JIM: Aw right, Shorty.

LITTLE GIRLS: Hurry! Come on, come on!

[*The six start off together. Then they notice that* JIM *and* ELLA *are hesitating, standing awkwardly and shyly together. They turn to mock.*]

JOE: Look at dat Jim Crow! Land sakes, he got a gal! [*He laughs. They all laugh.*]

JIM [*ashamed*]: Ne're mind, you Chocolate!

MICKEY: Look at de two softies, will yeh! Mush! Mush! [*He and the two other boys take this up.*]

LITTLE GIRLS [*pointing their fingers at Ella*]: Shame! Shame! Everybody knows your name! Painty Face! Painty Face!

ELLA [*hanging her head*]: Shut up!

LITTLE WHITE GIRL: He's been carrying her books!

COLOURED GIRL: Can't you find nuffin' better'n him, Ella? Look at de big feet he got! [*She laughs. They all laugh.* JIM *puts one foot on top of the other, looking at* ELLA.]

ELLA: Mind yer own business, see! [*She strides toward them angrily. They jump up and dance in an ecstasy, screaming and laughing.*]

ALL: Found yeh out! Found yeh out!

MICKEY: Mush-head! Jim Crow de Sissy! Stuck on Painty Face!

JOE: Will Painty Face let you hold her doll, boy?

SHORTY: Sissy! Softy! [ELLA *suddenly begins to cry. At this they all howl.*]

ALL: Cry-baby! Cry-baby! Look at her! Painty Face!

JIM [*suddenly rushing at them, with clenched fists, furiously*]: Shut yo' moufs! I kin lick de hull of you! [*They all run away, laughing, shouting, and jeering, quite triumphant now that they have made him, too, lose his temper. He comes back to* ELLA, *and stands beside her sheepishly, stepping on one foot after the other. Suddenly he blurts out:*] Don't bawl no more. I done chased 'em.

ELLA [*comforted, politely*]: T'anks.

JIM [*swelling out*]: It was a cinch. I kin wipe up de street wid any one of dem. [*He stretches out his arms, trying to bulge out his biceps.*] Feel dat muscle!

ELLA [*does so gingerly – then with admiration*]: My!

JIM [*protectingly*]: You mustn't never be scared when I'm hanging round, Painty Face.

ELLA: Don't call me that, Jim – please!

JIM [*contritely*]: I didn't mean nuffin'. I didn't know you'd mind.

ELLA: I do – more'n anything.

JIM: You oughtn't to mind. Dey's jealous, dat's what.

ELLA: Jealous? Of what?

JIM [*pointing to her face*]: Of dat. Red 'n' white. It's purty.

ELLA: I hate it!

JIM: It's purty. Yes, it's – it's purty. It's – outa sight!

ELLA: I hate it. I wish I was black like you.

JIM [*sort of shrinking*]: No, you don't. Dey'd call you Crow, den – or Chocolate – or Smoke.

ELLA: I wouldn't mind.

JIM [*sombrely*]: Dey'd call you nigger sometimes, too.

ELLA: I wouldn't mind.

JIM [*humbly*]: You wouldn't mind?

ELLA: No, I wouldn't mind. [*An awkward pause.*]

JIM [*suddenly*]: You know what, Ella? Since I been tuckin' yo' books to school and back, I been drinkin' lots o' chalk 'n' water three times a day. Dat Tom, de barber, he tole me dat make me white, if I drink enough. [*Pleadingly*] Does I look whiter?

ELLA [*comfortingly*]: Yes – maybe – a little bit –

JIM [*trying a careless tone*]: Reckon dat Tom's a liar, an' de joke's on me! Dat chalk only makes me feel kinder sick inside.

ELLA [*wonderingly*]: Why do you want to be white?

JIM: Because – just because – I lak dat better.

ELLA: I wouldn't. I like black. Let's you and me swap. I'd like to be black. [*Clapping her hands*] Gee, that'd be fun, if we only could!

JIM [*hesitatingly*]: Yes – maybe –

ELLA: Then they'd call me Crow, and you'd be Painty Face!

JIM: They wouldn't never dast call you nigger, you bet! I'd kill 'em! [*A long pause. Finally she takes his hand shyly. They both keep looking as far away from each other as possible.*]

ELLA: I like you.

JIM: I like you.

ELLA: Do you want to be my feller?

JIM: Yes.

ELLA: Then I'm your girl.

JIM: Yes. [*Then grandly*] You kin bet none o' de gang gwine call you Painty Face from dis out! I lam' 'em good! [*The sun has set. Twilight has fallen on the street. An organ-grinder comes up to the corner and plays 'Annie Rooney'. They stand hand-in-hand and listen. He goes away. It is growing dark.*]

ELLA [*suddenly*]: Golly, it's late! I'll git a lickin'!

JIM: Me, too.

ELLA: I won't mind it much.

JIM: Me nuther.

ELLA: See you going to school tomorrow?

JIM: Sure.

ELLA: I gotta skip now.

JIM: Me, too.

ELLA: I like you, Jim.

JIM: I like you.

ELLA: Don't forget.

JIM: Don't you.

ELLA: Good-bye.

JIM: So long. [*They run away from each other – then stop abruptly, and turn as at a signal.*]

ELLA: Don't forget.

JIM: I won't, you bet!

ELLA: Here! [*She kisses her hand at him, then runs off in frantic embarrassment.*]

JIM [*overcome*]: Gee! [*Then he turns and darts away, as*]

THE CURTAIN FALLS

SCENE 2

[*The same corner. Nine years have passed. It is again late spring at a time in the evening which immediately follows the hour of Scene 1. Nothing has changed much. One street is still all white, the other all black. The fire escapes are laden with drooping human beings. The grocery store is still at the corner. The street noises are now more rhythmically mechanical, electricity having taken the place of horse and steam. People pass, white and black. They laugh as in Scene 1. From the street of the whites the high pitched nasal tenor sings, 'Gee, I Wish I Had a Girl', and the Negro replies with, 'All I Got Was Sympathy'. The singing is followed again by laughter from both streets. Then silence. The dusk grows darker. With a spluttering flare the arc-lamp at the corner is lit and sheds a pale glare over the street. Two young roughs slouch up to the corner, as tough in manner as they can make themselves. One is the* SHORTY *of Scene 1; the other the Negro,* JOE. *They stand loafing. A boy of seventeen or so passes by, escorting a girl of about the same age. Both are dressed in their best, the boy in black with stiff collar, the girl in white.*]

SHORTY [*scornfully*]: Hully cripes! Pipe who's here. [*To the girl, sneeringly*] Wha's matter, Liz? Don't yer recernize yer old fr'en's?

GIRL [*frightenedly*]: Hello, Shorty.

SHORTY: Why de glad rags? Goin' to graduation? [*He tries to obstruct their way, but, edging away from him, they turn and run.*]

JOE: Har-har! Look at dem scoot, will you! [*Shorty grins with satisfaction.*]

SHORTY [*looking down other street*]: Here comes Mickey.

JOE: He won de semi-final last night easy?

SHORTY: Knocked de bloke out in de thoid.

JOE: Dat boy's suah a-comin'! He'll be de champeen yit.

SHORTY [*judicially*]: Got a good chanct – if he leaves de broads alone. Dat's where he's wide open.

[MICKEY *comes in from left. He is dressed loudly, a straw hat with a gaudy band cocked over one cauliflower ear. He has acquired a typical 'pug's' face, with the added viciousness of a natural bully. One of his eyes is puffed, almost closed, as a result of his battle the night before. He swaggers up.*]

BOTH: Hello, Mickey!

MICKEY: Hello!

JOE: Hear you knocked him col'.

MICKEY: Sure. I knocked his block off. [*Changing the subject*] Say. Seen 'em goin' past to de graduation racket?

SHORTY [*with a wink*]: Why? You int'rested?

JOE [*chuckling*]: Mickey's gwine roun' git a good conduct medal.

MICKEY: Sure. Dey kin pin it on de seat o' me pants. [*They laugh.*] Listen. Seen Ella Downey goin'?

SHORTY: Painty Face? No, she ain't been along.

MICKEY [*with authority*]: Can dat name, see! Want a bunch o' fives in yer kisser? Den nix! She's me goil, understan'?

JOE [*venturing to joke*]: Which one? Yo' number ten?

MICKEY [*flattered*]: Sure. De real K.O. one.

SHORTY [*pointing right – sneeringly*]: Gee! Pipe Jim Crow all dolled up for de racket.

JOE [*with disgusted resentment*]: You mean tell me dat nigger's graduatin'?

SHORTY: Ask him. [JIM HARRIS *comes in. He is dressed in black, stiff white collar, etc. – a quiet-mannered Negro boy with a queerly-baffled, sensitive face.*]

JIM [*pleasantly*]: Hello, fellows! [*They grunt in reply, looking over him scornfully.*]

JOE [*staring resentfully*]: Is you graduatin' tonight?

JIM: Yes.

JOE [*spitting disgustedly*]: Fo' Gawd's sake! You *is* gittin' high falutin'!

JIM [*smiling deprecatingly*]: This is my second try. I didn't pass last year.

JOE: What de hell does it git you, huh? Whatever is you gwine do wid it now you gits it? Live lazy on yo' ol' woman?

JIM [*assertively*]: I'm going to study and become a lawyer.

JOE [*with a snort*]: Fo' Chris' sake, nigger!

JIM [*fiercely*]: Don't you call me that – not before them!

JOE [*pugnaciously*]: Does you deny you's a nigger? I shows you –

MICKEY [*gives them both a push – truculently*]: Cut it out, see! I'm runnin' dis corner. [*Turning to* JIM *insultingly*] Say, you! Painty Face's gittin' her ticket tonight, ain't she?

JIM: You mean Ella –

MICKEY: Painty Face Downey, dat's who I mean! I don't have to be perlite wit' her. She's me goil!

JIM [*glumly*]: Yes, she's graduating.

SHORTY [*winks at* MICKEY]: Smart, huh?

MICKEY [*winks back – meaningly*]: Willin' to loin, take it from me! [JIM *stands tensely as if a struggle were going on in him.*]

JIM [*finally blurts out*]: I want to speak to you, Mickey – alone.

MICKEY [*surprised – insultingly*]: Aw, what de hell – !

JIM [*excitedly*]: It's important, I tell you!

MICKEY: Huh? [*Stares at him inquisitively – then motions the others back carelessly and follows* JIM *down front.*]

SHORTY: Some noive!

JOE [*vengefully*]: I gits dat Jim alone, you wait!

MICKEY: Well, spill de big news. I ain't got all night. I got a date.

JIM: With – Ella?

MICKEY: What's dat to you?

JIM [*the words tumbling out*]: What – I wanted to say! I know – I've heard – all the stories – what you've been doing around the ward – with other girls – it's none of my business, with them – but she – Ella – it's different – she's not that kind –

MICKEY [*insultingly*]: Who told yuh so, huh?

JIM [*draws back his fist threateningly*]: Don't you dare – ! [MICKEY *is so paralysed by this effrontery that he actually steps back.*]

MICKEY: Say, cut de comedy! [*Beginning to feel insulted*] Listen, you Jim Crow! Ain't you wise I could give yuh one poke dat'd knock yuh into next week?

JIM: I'm only asking you to act square, Mickey.

MICKEY: What's it to yuh? Why, yuh lousy goat, she wouldn't spit on yuh even! She hates de sight of a coon.

JIM [*in agony*]: I – I know – but once she didn't mind – we were kids together –

MICKEY: Aw, ferget dat! Dis is *now*!

JIM: And I'm still her friend always – even if she don't like coloured people –

MICKEY: *Coons*, why don't yuh say it right! De trouble wit' yoh is yuh're gittin' stuck up, dat's what! Stay where yeh belong, see! Yer old man made coin at de truckin' game and yuh're tryin' to buy yerself white – graduatin' and law, for hell's sake! Yuh're gittin' yerself in Dutch wit' everyone in de ward – and it ain't cause yer a coon neider. Don't de gang all train wit' Joe dere and lots of others? But yuh're tryin' to buy white and it won't git yuh no place, see!

JIM [*trembling*]: Some day – I'll show you –

MICKEY [*turning away*]: Aw, gwan!

JIM: D'you think I'd change – be you – your dirty white – !

MICKEY [*whirling about*]: What's dat?

JIM [*with hysterical vehemence*]: You act square with her – or I'll show you up – I'll report you – I'll write to the papers – the sporting writers – I'll let them know how white you are!

MICKEY [*infuriated*]: Yuh damn nigger, I'll bust yer jaw in! [*Assuming his ring pose he weaves toward* JIM, *his face set in a cruel scowl.* JIM *waits helplessly but with a certain dignity.*]

SHORTY: Cheese it! A couple of bulls! And here's de Downey skoit comin', too.

MICKEY: I'll get yuh de next time!

[ELLA DOWNEY *enters from the right. She is seventeen, still has the same rose-and-white complexion, is pretty but with a rather repelling bold air about her.*]

ELLA [*smiles with pleasure when she sees* MICKEY]: Hello, Mick! Am I late? Say, I'm so glad you won last night. [*She glances from one to the other as she feels something in the air.*] Hello! What's up?

MICKEY: Dis boob. [*He indicates* JIM *scornfully.*]

JIM [*diffidently*]: Hello, Ella!

ELLA [*shortly, turning away*]: Hello! [*Then to* MICKEY.] Come on, Mick. Walk down with me. I got to hurry.

JIM [*blurts out*]: Wait – just a second. [*Painfully*] Ella, do you hate – coloured people?

MICKEY: Aw, shut up!

JIM: Please answer.

ELLA [*forcing a laugh*]: Say! What is this – another exam?

JIM [*doggedly*]: Please answer.

ELLA [*irritably*]: Of course I don't! Haven't I been brought up alongside – Why, some of my oldest – the girls I've been to public school the longest with –

JIM: Do you hate me, Ella?

ELLA [*confusedly and more irritably*]: Say, is he drunk? Why should I? I don't hate anyone.

JIM: Then why haven't you ever hardly spoken to me – for years?

ELLA [*resentfully*]: What would I speak about? You and me've got nothing in common any more.

JIM [*desperately*]: Maybe not any more – but – right on this corner – do you remember once – ?

ELLA: I don't remember nothing! [*Angrily*] Say! What's got into you to be butting into my business all of a sudden like this? Because you finally managed to graduate, has it gone to your head?

JIM: No, I – only want to help you, Ella.

ELLA: Of all the nerve! You're certainly forgetting your place! Who's asking you for help, I'd like to know? Shut up and stop bothering me!

JIM [*insistently*]: If you ever need a friend – a true friend –

ELLA: I've got lots of friends among my own – kind, I can tell you. [*Exasperatedly*] You make me sick! Go to – hell! [*She flounces off. The three men laugh.* MICKEY *follows her.* JIM *is stricken. He goes and sinks down limply on a box in front of the grocery store.*]

SHORTY: I'm going to shoot a drink. Come on, Joe, and I'll blow yuh.

JOE [*who has never ceased to follow every move of Jim's with angry, resentful eyes*]: Go long. I'se gwine stay here a secon'. I got a li'l argyment. [*He points to* JIM.]

SHORTY: Suit yerself. Do a good job. See yuh later. [*He goes, whistling.*]

JOE [*stands for a while glaring at* JIM, *his fierce little eyes peering out of his black face. Then he spits on his hands aggressively and strides up to the oblivious Jim. He stands in front of him, gradually working himself into a fury at the other's seeming indifference to his words*]: Listen to me, nigger: I got a heap to whisper in yo' ear! Who is you, anyhow? Who does you think you is? Don't yo' old man and mine work on de docks togidder befo' yo old man gits his own truckin' business? Yo' ol' man swallers his nickels, my ol man buys him beer wid dem and swallers dat – dat's the on'y diff'rence. Don't you 'n' me drag up togidder?

JIM [*dully*]: I'm your friend, Joe.

JOE: No, you isn't! I ain't no fren' o' yourn! I don't even know who you is! What's all dis schoolin' you doin'? What's all dis dressin' up and graduatin' an' sayin' you gwine study to be a lawyer? What's all dis fakin' an' pretendin' and swellin' out grand an' talkin' soft and perlite? What's all dis denyin' you's a nigger – an' wid de white boys listenin' to you say it! Is you aimin' to buy white wid yo' ol' man's dough like Mickey say? What is you? [*In a rage at the other's silence*] You don't talk? Den I takes it out o' yo' hide! [*He grabs Jim by the throat with one hand and draws the other fist back.*] Tell me befo' I wrecks yo' face in! Is you a nigger or isn't you? [*Shaking him*] Is you a nigger, nigger? Nigger, is you a nigger?

JIM [*looking into his eyes – quietly*]: Yes. I'm a nigger. We're both niggers. [*They look at each other for a moment.* JOE'S *rage vanishes. He slumps on to a box beside* JIM'S. *He offers him a cigarette.* JIM *takes it.* JOE *scratches a match and lights both their cigarettes.*]

JOE [*after a puff, with full satisfaction*]: Man, why didn't you 'splain dat in de fust place?

JIM: We're both niggers. [*The same hand-organ man of Scene 1 comes to the corner. He plays the chorus of 'Bonbon Buddie', the 'Chocolate Drop'. They both stare straight ahead listening. Then the organ man goes away. A silence.* JOE *gets to his feet.*]

JOE: I'll go get me a cold beer. [*He starts to move off – then turns.*] Time you was graduatin', ain't it? [*He goes,* JIM *remains sitting on his box staring straight before him as*]

THE CURTAIN FALLS

SCENE 3

[*The same corner five years later. Nothing has changed much. It is a night in spring. The arc-lamp discovers faces with a favourless cruelty. The street noises are the same but more intermittent and dulled with a quality of fatigue. Two people pass, one black and one white. They are tired. They both yawn, but neither laughs. There is no laughter from the two streets. From the street of the whites the tenor, more nasal than ever and a bit drunken, wails in high barber-shop falsetto the last half of the chorus of 'When I Lost You'. The Negro voice, a bit maudlin in turn, replies with the last half of 'Waiting for the Robert E. Lee'. Silence.* SHORTY *enters. He looks tougher than ever, the typical gangster. He stands waiting, singing a bit drunkenly, peering down the street.*]

SHORTY [*indignantly*]: Yuh bum! Ain't yuh ever comin'? [*He begins to sing: 'And sewed up in her yeller kimona, She had a blue-barrelled forty-five gun, For to get her man Who'd done her wrong'. Then he comments scornfully:*] Not her, dough! No gat for her. She ain't got de noive. A little sugar. Dat'll fix her.

[ELLA *enters. She is dressed poorly, her face is pale and hollow-eyed, her voice cold and tired.*]

SHORTY: Yuh got de message?

ELLA: Here I am.

SHORTY: How yuh been?

ELLA: All right. [*A pause. He looks at her puzzledly.*]

SHORTY [*a bit embarrassedly*]: Well, I s'pose yuh'd like me to give yuh some dope on Mickey, huh?

ELLA: No.

SHORTY: Mean to say yuh don't wanter know where he is or what he's doin'?

ELLA: No.

SHORTY: Since when?

ELLA: A long time.

SHORTY [*after a pause – with a rat-like viciousness*]: Between you'n me, kid, you'll get even soon – you'n all de odder dames he's tossed. I'm on de inside. I've watched him trainin'. His next scrap, watch it! He'll go! It won't be de odder guy. It'll be all youse dames he's kidded – and de ones what's kidded him. Youse'll all be in de odder guy's corner. He won't need no odder seconds. Youse'll trow water on him, and sponge his face, and take de kinks out of his socker – and Mickey'll catch it on de button – and he won't be able to take it no more – 'cause all your weight – you and de odders – 'll be behind dat punch. Ha, ha! [*He laughs an evil laugh.*] And Mickey'll go – down to his knees first – [*He sinks to his knees in the attitude of a groggy boxer.*]

ELLA: I'd like to see him on his knees!

SHORTY: And den – flat on his pan – dead to de world – de

boidies singin' in de trees – ten – out! [*He suits his action to the words, sinking flat on the pavement, then rises and laughs the same evil laugh.*]

ELLA: He's been out – for me – a long time. [*A pause*] Why did you send for me?

SHORTY: He sent me.

ELLA: Why?

SHORTY: To slip you this wad o' dough. [*He reluctantly takes a roll of bills from his pocket and holds it out to her.*]

ELLA [*looks at the money indifferently*]: What for?

SHORTY: For you.

ELLA: No.

SHORTY: For de kid den.

ELLA: The kid's dead. He took diphtheria.

SHORTY: Hell yuh say! When?

ELLA: A long time.

SHORTY: Why didn't you write Mickey – ?

ELLA: Why should I? He'd only be glad.

SHORTY [*after a pause*]: Well – it's better.

ELLA: Yes.

SHORTY: You made up wit yer family?

ELLA: No chance.

SHORTY: Livin' alone?

ELLA: In Brooklyn.

SHORTY: Workin'?

ELLA: In a factory.

SHORTY: You're a sucker. There's lots of softer snaps for you, kid –

ELLA: I know what you mean. No.

SHORTY: Don't yuh wanter step out no more – have fun – live?

ELLA: I'm through.

SHORTY [*mockingly*]: Jump in de river, huh? T'ink it over, baby. I kin start yuh right in my stable. No one'll bodder yoh den. I got influence.

ELLA [*without emphasis*]: You're a dirty dog. Why doesn't someone kill you?

SHORTY: Is dat so! What're you? They say you been travellin' round with Jim Crow.

ELLA: He's been my only friend.

SHORTY: A nigger!

ELLA: The only white man in the world! Kind and white. You're all black – black to the heart.

SHORTY: Nigger-lover! [*He throws the money in her face. It falls to the street.*] Listen, you! Mickey says he's off of yuh for keeps. Dis is de finish! Dat's what he sent me to tell you. [*Glances at her searchingly – a pause*] Yuh won't make no trouble?

ELLA: Why should I? He's free. The kid's dead. I'm free. No hard feelings – only – I'll be there in spirit at his next fight, tell him! I'll take your tip – the other corner – second the punch – nine – ten – out! He's free! That's all. [*She grins horribly at* SHORTY.] Go away, Shorty.

SHORTY [*looking at her and shaking his head – maudlinly*]: Groggy! Groggy! We're all groggy! Gluttons for punishment! Me for a drink. So long.

[*He goes. A Salvation Army band comes toward the corner. They are playing and singing 'Till We Meet at Jesus' Feet'. They reach the end as they enter and stop before* ELLA. *The* CAPTAIN *steps forward.*]

CAPTAIN: Sister –

ELLA [*picks up the money and drops it in his hat – mockingly*]: Here. Go save yourself. Leave me alone.

A WOMAN SALVATIONIST: Sister –

ELLA: Never mind that. I'm not in your line – yet. [*As they hesitate, wonderingly*] I want to be alone.

[*To the thud of the big drum they march off.* ELLA *sits down on a box, her hands hanging at her sides. Presently* JIM HARRIS *comes in. He has grown into a quietly-dressed, studious-looking Negro with an intelligent yet queerly-baffled face.*]

JIM [*with a joyous but bewildered cry*]: Ella! I just saw Shorty –

ELLA [*smiling at him with frank affection*]: He had a message from Mickey.

JIM [*sadly*]: Ah!

ELLA [*pointing to the box behind her*]: Sit down. [*He does so. A pause – then she says indifferently*] It's finished. I'm free, Jim.

JIM [*wearily*]: We're never free – except to do what we have to do.

ELLA: What are you getting gloomy about all of a sudden?

JIM: I've got the report from the school. I've flunked again.

ELLA: Poor Jim!

JIM: Don't pity me. I'd like to kick myself all over the block. Five years – and I'm still plugging away where I ought to have been at the end of two.

ELLA: Why don't you give it up?

JIM: No!

ELLA: After all, what's being a lawyer?

JIM: A lot – to me – what it means. [*Intensely*] Why, if I was a Member of the Bar right now, Ella, I believe I'd almost have the courage to –

ELLA: What?

JIM: Nothing. [*After a pause – gropingly*] I can't explain – just – but it hurts like fire. It brands me in my pride. I swear I know more'n any member of my class. I ought to, I study harder. I work like the devil. It's all in my head – all fine and correct to a T. Then when I'm called on – I stand up – all the white faces looking at me – and I can feel their eyes – I hear my own voice sounding funny, trembling – and all of a sudden it's all gone in my head – there's nothing remembered – and I hear myself stuttering – and give up – sit down – They don't laugh, hardly ever. They're kind. They're good people. [*In a frenzy*] They're considerate, damn them! But I feel branded!

ELLA: Poor Jim!

JIM [*going on painfully*]: And it's the same thing in the written exams. For weeks before I study all night. I can't sleep, anyway. I learn it all, I see it, I understand it. Then they give me the paper in the exam room. I look it over, I know each answer – perfectly. I take up my pen. On all sides are white men starting to write. They're so sure – even the ones that I know know nothing. But I know it all – but I can't remember any more – it fades – it goes – it's gone. There's a blank in my head – stupidity – I sit like a fool fighting to remember a little bit here, a little bit there – not enough to pass – not enough for anything – when I know it all!

ELLA [*compassionately*]: Jim, it isn't worth it. You don't need to –

JIM: I need it more than anyone ever needed anything. I need it to live.

ELLA: What'll it prove?

JIM: Nothing at all much – but everything to me.

ELLA: You're so much better than they are in every other way.

JIM [*looking up at her*]: Then – you understand?

ELLA: Of course. [*Affectionately*] Don't I know how fine you've been to me! You've been the only one in the world who's stood by me – the only understanding person – and all after the rotten way I used to treat you.

JIM: But before that – way back so high – you treated me good. [*He smiles.*]

ELLA: You've been white to me, Jim. [*She takes his hand.*]

JIM: White – to you!

ELLA: Yes.

JIM: All love is white. I've always loved you. [*This with the deepest humility.*]

ELLA: Even now – after all that's happened!

JIM: Always.

ELLA: I like you, Jim – better than anyone else in the world.

JIM: That's more than enough, more than I ever hoped for. [*The organ-grinder comes to the corner. He plays the chorus of*

'Annie Laurie'. They sit listening, hand-in-hand.] Would you ever want to marry me, Ella?

ELLA: Yes, Jim.

JIM [*as if this quick consent alarmed him*]: No, no, don't answer now. Wait! Turn it over in your mind! Think what it means to you! Consider it – over and over again! I'm in no hurry, Ella. I can wait months – years –

ELLA: I'm alone. I've got to be helped. I've got to help someone – or it's the end – one end or another.

JIM [*eagerly*]: Oh, I'll help – I know I can help – I'll give my life to help you – that's what I've been living for –

ELLA: But can I help you? Can I help you?

JIM: Yes! Yes! We'll go abroad where a man is a man – where it don't make that difference – where people are kind and wise to see the soul under skins. I don't ask you to love me – I don't dare to hope nothing like that! I don't want nothing – only to wait – to know you like me – to be near you – to keep harm away – to make up for the past – to never let you suffer any more – to serve you – to lie at your feet like a dog that loves you – to kneel by your bed like a nurse that watches over you sleeping – to preserve and protect and shield you from evil and sorrow – to give my life and my blood and all the strength that's in me to give you peace and joy – to become your slave! – yes, be your slave – your black slave that adores you as sacred!

[*He has sunk to his knees. In a frenzy of self-abnegation, as he says the last words he beats his head on the flagstones.*]

ELLA [*overcome and alarmed*]: Jim! Jim! You're crazy! I want to help you, Jim – I want to help –

THE CURTAIN FALLS

SCENE 4

Some weeks or so later. A street in the same ward in front of an old brick church. The church stands back from the sidewalk in a yard enclosed by a rusty iron railing with a gate at centre. On each side of this yard are tenements. The buildings have a stern, forbidding look. All the shades on the windows are drawn down, giving an effect of staring, brutal eyes that pry callously at human beings without acknowledging them. Even the two tall, narrow church windows on either side of the arched door are blanked with dull green shades. It is a bright sunny morning. The district is unusually still, as if it were waiting, holding its breath.

[*From the street of the blacks to the right a Negro tenor sings in a voice of shadowy richness – the first stanza with a contented, childlike melancholy –*]

Sometimes I feel like a mourning dove,
Sometimes I feel like a mourning dove,
I feel like a mourning dove.

[*The second with a dreamy, boyish exultance –*]

Sometimes I feel like an eagle in the air,
Sometimes I feel like an eagle in the air,
I feel like an eagle in the air.

[*The third with a brooding, earthbound sorrow*]

Sometimes I wish that I'd never been born,
Sometimes I wish that I'd never been born,
I wish that I'd never been born.

[*As the music dies down there is a pause of waiting stillness. This is broken by one startling, metallic clang of the church bell. As if it were a signal, people – men, women, children – pour from the two tenements, whites from the tenement to the left, blacks from the one to the right. They hurry to form into two racial lines on each side of the gate, rigid and unyielding, staring across at each other with bitter hostile eyes. The halves of the big church door swing open and* JIM *and* ELLA *step out from the darkness within into the sunlight. The doors slam behind them like wooden lips of an idol that has spat them out.* JIM *is dressed in black,* ELLA *in white, both with extreme plainness. They stand in the sunlight, shrinking and confused. All the hostile eyes are now concentrated on them. They become aware of the two lines through which they must pass; they hesitate and tremble; then stand there staring back at the people as fixed and immovable as they are. The organ-grinder comes in from the right. He plays the chorus of 'Old Black Joe'. As he finishes the bell of the church clangs one more single stroke, insistently dismissing.*]

JIM [*as if the sound had awakened him from a trance, reaches out and takes her hand*]: Come. Time we got to the steamer. Time we sailed away over the sea. Come, Honey! [*She tries to answer, but her lips tremble; she cannot take her eyes off the eyes of the people; she is unable to move. He sees this and, keeping the same tone of profound, affectionate kindness, he points upward in the sky, and gradually persuades her eyes to look up.*] Look up, Honey! See the sun! Feel his warm eye lookin' down! Feel how kind he looks! Feel his blessing deep in your heart, your bones! Look up, Honey! [*Her eyes are fixed on the sky now. Her face is calm. She tries to smile bravely back at the sun. Now he pulls her by the hand, urging her gently to walk with him down through the yard and gate, through the lines of people. He is maintaining an attitude to support them through the ordeal only by a terrible effort, which manifests itself in the hysteric quality of ecstasy which breaks into his voice.*] And look at the sky! Ain't it kind and blue? Blue for hope. Don't they say blue's for hope? Hope! That's for us, Honey. All those blessings in the sky! What's it the Bible says? Falls on just and unjust alike? No, that's the sweet rain. Pshaw, what am I saying! All mixed up. There's no unjust about it. We're all the same – equally just – under the sky – under the sun – under God – sailing over the sea – to the other side of the world – the side where Christ was born – the kind side that takes count of the soul – over the sea – the sea's blue, too – Let's not be late – let's get that steamer! [*They have reached the kerb now, passed the lines of people. She is looking up to the sky with an expression of trance-like calm and peace. He is on the verge of collapse, his face twitching, his eyes staring. He calls hoarsely:*] Taxi! Where is he? Taxi!

THE CURTAIN FALLS

ACT TWO

SCENE 1

Two years later. A flat of the better sort in the Negro district near the corner of Act One. This is the parlour. Its furniture is a queer clash. The old pieces are cheaply ornate, naïvely, childishly gaudy – the new pieces give evidence of a taste that is diametrically opposed, severe to the point of sombreness. On one wall, in a heavy gold frame, is a coloured photograph – the portrait of an elderly Negro with an able, shrewd face, but dressed in outlandish lodge regalia, a get-up adorned with medals, sashes, a cocked hat with frills – the whole effect as absurd to contemplate as one of Napoleon's Marshals in full uniform. In the left corner, where a window lights it effectively, is a Negro primitive mask from the Congo – a grotesque face, inspiring obscure, dim connotations in one's mind, but beautifully done, conceived in a true religious spirit. In this room, however, the mask acquires an arbitrary accentuation. It dominates by a diabolical quality that contrast imposes upon it.

There are two windows on the left looking out in the street. In the rear, a door to the hall of the building. In the right, a doorway with red and gold portières, leading into the bedroom and the rest of the flat. Everything is cleaned and polished. The dark brown wall-paper is new, the brilliantly figured carpet also. There is a round mahogany table at centre.

[*In a rocking-chair by the table* MRS HARRIS *is sitting. She is a mild-looking, grey-haired Negress of sixty-five, dressed in an old-fashioned Sunday-best dress. Walking about the room nervously is* HATTIE, *her daughter, Jim's sister, a woman of about thirty with a high-strung, defiant face – an intelligent head showing both power and courage. She is dressed severely, mannishly.*

It is a fine morning in spring. Sunshine comes through the windows at the left.]

MRS HARRIS: Time dey was here, ain't it?

HATTIE [*impatiently*]: Yes.

MRS HARRIS [*worriedly*]: You ain't gwine ter kick up a fuss, is you – like you done wid Jim befo' de weddin'?

HATTIE: No. What's done is done.

MRS HARRIS: We mustn't let her see we hold it agin' her – de bad dat happened to her wid dat no-count fighter.

HATTIE: I certainly never give that a thought. It's what she's done to Jim – making him run away and give up his fight – !

MRS HARRIS: Jim loves her a powerful lot, must be.

HATTIE [*after a pause – bitterly*]: I wonder if she loves Jim!

MRS HARRIS: She must, too. Yes, she must, too. Don't you forget dat it was hard for her – mighty, mighty hard – harder for de white dan for de black!

HATTIE [*indignantly*]: Why should it be?

MRS HARRIS [*shaking her head*]: I ain't talkin' of shoulds. It's too late for shoulds. Dey's on'y one should. [*Solemnly*] De white and de black shouldn't mix dat close. Dere's one road where de white goes on alone; dere's anudder road where de black goes on alone –

HATTIE: Yes, if they'd only leave us alone!

MRS HARRIS: Dey leaves your Pa alone. He comes to de top till he's got his own business, lots o' money in de bank, he owns a building even befo' he die. [*She looks up proudly at the picture.* HATTIE *sighs impatiently – then her mother goes on.*] Dey leaves me alone. I bears four children into dis worl', two dies, two lives. I helps you two grow up fine an' healthy and eddicated wid schoolin' and money fo' yo' comfort –

HATTIE [*impatiently*]: Ma!

MRS HARRIS: I does de duty God set for me in dis worl'. Dey leaves me alone. [HATTIE *goes to the window to hide her exasperation. The mother broods for a minute – then goes on.*] The worl' done change. Dey ain't no satisfaction wid nuffin' no more.

HATTIE: Oh! [*Then after a pause*] They'll be here any minute now.

MRS HARRIS: Why didn't you go meet 'em at de dock like I axed you?

HATTIE: I couldn't. My face and Jim's among those hundreds of white faces – [*With a harsh laugh*] It would give her too much advantage!

MRS HARRIS [*impatiently*]: Don't talk dat way! What makes you so proud? [*Then after a pause – sadly*] Hattie!

HATTIE [*turning*]: Yes, Ma.

MRS HARRIS: I want to see Jim again – my only boy – but – all de same I'd ruther he stayed away. He say in his letter he's happy, she's happy, dey likes it dere, de folks don't think nuffin' but what's natural at seeing 'em married. Why don't dey stay?

HATTIE [*vehemently*]: No! They were cowards to run away. If they believe in what they've done, then let them face it out, live it out here, be strong enough to conquer all prejudice!

MRS HARRIS: Strong? Dey ain't many strong. Dey ain't many happy neider. Dey was happy ovah yondah.

HATTIE: We don't deserve happiness till we've fought the fight of our race and won it! [*In the pause that follows there is a ring from back in the flat.*] It's the door bell! You go, Ma. I – I – I'd rather not. [*Her mother looks at her rebukingly and goes out agitatedly through the portières.* HATTIE *waits, nervously walking about, trying to compose herself. There is a long pause. Finally the portières are parted and* JIM *enters. He looks much older, graver, worried.*]

JIM: Hattie!

HATTIE: Jim! [*They embrace with great affection.*]

JIM: It's great to see you again! You're looking fine.

HATTIE [*looking at him searchingly*]: You look well, too – thinner maybe – and tired. [*Then as she sees him frowning*] But where's Ella?

JIM: With Ma. [*Apologetically*] She sort of – broke down – when we came in. The trip wore her out.

HATTIE [*coldly*]: I see.

JIM: Oh, it's nothing serious. Nerves. She needs a rest.

HATTIE: Wasn't living in France restful?

JIM: Yes, but – too lonely – especially for her.

HATTIE [*resentfully*]: Why? Didn't the people there want to associate – ?

JIM [*quickly*]: Oh, no indeed, they didn't think anything of that. [*After a pause*] But – she did. For the first year it was all right. Ella liked everything a lot. She went out with French folks and got so she could talk a little – and I learned it – a little. We were having a right nice time. I never thought then we'd ever want to come back here.

HATTIE [*frowning*]: But – what happened to change you?

JIM [*after a pause – haltingly*]: Well – you see – the first year – she and I were living around – like friends – like a brother and sister – like you and I might.

HATTIE [*her face becoming more and more drawn and tense*]: You mean – then – ? [*She shudders – then after a pause.*] She loves you, Jim?

JIM: If I didn't know that I'd have to jump in the river.

HATTIE: Are you sure she loves you?

JIM: Isn't that why she's suffering?

HATTIE [*letting her breath escape through her clenched teeth*]: Ah!

JIM [*suddenly springs up and shouts almost hysterically*]: Why d'you ask me all those damn questions? Are you trying to make trouble between us?

HATTIE [*controlling herself – quietly*]: No, Jim.

JIM [*after a pause – contritely*]: I'm sorry, Hattie. I'm kind of on edge today. [*He sinks down on his chair – then goes on as if something forced him to speak.*] After that we got to living housed in. Ella didn't want to see nobody, she said just the two of us was enough. I was happy then – and I really guess she was happy, too – in a way – for a while. [*Again a pause*]

But she never did get to wanting to go out any place again. She got to saying she felt she'd be sure to run into someone she knew – from over here. So I moved us out to the country where no tourist ever comes – but it didn't make any difference to her. She got to avoiding the French folks the same as if they were Americans and I couldn't get it out of her mind. She lived in the house and got paler and paler, and more and more nervous and scarey, always imagining things – until I got to imagining things, too. I got to feeling blue. Got to sneering at myself that I wasn't any better than a quitter because I sneaked away right after getting married, didn't face nothing, gave up trying to become a Member of the Bar – and I got to suspecting Ella must feel that way about me, too – that I wasn't a *real man*!

HATTIE [*indignantly*]: She couldn't!

JIM [*with hostility*]: You don't need to tell me! All this was only in my own mind. We never quarrelled a single bit. We never said a harsh word. We were as close to each other as could be. We were all there was in the world to each other. We were alone together! [*A pause*] Well, one day I got so I couldn't stand it. I could see she couldn't stand it. So I just up and said: Ella, we've got to have a plain talk, look everything straight in the face, hide nothing, come out with the exact truth of the way we feel.

HATTIE: And you decided to come back!

JIM: Yes. We decided the reason we felt sort of ashamed was we'd acted like cowards. We'd run away from the thing – and taken it with us. We decided to come back and face it and live it down in ourselves, and prove to ourselves we were strong in our love – and then, and that way only, by being brave we'd free ourselves, and gain confidence, and be really free inside and able then to go anywhere and live in peace and equality with ourselves and the world without any guilty uncomfortable feeling coming up to rile us. [*He has talked himself now into a state of happy confidence.*]

HATTIE [*bending over and kissing him*]: Good for you! I admire you so much, Jim! I admire both of you! And are you going to begin studying right away and get admitted to the Bar?

JIM: You bet I am!

HATTIE: You must, Jim! Our race needs men like you to come to the front and help – [*As voices are heard approaching she stops, stiffens, and her face grows cold.*]

JIM [*noticing this – warningly*]: Remember Ella's been sick! [*Losing control – threateningly*] You be nice to her, you hear!

[MRS HARRIS *enters, showing* ELLA *the way. The coloured woman is plainly worried and perplexed.* ELLA *is pale, with a strange, haunted expression in her eyes. She runs to* JIM *as to a refuge, clutching his hands in both of hers, looking from* MRS HARRIS *to* HATTIE *with a frightened defiance.*]

MRS HARRIS: Dere he is, child, big's life! She was afraid we'd done kidnapped you away, Jim.

JIM [*patting her hand*]: This place ought to be familiar, Ella. Don't you remember playing here with us sometimes as a kid?

ELLA [*queerly – with a frown of effort*]: I remember playing marbles one night – but that was on the street.

JIM: Don't you remember Hattie?

HATTIE [*coming forward with a forced smile*]: It was a long time ago – but I remember Ella. [*She holds out her hand.*]

ELLA [*taking it – looking at* HATTIE *with the same queer defiance*]: I remember. But you've changed so much.

HATTIE [*stirred to hostility by* ELLA's *manner – condescendingly*]: Yes, I've grown older, naturally. [*Then in a tone which, as if in spite of herself, becomes bragging*] I've worked so hard. First I went away to college, you know – then I took up post-graduate study – when suddenly I decided I'd accomplish more good if I gave up learning and took up teaching. [*She suddenly checks herself, ashamed, and stung by Ella's indifference.*] But this sounds like stupid boasting. I don't mean that. I was only explaining –

ELLA [*indifferently*]: I didn't know you'd been to school so long. [*A pause*] Where are you teaching? In a coloured school, I suppose. [*There is an indifferent superiority in her words that is maddening to* HATTIE.]

HATTIE [*controlling herself*]: Yes. A private school endowed by some wealthy members of our race.

ELLA [*suddenly – even eagerly*]: Then you must have taken lots of examinations and managed to pass them, didn't you?

HATTIE [*biting her lips*]: I always passed with honours!

ELLA: Yes, we both graduated from the same High School, didn't we? That was dead easy for me. Why, I hardly even looked at a book. But Jim says it was awfully hard for him. He failed one year, remember?

[*She turns and smiles at* JIM *– a tolerant, superior smile, but one full of genuine love.* HATTIE *is outraged, but* JIM *smiles.*]

JIM: Yes, it was hard for me, Honey.

ELLA: And the law school examinations Jim hardly ever could pass at all. Could you? [*She laughs lovingly.*]

HATTIE [*harshly*]: Yes, he could! He can! He'll pass them now – if you'll give him a chance!

JIM [*angrily*]: Hattie!

MRS HARRIS: Hold yo' fool tongue!

HATTIE [*sullenly*]: I'm sorry.

[ELLA *has shrunk back against* JIM. *She regards* HATTIE *with a sort of wondering hatred. Then she looks away about the room. Suddenly her eyes fasten on the primitive mask and she gives a stifled scream.*]

JIM: What's the matter, Honey?

ELLA [*pointing*]: That! For God's sake, what is it?

HATTIE [*scornfully*]: It's a Congo mask. [*She goes and picks it up.*] I'll take it away if you wish. I thought you'd like it. It was my wedding present to Jim.

ELLA: What is it?

HATTIE: It's a mask which used to be worn in religious ceremonies by my people in Africa. But, aside from that, it's beautifully made, a work of Art by a real artist – as real in his way as your Michelangelo. [*Forces* ELLA *to take it.*] Here. Just notice the workmanship.

ELLA [*defiantly*]: I'm not scared of it if you're not. [*Looking at it with disgust*] Beautiful? Well, some people certainly have queer notions! It looks ugly to me and stupid – like a kid's game – making faces! [*She slaps it contemptuously.*] Pooh! You needn't look hard at me. I'll give you the laugh. [*She goes to put it back on the stand.*]

JIM: Maybe, if it disturbs you, we better put it in some other room.

ELLA [*defiantly aggressive*]: No. I want it here where I can give it the laugh! [*She sets it there again – then turns suddenly on* HATTIE *with aggressive determination.*] Jim's not going to take any more examinations! I won't let him!

HATTIE [*bursting forth*]: Jim! Do you hear that? There's white justice! – their fear for their superiority – !

ELLA [*with terrified pleading*]: Make her go away, Jim!

JIM [*losing control – furiously to his sister*]: Either you leave here – or we will!

MRS HARRIS [*weeping – throws her arms around* HATTIE]: Let's go, chile! Let's go!

HATTIE [*calmly now*]: Yes, Ma. All right.

[*They go through the portières. As soon as they are gone,* JIM *suddenly collapses into a chair and hides his head in his hands.* ELLA *stands beside him for a moment. She stares distractedly about her, at the portrait, at the mask, at the furniture, at* JIM. *She seems fighting to escape from some weight on her mind. She throws this off and, completely her old self for the moment, kneels by* JIM *and pats his shoulder.*]

ELLA [*with kindness and love*]: Don't, Jim! Don't cry, please! You don't suppose I really meant that about the examinations, do you? Why, of course, I didn't mean a word! I couldn't mean it! I want you to take the examinations! I want you to pass! I want you to be a lawyer! I want you to be the best lawyer in the country! I want you to show 'em – all the dirty sneaking, gossiping liars that talk behind our backs – what a man I married. I want the whole world to know you're the whitest of the white! I want you to climb and climb – and step on 'em, stamp right on their mean faces! I love you, Jim. You know that!

JIM [*calm again – happily*]: I hope so, Honey – and I'll make myself worthy.

HATTIE [*appears in the doorway – quietly*]: We're going now, Jim.

ELLA: No. Don't go.

HATTIE: We were going to, anyway. This is your house – Mother's gift to you, Jim.

JIM [*astonished*]: But I can't accept – Where are you going?

HATTIE: We've got a nice flat in the Bronx – [*with bitter pride*] in the heart of the Black Belt – the Congo – among our own people!

JIM [*angrily*]: You're crazy – I'll see Ma –

[*He goes out.* HATTIE *and* ELLA *stare at each other with scorn and hatred for a moment, then* HATTIE *goes.* ELLA *remains kneeling for a moment by the chair, her eyes dazed and strange as she looks about her. Then she gets to her feet and stands before the portrait of Jim's father – with a sneer.*]

ELLA: It's his Old Man – all dolled up like a circus horse! Well, they can't help it. It's in the blood, I suppose. They're ignorant, that's all there is to it. [*She moves to the mask – forcing a mocking tone.*] Hello, sport! Who d'you think you're scaring? Not me! I'll give you the laugh. He won't pass, you wait and see. Not in a thousand years! [*She goes to the window and looks down at the street and mutters.*] All black! Every one of them! [*Then with sudden excitement*] No, there's one. Why, it's Shorty! [*She throws the window open and calls.*] Shorty! Shorty! Hello, Shorty! [*She leans out and waves – then stops, remains there for a moment looking down, then comes back into the room suddenly as if she wanted to hide – her whole face in an anguish.*] Say! Say! I wonder? –

No, he didn't hear you. Yes, he did, too! He must have! I yelled so loud you could hear me in Jersey! No, what are you talking about? How would he hear with all kids yelling down there? He never heard a word, I tell you! He did, too! He didn't want to hear you! He didn't want to let anyone know he knew you! Why don't you acknowledge it? What are you lying about? I'm not! Why shouldn't he? Where does he come in to – for God's sake, who is Shorty, anyway? A pimp! Yes, and a dope-pedlar, too! D'you mean to say he'd have the nerve to hear me call him and then deliberately – ? Yes, I mean to say it! I do say it! And it's true, and you know it, and you might as well be honest for a change and admit it! He heard you, but he didn't want to hear you! He doesn't want to know you any more. No, not even him! He's afraid it'd get him in wrong with the old gang. Why? You know well enough! Because you married a – a – a – well, I won't say it, but you know without my mentioning names! [ELLA *springs to her feet in horror and shakes off her obsession with a frantic effort.*] Stop! [*Then whimpering like a frightened child*] Jim! Jim! Jim! Where are you? I want you, Jim! [*She runs out of the room as*]

THE CURTAIN FALLS

SCENE 2

The same. Six months later. It is evening. The walls of the room appear shrunken in, the ceiling lowered, so that the furniture, the portrait, the mask, look unnaturally large and domineering.

[JIM *is seated at the table studying, law books piled by his elbows. He is keeping his attention concentrated only by a driving physical effort which gives his face the expression of a runner's near the tape. His forehead shines with perspiration. He mutters one sentence from Blackstone over and over again, tapping his forehead with his fist in time to the rhythm he gives the stale words. But, in spite of himself, his attention wanders, his eyes have an uneasy, hunted look, he starts at every sound in the house or from the street. Finally, he remains rigid, Blackstone forgotten, his eyes fixed on the portières with tense grief. Then he groans, slams the book shut, goes to the window and throws it open and sinks down beside it, his arms on the sill, his head resting wearily on his arms, staring out into the night, the pale glare from the arc-lamp on the corner throwing his face into relief. The portières on the right are parted and* HATTIE *comes in.*]

HATTIE [*not seeing him at the table*]: Jim! [*Discovering him*] Oh, there you are! What're you doing?

JIM [*turning to her*]: Resting. Cooling my head. [*Forcing a smile*] These law books certainly are a sweating proposition! [*Then anxiously*] How is she?

HATTIE: She's asleep now. I felt it was safe to leave her for a minute. [*After a pause*] What did the doctor tell you, Jim?

JIM: The same old thing. She must have rest, he says, her mind needs rest – [*Bitterly*] But he can't tell me any prescription for that rest – leastways not any that'd work.

HATTIE [*after a pause*]: I think you ought to leave her, Jim – or let her leave you – for a while, anyway.

JIM [*angrily*]: You're like the doctor. Everything's so simple and easy. Do this and that happens. Only it don't. Life isn't simple like that – not in this case, anyway – no, it isn't simple a bit. [*After a pause*] I can't leave her. She can't leave me. And there's a million little reasons combining to make one big reason why we can't. [*A pause*] For her sake – if it'd do her good – I'd go – I'd leave – I'd do anything – because I love her. I'd kill myself even – jump out of this window this second – I've thought it over, too – but that'd only make matters worse for her. I'm all she's got in the world! Yes, that isn't bragging or fooling myself. I know that for a fact! Don't you know that's true? [*There is a pleading or the certainty he claims.*]

HATTIE: Yes, I know she loves you, Jim. I know that now.

JIM [*simply*]: Then we've got to stick together to the end, haven't we, whatever comes – and hope and pray for the best? [*A pause – then hopefully*] I think maybe this is the crisis in her mind. Once she settles this in herself, she's won to the other side. And me – once I become a Member of the Bar – then I win, too! We're both free – by our own fighting down our own weakness! We're both really, truly free! Then we can be happy with ourselves here or anywhere. She'll be proud then! Yes, she's told me again and again, she says she'll be actually proud!

HATTIE [*turning away to conceal her emotion*]: Yes, I'm sure – but you mustn't study too hard, Jim! You mustn't study too awfully hard!

JIM [*gets up and goes to the table and sits down wearily*]: Yes, I know. Oh, I'll pass easily. I haven't got any scarey feeling about that any more. And I'm doing two years' work in one here alone. That's better than schools, eh?

HATTIE [*doubtfully*]: It's wonderful, Jim.

JIM [*his spirit evaporating*]: If I can only hold out! It's hard! I'm worn out. I don't sleep. I get to thinking and thinking. My head aches and burns like fire with thinking. Round and round my thoughts go chasing like crazy chickens hopping and flapping before the wind. It gets me crazy mad – 'cause I can't stop!

HATTIE [*watching him for a while and seeming to force herself to speak*]: The doctor didn't tell you all, Jim.

JIM [*dully*]: What's that?

HATTIE: He told me you're liable to break down too, if you don't take care of yourself.

JIM [*abjectly weary*]: Let 'er come! I don't care what happens to me. Maybe if I get sick she'll get well. There's only so much bad luck allowed to one family, maybe. [*He forces a wan smile.*]

HATTIE [*hastily*]: Don't give in to that idea, for the Lord's sake!

JIM: I'm tired – and blue – that's all.

HATTIE [*after another long pause*]: I've got to tell you something else, Jim.

JIM [*dully*]: What?

HATTIE: The doctor said Ella's liable to be sick like this a very long time.

JIM: He told me that, too – that it'd be a long time before she got back her normal strength. Well, I suppose that's got to be expected.

HATTIE [*slowly*]: He didn't mean convalescing – what he told me. [*A long pause.*]

JIM [*evasively*]: I'm going to get other doctors in to see Ella – specialists. This one's a damn fool.

HATTIE: Be sensible, Jim. You'll have to face the truth – sooner or later.

JIM [*irritably*]: I know the truth about Ella better'n any doctor.

HATTIE [*persuasively*]: She'd get better so much sooner if you'd send her away to some nice sanatorium –

JIM: No! She'd die of shame there!

HATTIE: At least until after you've taken your examinations –

JIM: To hell with me!

HATTIE: Six months. That wouldn't be long to be parted.

JIM: What are you trying to do – separate us? [*He gets to his feet – furiously.*] Go on out! Go on out!

HATTIE [*calmly*]: No, I won't. [*Sharply*] There's something that's got to be said to you and I'm the only one with the courage – [*Intensely*] Tell me, Jim, have you heard her raving when she's out of her mind?

JIM [*with a shudder*]: No!

HATTIE: You're lying, Jim. You must have – if you don't stop your ears – and the doctor says she may develop a violent mania, dangerous for you – get worse and worse until – Jim, you'll go crazy, too – living this way. Today she raved on about 'Black! Black!' and cried because she said her skin was turning black – that you had poisoned her –

JIM [*in anguish*]: That's only when she's out of her mind.

HATTIE: And then she suddenly called me a dirty nigger.

JIM: No! She never said that ever! She never would!

HATTIE: She did – and kept on and on! [*A tense pause*] She'll be saying that to you soon.

JIM [*torturedly*]: She don't mean it! She isn't responsible for what she's saying!

HATTIE: I know she isn't – yet she is just the same. It's deep down in her or it wouldn't come out.

JIM: Deep down in her people – not deep in her.

HATTIE: I can't make such distinctions. The race in me, deep in me, can't stand it. I can't play nurse to her any more, Jim – not even for your sake. I'm afraid – afraid of myself – afraid sometime I'll kill her dead to set you free! [*She loses control and begins to cry.*]

JIM [*after a long pause – sombrely*]: Yes, I guess you'd better stay away from here. Good-bye.

HATTIE: Who'll you get to nurse her, Jim – a white woman?

JIM: Ella'd die of shame. No, I'll nurse her myself.

HATTIE: And give up your studies?

JIM: I can do both.

HATTIE: You can't! You'll get sick yourself! Why, you look terrible even as it is – and it's only beginning!

JIM: I can do anything for her! I'm all she's got in the world! I've got to prove I can be all to her! I've got to prove worthy! I've got to prove she can be proud of me! I've got to prove I'm the whitest of the white!

HATTIE [*stung by this last – with rebellious bitterness*]: Is that the ambition she's given you? Oh, you soft, weak-minded fool, you traitor to your race! And the thanks you'll get – to be called a dirty nigger – to hear her cursing you because she can never have a child because it'll be born black – !

JIM [*in a frenzy*]: Stop!

HATTIE: I'll say what must be said even though you kill me, Jim. Send her to an asylum before you both have to be sent to one together.

JIM [*with a sudden wild laugh*]: Do you think you're threatening me with something dreadful now? Why, I'd like that. Sure, I'd like that! Maybe she'd like it better, too. Maybe we'd both find it all simple then – like you think it is now. Yes. [*He laughs again.*]

HATTIE [*frightenedly*]: Jim!

JIM: Together! You can't scare me even with hell fire if you say she and I go together. It's heaven then for me! [*With sudden savagery*] You go out of here! All you've ever been aiming to do is to separate us so we can't be together!

HATTIE: I've done what I did for your own good.

JIM: I have no own good. I only got a good together with her. I'm all she's got in the world! Let her call me nigger! Let her call me the whitest of the white! I'm all she's got in the world, ain't I? She's all I've got! You with your fool talk of the black race and the white race! Where does the human race get a chance to come in? I suppose that's simple for you. You lock it up in asylums and throw away the key! [*With fresh violence*] Go along! There isn't going to be no more people coming in here to separate – excepting the doctor. I'm going to lock the door, and it's going to stay locked, you hear? Go along, now!

HATTIE [*confusedly*]: Jim!

JIM [*pushes her out gently and slams the door after her – vaguely*]: Go along! I got to study. I got to nurse Ella, too. Oh, I can do it! I can do anything for her!

[*He sits down at the table and, opening the book, begins again to recite the lines from Blackstone in a meaningless rhythm, tapping his forehead with his fist.* ELLA *enters noiselessly through the portières. She wears a red dressing-gown over her night-dress but is in her bare feet. She has a carving-knife in her right hand. Her eyes fasten on* JIM *with a murderous mania. She creeps up behind him. Suddenly he senses something and turns. As he sees her he gives a cry, jumping up and catching her wrist. She stands fixed, her eyes growing bewildered and frightened.*]

JIM [*aghast*]: Ella! For God's sake! Do you want to murder me? [*She does not answer. He shakes her.*]

ELLA [*whimperingly*]: They kept calling me names as I was walking along – I can't tell you what, Jim – and then I grabbed a knife –

JIM: Yes! See! This! [*She looks at it frightenedly.*]

ELLA: Where did I – ? I was having a nightmare – Where did they go – I mean, how did I get here? [*With sudden terrified pleading – like a little girl*] Oh, Jim – don't ever leave me alone! I have such terrible dreams, Jim – promise you'll never go away!

JIM: I promise, Honey.

ELLA [*her manner becoming more and more childishly silly*]: I'll be a little girl – and you'll be old Uncle Jim who's been with us for years and years – Will you play that?

JIM: Yes, Honey. Now you better go back to bed.

ELLA [*like a child*]: Yes, Uncle Jim. [*She turns to go. He pretends to be occupied by his book. She looks at him for a second – then suddenly asks in her natural woman's voice.*] Are you studying hard, Jim?

JIM: Yes, Honey. Go to bed now. You need to rest, you know.

ELLA [*stands looking at him, fighting with herself. A startling transformation comes over her face. It grows mean, vicious, full of jealous hatred. She cannot contain herself, but breaks out harshly with a cruel, venomous grin*]: You dirty nigger!

JIM [*starting as if he'd been shot*]: Ella! For the good Lord's sake!

ELLA [*coming out of her insane mood for a moment, aware of something terrible, frightened*]: Jim! Jim! Why are you looking at me like that?

JIM: What did you say to me just then?

ELLA [*gropingly*]: Why, I – I said – I remember saying, are you studying hard, Jim? Why? You're not mad at that, are you?

JIM: No, Honey. What made you think I was mad? Go to bed now.

ELLA [*obediently*]: Yes, Jim. [*She passes behind the portières.* JIM *stares before him. Suddenly her head is thrust out at the side of the portières. Her face is again that of a vindictive maniac.*] Nigger! [*The face disappears – she can be heard running away, laughing with cruel satisfaction.* JIM *bows his head on his outstretched arms, but he is too stricken for tears.*]

THE CURTAIN FALLS

SCENE 3

The same, six months later. The sun has just gone down. The spring twilight sheds a vague, grey light about the room, picking out the Congo mask on the stand by the window. The walls have shrunken in still more, the ceiling now barely clears the people's heads, the furniture and the characters appear enormously magnified. Law books are stacked in two great piles on each side of the table.

[ELLA *comes in from the right, the carving-knife in her hand. She is pitifully thin, her face is wasted, but her eyes glow with a mad energy, her movements are abrupt and spring-like. She looks stealthily about the room, then advances and stands before the mask, her arms akimbo, her attitude one of crazy mockery, fear, and bravado. She is dressed in the red dressing-gown, grown dirty and ragged now, and is in her bare feet.*]

ELLA: I'll give you the laugh, wait and see! [*Then in a confidential tone*] He thought I was asleep! He called, Ella, Ella

– but I kept my eyes shut, I pretended to snore. I fooled him good. [*She gives a little hoarse laugh.*] This is the first time he's dared to leave me alone for months and months. I've been wanting to talk to you every day, but this is the only chance – [*With sudden violence – flourishing her knife*] What're you grinning about, you dirty nigger, you? How dare you grin at me? I guess you forget what you are! That's always the way. Be kind to you, treat you decent, and in a second you've got a swelled head, you think you're somebody, you're all over the place putting on airs. Why, it's got so I can't even walk down the street without seeing niggers, niggers everywhere. Hanging around, grinning, grinning – going to school – pretending they're white – taking examinations – [*She stops, arrested by the word, then suddenly.*] That's where he's gone – down to the mail-box – to see if there's a letter from the Board – telling him – But why is he so long? [*She calls pitifully.*] Jim! [*Then in a terrified whimper*] Maybe he's passed! Maybe he's passed! [*In a frenzy*] No! No! He can't! I'd kill him! I'd kill myself! [*Threatening the Congo mask*] It's you who're to blame for this! Yes, you! Oh, I'm on to you! [*Then appealingly*] But why d'you want to do this to us? What have I ever done wrong to you? What have you got against me? I married you, didn't I? Why don't you let Jim alone? Why don't you let him be happy as he is – with me? Why don't you let me be happy? He's white, isn't he – the whitest man that ever lived? Where do you come in to interfere? Black! Black! Black as dirt! You've poisoned me! I can't wash myself clean! Oh, I hate you! I hate you! Why don't you let Jim and I be happy?

[*She sinks down in his chair, her arms outstretched on the table. The door from the hall is slowly opened and* JIM *appears. His bloodshot, sleepless eyes stare from deep hollows. His expression is one of crushed numbness. He holds an open letter in his hand.*]

JIM [*seeing Ella – in an absolutely dead voice*]: Honey – I thought you were asleep.

ELLA [*starts and wheels about in her chair*]: What's that? You got – you got a letter – ?

JIM [*turning to close the door after him*]: From the Board of Examiners for admission to the Bar, State of New York – God's country! [*He finishes up with a chuckle of ironic self-pity so spent as to be barely audible.*]

ELLA [*writhing out of her chair like some fierce animal, the knife held behind her – with fear and hatred*]: You didn't – you didn't – you didn't pass, did you?

JIM [*looking at her wildly*]: Pass? Pass? [*He begins to chuckle and laugh between sentences and phrases, rich, Negro laughter, but heart-breaking in its mocking grief.*] Good Lord, child, how come you can ever imagine such a crazy idea? Pass? Me? Jim Crow Harris? Nigger Jim Harris – become a full-fledged Member of the Bar! Why, the mere notion of it is enough to kill you with laughing! It'd be against all natural laws, all human right and justice. It'd be miraculous, there'd be earthquakes and catastrophes, the Seven Plagues'd come again and locusts'd devour all the money in the banks, the second Flood'd come roaring and Noah'd fall overboard, the sun'd drop out of the sky like a ripe fig, and the Devil'd perform miracles, and God'd be tipped head first right out of the Judgement Seat! [*He laughs, maudlinly uproarious.*]

ELLA [*her face beginning to relax, to light up*]: Then you – you didn't pass?

JIM [*spent – giggling and gasping idiotically*]: Well, I should say not! I should certainly say not!

ELLA [*with a cry of joy, pushes all the law books crashing to the floor – then with childish happiness she grabs* JIM *by both hands and dances up and down*]: Oh, Jim, I knew it! I knew you couldn't! Oh, I'm so glad, Jim! I'm so happy! You're still my old Jim – and I'm so glad! [*He looks at her dazedly, a fierce rage slowly gathering on his face. She dances away from him. His eyes follow her. His hands clench. She stands in front of the mask – triumphantly.*] There! What did I tell you? I told you I'd give you the laugh! [*She begins to laugh with wild unrestraint, grabs the mask from its place, sets it in the middle of the table and plunging the knife down through it pins it to the table.*] There! Who's got the laugh now?

JIM [*his eyes bulging – hoarsely*]: You devil! You white devil woman! [*In a terrible roar, raising his fists above her head*] You devil!

ELLA [*looking up at him with a bewildered cry of terror*]: Jim! [*Her appeal recalls him to himself. He lets his arms slowly drop to his sides, bowing his head.* ELLA *points tremblingly to the mask.*] It's all right, Jim! It's dead. The devil's dead. See! It couldn't live – unless you passed. If you'd passed it would have lived in you. Then I'd have had to kill you, Jim, don't you see – or it would have killed me. But now I've killed it. [*She pats his hand.*] So you needn't ever be afraid any more, Jim.

JIM [*dully*]: I've got to sit down, Honey. I'm tired. I haven't had much chance for sleep in so long – [*He slumps down in the chair by the table.*]

ELLA [*sits down on the floor beside him and holds his hand. Her face is gradually regaining an expression that is happy, childlike, and pretty*]: I know, Jim! That was my fault. I wouldn't let you sleep. I couldn't let you. I kept thinking if he sleeps good then he'll be sure to study good and then he'll pass – and the devil'll win!

JIM [*with a groan*]: Don't, Honey!

ELLA [*with a childish grin*]: That was why I carried that knife around – [*she frowns – puzzled*] – one reason – to keep you from studying and sleeping by scaring you.

JIM: I wasn't scared of being killed. I was scared of what they'd do to you after.

ELLA [*after a pause – like a child*]: Will God forgive me, Jim?

JIM: Maybe He can forgive what you've done to me; and maybe He can forgive what I've done to you; but I don't see how He's going to forgive – Himself.

ELLA: I prayed and prayed. When you were away taking the examinations and I was alone with the nurse, I closed my eyes and pretended to be asleep, but I was praying with all my might: O God, don't let Jim pass!

JIM [*with a sob*]: Don't, Honey, don't! For the good Lord's sake! You're hurting me!

ELLA [*frightenedly*]: How, Jim? Where? [*Then after a pause – suddenly*] I'm sick, Jim. I don't think I'll live long.

JIM [*simply*]: Then I won't either. Somewhere yonder maybe – together – our luck'll change. But I wanted – here and now – before you – we – I wanted to prove to you – to myself – to become a full-fledged Member – so you could be proud – [*He stops. Words fail and he is beyond tears.*]

ELLA [*brightly*]: Well, it's all over, Jim. Everything'll be all right now. [*Chattering along*] I'll be just your little girl, Jim – and you'll be my little boy – just as we used to be, remember, when we were beaux; and I'll put shoe blacking on my face and pretend I'm black, and you can put chalk on your face and pretend you're white, just as we used to do – and we can play marbles – only you mustn't all the time be a boy. Sometimes you must be my old kind Uncle Jim who's been with us for years and years. Will you, Jim?

JIM [*with utter resignation*]: Yes, Honey.

ELLA: And you'll never, never, never, never leave me, Jim?

JIM: Never, Honey.

ELLA: 'Cause you're all I've got in the world – and I love you, Jim. [*She kisses his hand as a child might, tenderly and gratefully.*]

JIM [*suddenly throws himself on his knees and raises his shining eyes, his transfigured face*]: Forgive me, God – and make me worthy! Now I see Your Light again! Now I hear Your Voice! [*He begins to weep in an ecstasy of religious humility.*] Forgive me, God, for blaspheming You! Let this fire of burning suffering purify me of selfishness and make me worthy of the child You send me for the woman You take away!

ELLA [*jumping to her feet – excitedly*]: Don't cry, Jim! You mustn't cry! I've got only a little time left and I want to play. Don't be old Uncle Jim now. Be my little boy, Jim. Pretend you're Painty Face and I'm Jim Crow. Come and play!

JIM [*still deeply exalted*]: Honey, Honey, I'll play right up to the gates of heaven with you! [*She tugs at one of his hands, laughingly trying to pull him up from his knees as*]

THE CURTAIN FALLS

THE EMPEROR JONES

CHARACTERS

BRUTUS JONES, Emperor
HENRY SMITHERS, A Cockney Trader
AN OLD NATIVE WOMAN
LEM, A Native Chief
SOLDIERS, Adherents of Lem
The Little Formless Fears; Jeff; the Negro Convicts; the Prison Guard; the Planters; the Auctioneer; the Slaves; the Congo Witch-Doctor; the Crocodile God

The action of the play takes place on an island in the West Indies as yet not self-determined by White Mariners. The form of native government is, for the time being, an Empire

SCENE ONE

The audience chamber in the palace of the Emperor – a spacious, high-ceilinged room with bare, whitewashed walls. The floor is of white tiles. In the rear, to the left of centre, a wide archway giving out on a portico with white pillars. The palace is evidently situated on high ground, for beyond the portico nothing can be seen but a vista of distant hills, their summits crowned with thick groves of palm trees. In the right wall, centre, a smaller arched doorway leading to the living quarters of the palace. The room is bare of furniture with the exception of one huge chair made of uncut wood which stands at centre, its back to rear. This is very apparently the Emperor's throne. It is painted a dazzling, eye-smiting scarlet. There is a brilliant orange cushion on the seat and another smaller one is placed on the floor to serve as a footstool. Strips of matting, dyed scarlet, lead from the foot of the throne to the two entrances.

It is late afternoon, but the yellow sunlight still blazes beyond the portico and there is an oppressive burden of exhausting heat in the air.

[*As the curtain rises, a native* NEGRO WOMAN *sneaks in cautiously from the entrance on the right. She is very old, dressed in cheap calico, bare-footed, a red bandana handkerchief covering all but a few stray wisps of white hair. A bundle bound in coloured cloth is carried over her shoulder on the end of a stick. She hesitates beside the doorway, peering back as if in extreme dread of being discovered. Then she begins to glide noiselessly, a step at a time, towards the doorway in the rear. At this moment* SMITHERS *appears beneath the portico.*

SMITHERS *is a tall man, round-shouldered, about forty. His bald head, perched on a long neck with an enormous Adam's apple, looks like an egg. The tropics have tanned his naturally pasty face with its small, sharp features to a sickly yellow, and native rum has painted his pointed nose to a startling red. His little washy-blue eyes are red-rimmed and dart about him like a ferret's. His expression is one of unscrupulous meanness, cowardly and dangerous. He is dressed in a worn riding suit of dirty white drill, puttees, and spurs, and wears a white cork helmet. A cartridge belt with an automatic revolver is around his waist. He carries a riding whip in his hand. He sees the woman and stops to watch her suspiciously. Then, making up his mind, he steps quickly on tiptoe into the room. The* WOMAN, *looking back over her shoulder continually, does not see him until it is too late. When she does* SMITHERS *springs forward and grabs her firmly by the shoulder. She struggles to get away, fiercely but silently.*]

SMITHERS [*tightening his grasp – roughly*]: Easy! None o' that, me birdie. You can't wriggle out now. I got me 'ooks on yer.

WOMAN [*seeing the uselessness of struggling, gives way to frantic terror, and sinks to the ground, embracing his knees supplicatingly*]: No tell him! No tell him, Mister!

SMITHERS [*with great curiosity*]: Tell 'im? [*Then scornfully*] Oh, you mean 'is bloomin' Majesty. What's the game, any 'ow? What are you sneakin' away for? Been stealin' a bit, I s'pose. [*He taps her bundle with his riding whip significantly.*]

WOMAN [*shaking her head vehemently*]: No, me no steal.

SMITHERS: Bloody liar! But tell me what's up. There's somethin' funny goin' on. I smelled it in the air first thing I got up this mornin'. You blacks are up to some devilment. This palace of 'is is like a bleedin' tomb. Where's all the 'ands? [*The* WOMAN *keeps sullenly silent.* SMITHERS *raises his whip threateningly.*] Ow, yer won't, won't yer? I'll show yer what's what.

WOMAN [*coweringly*]: I tell, Mister. You no hit. They go – all go. [*She makes a sweeping gesture towards the hills in the distance.*]

SMITHERS: Run away – to the 'ills?

WOMAN: Yes, Mister. Him Emperor – Great Father. [*She touches her forehead to the floor with a quick mechanical jerk.*] Him sleep after eat. Then they go – all go. Me old woman. Me left only. Now me go too.

SMITHERS [*his astonishment giving way to an immense, mean satisfaction*]: Ow! So that's the ticket! Well, I know bloody well wot's in the air – when they runs orf to the 'ills. The tom-tom'll be thumping out there bloomin' soon. [*With extreme vindictiveness*] And I'm bloody glad of it, for one! Serve 'im right! Puttin' on airs, the stinkin' nigger! 'Is Majesty! Gawd blimey! I only 'opes I'm there when they takes 'im out to shoot 'im. [*Suddenly*] 'E's still 'ere all right, ain't 'e?

WOMAN: Yes. Him sleep.

SMITHERS: 'E's bound to find out soon as 'e wakes up. 'E's cunnin' enough to know when 'is time's come. [*He goes to the doorway on right and whistles shrilly with his fingers in his mouth. The* OLD WOMAN *springs to her feet and runs out of the doorway, rear.* SMITHERS *goes after her, reaching for his revolver.*] Stop or I'll shoot! [*Then stopping – indifferently*] Pop orf then, if yer like, yer black cow. [*He stands in the doorway, looking after her.*]

[JONES *enters from the right. He is a tall, powerfully built, full-blooded Negro of middle age. His features are typically negroid, yet there is something decidedly distinctive about his face – an underlying strength of will, a hardy, self-reliant confidence in himself that inspires respect. His eyes are alive with a keen, cunning intelligence. In manner he is shrewd, suspicious, evasive. He wears a light blue uniform coat, sprayed with brass buttons, heavy gold chevrons on his shoulders, gold braid on the collar, cuffs, etc. His trousers are bright red with a light blue stripe down the side. Patent-leather laced boots with brass spurs, and a belt with a long-barrelled, pearl-handled revolver in a holster complete his attire. Yet there is something not altogether ridiculous about his grandeur. He has a way of carrying it off.*]

JONES [*not seeing anyone – greatly irritated and blinking sleepily – shouts*]: Who dare whistle dat way in my palace? Who dare wake up de Emperor? I'll git de hide flayed off some o' you niggers sho'!

SMITHERS [*showing himself – in a manner half-afraid and half-defiant*]: It was me whistled to yer. [*As* JONES *frowns angrily*] I got news for yer.

JONES [*putting on his suavest manner, which fails to cover up his contempt for the white man*]: Oh, it's you, Mister Smithers. [*He sits down on his throne with easy dignity.*] What news you got to tell me?

SMITHERS [*coming close to enjoy his discomfiture*]: Don't yer notice nothin' funny today?

JONES [*coldly*]: Funny? No. I ain't perceived nothin' of de kind!

SMITHERS: Then yer ain't so foxy as I thought yer was. Where's all your court? [*Sarcastically*] The Generals and the Cabinet Ministers and all?

JONES [*imperturbably*]: Where dey mostly runs to minute I closes my eyes – drinkin' rum and talkin' big down in de town. [*Sarcastically*] How come you don't know dat? Ain't you carousing with 'em most every day?

SMITHERS [*stung, but pretending indifference – with a wink*]: That's part of the day's work. I got ter – ain't I – in my business?

JONES [*contemptuously*]: Yo' business!

SMITHERS [*imprudently enraged*]: Gawd blimey, you was glad enough for me ter take yer in on it when you landed 'ere first. You didn't 'ave no 'igh and mighty airs in them days!

JONES [*his hand going to his revolver like a flash – menacingly*]: Talk polite, white man! Talk polite, you heah me! I'm boss heah now, is you fergettin'?

[*The Cockney seems about to challenge this last statement with the facts, but something in the other's eyes holds and cows him.*]

SMITHERS [*in a cowardly whine*]: No 'arm meant, old top.

JONES [*condescendingly*]: I accepts yo' apology. [*Lets his hand fall from his revolver.*] No use'n you rakin' up ole times. What I was den is one thing. What I is now 's another. You didn't let me in on yo' crooked work out o' no kind feelin's dat time. I done de dirty work fo' you – and most o' de brain work, too, fo' dat matter – and I was wu'th money to you, dat's de reason.

SMITHERS: Well, blimey, I give yer a start, didn't I – when no one else would. I wasn't afraid to 'ire yer like the rest was – 'count of the story about your breakin' jail back in the States.

JONES: No, you didn't have no s'cuse to look down on me fo' dat. You been in jail you'self more'n once.

SMITHERS [*furiously*]: It's a lie! [*Then trying to pass it off by an attempt at scorn.*] Garn! Who told yer that fairy tale?

JONES: Dey's some tings I ain't got to be tole. I kin see 'em in folk's eyes. [*Then after a pause – meditatively*] Yes, you sho' give me a start. And it didn't take long from dat time to git dese fool woods' niggers right where I wanted dem. [*With pride*] From stowaway to Emperor in two years! Dat's goin' some!

SMITHERS [*with curiosity*]: And I bet you got yer pile o'money 'id safe some place.

JONES [*with satisfaction*]: I sho' has! And it's in a foreign bank where no pusson don't ever git it out but me no matter what come. You didn't s'pose I was holdin' down dis Emperor job for de glory in it, did you? Sho'! De fuss and glory part of it, dat's only to turn de heads o' de low-flung bush niggers dat's here. Dey wants de big circus show for deir money. I gives it to 'em an' I gits de money. [*With a grin*] De long green, dat's me every time! [*Then rebukingly*] But you ain't got no kick agin me, Smithers. I'se paid you back all you done for me many times. Ain't I pertected you and winked at all de crooked tradin' you been doin' right out in de broad day. Sho' I has – and me makin' laws to stop it at de same time! [*He chuckles.*]

SMITHERS [*grinning*]: But, meanin' no 'arm, you been grabbin' right and left yourself, ain't yer! Look at the taxes you've put on 'em! Blimey! You've squeezed 'em dry!

JONES [*chuckling*]: No, dey ain't *all* dry yet. I'se still heah, ain't I?

SMITHERS [*smiling at his secret thought*]: They're dry right now, you'll find out. [*Changing the subject abruptly*] And as for me breakin' laws, you've broke 'em all yerself just as fast as yer made 'em.

JONES: Ain't I de Emperor? De laws don't go for him. [*Judicially*] You heah what I tells you, Smithers. Dere's little stealin' like you does, and dere's big stealin' like I does. For de little stealin' dey gits you in jail soon or late. For de big stealin' dey makes you Emperor and puts you in de Hall o' Fame when you croaks. [*Reminiscently*] If dey's one thing I learns in ten years on de Pullman ca's listenin' to de white quality talk, it's dat same fact. And when I gits a chance to use it I winds up Emperor in two years.

SMITHERS [*unable to repress the genuine admiration of the small fry for the large*]: Yes, yer turned the bleedin' trick, all right. Blimey, I never seen a bloke 'as 'ad the bloomin' luck you 'as.

JONES [*severely*]: Luck? What you mean – luck?

SMITHERS: I suppose you'll say as that swank about the silver bullet ain't luck – and that was what first got the fool blacks on yer side the time of the revolution, wasn't it?

JONES [*with a laugh*]: Oh, dat silver bullet! Sho' was luck! But I makes dat luck, you heah? I loads de dice! Yessuh! When dat murderin' nigger ole Lem hired to kill me takes aim ten feet away and his gun misses fire and I shoots him dead, what you heah me say?

SMITHERS: You said yer'd got a charm so's no lead bullet'd kill yer. You was so strong only a silver bullet could kill yer, you told 'em. Blimey, wasn't that swank for yer, and plain, fat-'eaded luck?

JONES [*proudly*]: I got brains and I uses 'em quick. Dat ain't luck.

SMITHERS: Yer know they wasn't 'ardly liable to get no silver bullets. And it was luck 'e didn't 'it you that time.

JONES [*laughing*]: And dere all dem fool bush niggers was kneelin' down and bumpin' deir heads on de ground like I was a miracle out o' de Bible. Oh Lawd, from dat time on I has dem all eatin' out of my hand. I cracks de whip and dey jumps through.

SMITHERS [*with a sniff*]: Yankee bluff done it.

JONES: Ain't a man's talkin' big what makes him big – long as he makes folks believe it? Sho', I talks large when I ain't got nothin' to back it up, but I ain't talkin' wild just de same. I knows I kin fool 'em – I *knows* it – and dat's backin' enough fo' my game. And ain't I got to learn deir lingo and teach some of dem English befo' I kin talk to em? Ain't dat wuk? You ain't never learned any word of it, Smithers, in de ten years you been heah, dough you knows it's money in yo' pocket tradin' wid 'em if you does. But you'se too shiftless to take de trouble.

SMITHERS [*flushing*]: Never mind about me. What's this I've 'eard about yer really 'avin' a silver bullet moulded for yourself?

JONES: It's playin' out my bluff. I has de silver bullet moulded and I tells 'em when de time comes I kills myself wid it. I tells 'em dat's 'cause I'm de on'y man in de world big enuff to git me. No use'n deir tryin'. And dey falls down and bumps deir heads. [*He laughs.*] I does dat so's I kin take a walk in peace widout no jealous nigger gunnin' at me from behind de trees.

SMITHERS [*astonished*]: Then you 'ad it made – 'onest?

JONES: Sho' did. Heah she be. [*He takes out his revolver, breaks it, and takes the bullet out of one chamber.*] Five lead an' dis silver baby at de last. Don't she shine pretty? [*He holds it in his hand, looking at it admiringly, as if strangely fascinated.*]

SMITHERS: Let me see. [*Reaches out his hand for it.*]

JONES [*harshly*]: Keep yo' hands whar dey b'long, white man. [*He replaces it in the chamber and puts the revolver back on his hip.*]

SMITHERS [*snarling*]: Gawd blimey! Think I'm a bleedin' thief, you would.

JONES: No, 'tain't dat. I knows you'se scared to steal from me. On'y I ain't 'lowin' nary body to touch dis baby. She's my rabbit's foot.

SMITHERS [*sneering*]: A bloomin' charm, wot? [*Venomously*] Well, you'll need all the bloody charms you 'as before long, s' 'elp me!

JONES [*judicially*]: Oh, I'se good for six months yit 'fore dey gits sick o' my game. Den, when I sees trouble comin', I makes a move.

SMITHERS: Ho! You got it all planned, ain't yer?

JONES: I ain't no fool. I know dis Emperor's time is sho't. Dat why I make hay when de sun shine. Was you thinkin' I'se aimin' to hold down dis job for life? No, suh! What good is gittin' money if you stays back in dis raggedy country? I wants action when I spends. And when I sees dese niggers gittin' up deir nerve to tu'n me out, and I'se got all de money in sight, I resigns on de spot and gets away quick.

SMITHERS: Where to?

JONES: None o' yo' business.

SMITHERS: Not back to the bloody States, I'll lay my oath.

JONES [*suspiciously*]: Why don't I? [*Then with an easy laugh*] You mean 'count of dat story 'bout me breakin' from jail back dere? Dat's all talk.

SMITHERS [*sceptically*]: Ho, yes!

JONES [*sharply*]: You ain't 'sinuatin' I'se a liar, is you?

SMITHERS [*hastily*]: No, Gawd strike me! I was only thinkin' o' the bloody lies you told the blacks 'ere about killin' white men in the States.

JONES [*angered*]: How come dey're lies?

SMITHERS: You'd 'ave been in jail if you 'ad, wouldn't yer then? [*With venom*] And from what I've 'eard, it ain't 'ealthy for a black to kill a white man in the States. They burns 'em in oil, don't they?

JONES [*with cool deadliness*]: You mean lynchin' 'd scare me? Well, I tells you, Smithers, maybe I does kill one white man back dere. Maybe I does. And maybe I kills another right heah 'fore long if he don't look out.

SMITHERS [*trying to force a laugh*]: I was on'y spoofin' yer. Can't yer take a joke? And you was just sayin' you'd never been in jail.

JONES [*in the same tone – slightly boastful*]: Maybe I goes to jail dere for gettin' in an argument wid razors ovah a game of dice. Maybe I gits twenty years when dat coloured man die. Maybe I gits in 'nother argument wid de prison guard and de overseer ovah us when we're wukin' de roads. Maybe he hits me wid a whip and I splits his head wid a shovel and runs away and files de chain off my leg and gits away safe. Maybe I does all dat an' maybe I don't. It's a story I tells you so's you knows I'se de kind of man dat if you evah repeats one word of it, I ends yo' stealin' on dis yearth mighty damn quick!

SMITHERS [*terrified*]: Think I'd peach on yer? Not me! Ain't I always been yer friend?

JONES [*suddenly relaxing*]: Sho' you has – and you better be.

SMITHERS [*recovering his composure – and with it his malice*]: And just to show yer I'm yer friend, I'll tell yer that bit o' news I was goin' to.

JONES: Go ahead! Must be bad news from de happy way you look.

SMITHERS [*warningly*]: Maybe it's gettin' time for you to

resign – with that bloomin' silver bullet, wot? [*He finishes with a mocking grin.*]

JONES [*puzzled*]: What's dat you say? Talk plain.

SMITHERS: Ain't noticed any of the guards or servants about the place today, I 'aven't.

JONES [*carelessly*]: Dey're all out in de garden sleepin' under de trees. When I sleeps, dey sneaks a sleep too, and I pretends I never suspicions it. All I got to do is to ring de bell and dey come flyin', makin' a bluff dey was wukin' all de time.

SMITHERS [*in the same mocking tone*]: Ring the bell now an' you'll bloody well see what I mean.

JONES [*startled to alertness, but preserving the same careless tone*]: Sho' I rings.

[*He reaches below the throne and pulls out a big common dinner bell which is painted the same vivid scarlet as the throne. He rings this vigorously – then stops to listen. Then he goes to both doors, rings again, and looks out.*]

SMITHERS [*watching him with malicious satisfaction, after a pause – mockingly*]: The bloody ship is sinkin' an' the bleedin' rats 'as slung their 'ooks.

JONES [*in a sudden fit of anger flings the bell clattering into a corner*]: Low-flung bush niggers! [*Then catching* SMITHERS' *eye on him, he controls himself and suddenly bursts into a low chuckling laugh.*] Reckon I overplays my hand dis once! A man can't take de pot on a short-tailed flush all de time. Was I sayin' I'd sit it six months mo'? Well, I'se changed my mind den. I gives in and resigns de job of Emperor right dis minute.

SMITHERS [*with real admiration*]: Blimey, but you're a cool bird, and no mistake.

JONES: No use'n fussin'. When I knows de game's up I kisses it good-bye widout no long waits. Dey've all run off to de hills, ain't dey?

SMITHERS: Yes – every bleedin' man jack of 'em.

JONES: Den de revolution is at de door. And de Emperor better git his feet movin' up de trail. [*He starts for the door in rear.*]

SMITHERS: Goin' out to look for your 'orse? Yer won't find any. They steals the 'orses first thing. Mine was gone when I went for 'im this mornin'. That's wot first give me a suspicion of wot was up.

JONES [*alarmed for a second, scratches his head, then philosophically*]: Well, den I hoofs it. Feet, do yo' duty! [*He pulls out a gold watch and looks at it.*] Three-thuty. Sundown's at six-thuty or dereabouts. [*Puts his watch back – with cool confidence.*] I got plenty o' time to make it easy.

SMITHERS: Don't be so bloomin' sure of it. They'll be after you 'ot and 'eavy. Ole Lem is at the bottom o' this business an' 'e 'ates you like 'ell. 'E'd rather do for you than eat 'is dinner, 'e would!

JONES [*scornfully*]: Dat fool no-count nigger! Does you think I'se scared o' him? I stands him on his thick head more'n once befo' dis, and I does it again if he comes in my way – [*Fiercely*] And dis time I leave him a dead nigger fo' sho'!

SMITHERS: You'll 'ave to cut through the big forest – an' these blacks 'ere can sniff and follow a trail in the dark like 'ounds. You'd 'ave to 'ustle to get through that forest in twelve hours even if you knew all the bloomin' paths like a native.

JONES [*with indignant scorn*]: Look-a-heah, white man! Does you think I'se a natural bo'n fool? Give me credit fo' havin' some sense, fo' Lawd's sake! Don't you s'pose I'se looked ahead and made sho' of all de chances? I'se gone out in dat big forest, pretendin' to hunt, so many times dat I knows it high an' low like a book. I could go through on dem paths wid my eyes shut. [*With great contempt*] Think dese ig'nerent bush niggers dat ain't got brains enuff to know deir own names even, can catch Brutus Jones? Huh, I s'pects not! Not on yo' life! Why, man, de white men went after me wid bloodhounds, where I come from an' I jes' laughs at 'em. It's a shame to fool dese black trash around heah, dey're so easy. You watch me, man. I'll make dem look sick, I will. I'll be 'cross de plain to de edge of de forest by time dark comes. Once in de woods in de night, dey got a fine chance o' findin' dis baby! Dawn tomorrow I'll be out at de oder side and on de coast whar dat French gunboat is stayin'. She picks me up, take me to the Martinique when she go dar, and dere I is safe wid a mighty big bankroll in my pocket. It's easy as rollin' off a log.

SMITHERS [*maliciously*]: But s'posin' somethin' 'appens wrong an' they do nab yer?

JONES [*decisively*]: Dey don't – dat's de answer.

SMITHERS: But, just for argyment's sake – what'd you do?

JONES [*frowning*]: I'se got five lead bullets in dis gun good enuff fo' common bush niggers – and after dat I got de silver bullet left to cheat 'em out o' gittin' me.

SMITHERS [*jeeringly*]: Ho, I was fergettin' that silver bullet. You'll bump yourself orf in style, won't yer? Blimey!

JONES [*gloomily*]: You kin bet yo' whole money on one thing, white man. Dis baby plays out his string to de end and when he quits, he quits wid a bang de way he ought. Silver bullet ain't none too good for him when he go, dat's a fac'! [*Then shaking off his nervousness – with a confident laugh.*] Sho'! What is I talkin' about? Ain't come to dat yit and I never will – not wid trash niggers like dese yere. [*Boastfully*] Silver bullet bring me luck anyway. I kin outguess, outrun, outfight, an' outplay de whole lot o' dem all ovah de board any time o' de day er night! You watch me!

[*From the distant hills comes the faint, steady thump of a tom-tom, low and vibrating. It starts at a rate exactly corresponding to normal pulse beat – seventy-two to the minute – and continues at a gradually accelerating rate from this point uninterruptedly to the very end of the play.*]

JONES [*starts at the sound. A strange look of apprehension creeps into his face for a moment as he listens. Then he asks, with an attempt to regain his most casual manner*]: What's dat drum beatin' fo'?

SMITHERS [*with a mean grin*]: For you. That means the bleedin' ceremony 'as started. I've 'eard it before and I knows.

JONES: Cer'mony? What cer'mony?

SMITHERS: The blacks is 'oldin' a bloody meetin', 'avin' a war dance, gettin' their courage worked up b'fore they starts after you.

JONES: Let dem! Dey'll sho' need it!

SMITHERS: And they're there 'oldin' their 'eathen religious service – makin' no end of devil spells and charms to 'elp 'em against your silver bullet. [*He guffaws loudly.*] Blimey, but they're balmy as 'ell!

JONES [*a tiny bit awed and shaken in spite of himself*]: Huh! Takes more'n dat to scare dis chicken!

SMITHERS [*scenting the other's feeling – maliciously*]: Ternight when it's pitch black in the forest, they'll 'ave their pet devils and ghosts 'oundin' after you. You'll find yer bloody 'air 'll be standin' on end before termorrow mornin'. [*Seriously*] It's a bleedin' queer place, that stinkin' forest, even in daylight. Yer don't know what might 'appen in there, it's that rotten still. Always sends the cold shivers down my back minute I gets in it.

JONES [*with a contemptuous sniff*]: I ain't no white-liver like you is. Trees an' me, we'se friends, and dar's a full moon comin' bring me light. And let dem po' niggers make all de fool spells dey'se a min' to. Does yo' s'pect I'se silly enuff to b'lieve in ghosts an' ha'nts an' all dat ole woman's talk? G'long, white man! You ain't talkin' to me. [*With a chuckle*] Doesn't you know dey's got to do wid a man who was member in good standin' o' de Baptist Church? Sho' I was dat when I was porter on de Pullmans, befo' I gits into my little trouble. Let dem try deir heathen tricks. De Baptist Church done pertect me and land dem all in hell. [*Then with more confident satisfaction*] And I'se got little silver bullet o' my own, don't forgit.

SMITHERS: Ho! You 'aven't give much 'eed to your Baptist Church since you been down 'ere. I've 'eard myself you 'ad turned yer coat an' was takin' up with their blarsted witch-doctors, or whatever the 'ell yer calls the swine.

JONES [*vehemently*]: I pretends to! Sho' I pretends! Dat's part o' my game from de fust. If I finds out dem niggers believes dat black is white, den I yells it out louder 'n deir loudest. It don't git me nothin' to do missionary work for de Baptist Church. I'se after de coin, an' I lays my Jesus on de shelf for de time bein'. [*Stops abruptly to look at his watch – alertly.*] But I ain't got de time to waste no more fool talk wid you. I'se gwine away from heah dis secon'. [*He reaches in under the throne and pulls out an expensive Panama hat with a bright multi-coloured band and sets it jauntily on his head.*] So long, white man! [*With a grin*] See you in jail some time, maybe!

SMITHERS: Not me, you won't. Well, I wouldn't be in yer bloody boots for no bloomin' money, but 'ere's wishin' yer luck just the same.

JONES [*contemptuously*]: You're de frightenedest man evah I see! I tells you I'se safe's 'f I was in New York City. It takes dem niggers from now to dark to git up de nerve to start somethin'. By dat time, I'se got a head start dey never kotch up wid.

SMITHERS [*maliciously*]: Give my regards to any ghosts yer meets up with.

JONES [*grinning*]: If dat ghost got money, I'll tell him never ha'nt you less'n he wants to lose it.

SMITHERS [*flattered*]: Garn! [*Then curiously*] Ain't yer takin' no luggage with yer?

JONES: I travels light when I wants to move fast. And I got tinned grub buried on de edge o' de forest. [*Boastfully*] Now say dat I don't look ahead an' use my brains! [*With a wide, liberal gesture*] I will all dat's left in de palace to you – and you better grab all you kin sneak away wid befo' dey gits here.

SMITHERS [*gratefully*]: Righto – and thanks ter yer. [*As* JONES *walks towards the door in rear – cautioningly*] Say! Look 'ere, you ain't goin' out that way, are yer?

JONES: Does you think I'd slink out de back door like a common nigger? I'se Emperor yit, ain't I? And de Emperor Jones leaves de way he comes, and dat black trash don't dare stop him – not yit, leastways. [*He stops for a moment in the doorway, listening to the far-off but insistent beat of the tom-tom.*] Listen to dat roll-call, will you? Must be mighty big drum carry dat far. [*Then with a laugh*] Well, if dey ain't no whole brass band to see me off, I sho' got de drum part of it. So long, white man.

[*He puts his hands in his pockets and with studied carelessness, whistling a tune, he saunters out of the doorway and off to left.*]

SMITHERS [*looks after him with a puzzled admiration*]: 'E's got 'is bloomin' nerve with 'im, s'elp me! [*Then angrily*] Ho – the bleedin' nigger – puttin' on 'is bloody airs! I 'opes they nabs 'im an' gives 'im what's what! [*Then putting business before the pleasure of this thought, looking around him with cupidity*] A bloke ought to find a 'ole lot in this palace that'd go for a bit of cash. Let's take a look, 'Arry, me lad.

[*He starts for the doorway on right as the curtain falls.*]

SCENE TWO

NIGHTFALL

The end of the plain where the Great Forest begins. The foreground is sandy, level ground dotted by a few stones and clumps of stunted bushes cowering close against the earth to escape the buffeting of the trade wind. In the rear the forest is a wall of darkness dividing the world. Only when the eye becomes accustomed to the gloom can the outlines of separate trunks of the nearest trees be made out, enormous pillars of deeper blackness. A sombre monotone of wind lost in the leaves moans in the air. Yet this sound serves but to intensify the impression of the forest's relentless immobility, to form a background throwing into relief its brooding, implacable silence.

[JONES *enters from the left, walking rapidly. He stops as he nears the edge of the forest, looks around him quickly, peering into the dark as if searching for some familiar landmark. Then, apparently satisfied that he is where he ought to be, he throws himself on the ground, dog-tired.*]

JONES: Well, heah I is. In de nick o' time, too! Little mo' an' it'd be blacker'n de ace of spades heah-abouts. [*He pulls a bandana handkerchief from his hip pocket and mops off his perspiring face.*] Sho'! Gimme air! I'se done up sho' 'nuff. Dat soft Emperor job ain't no trainin' fo' a long dash ovah dat plain in de brilin' sun. [*Then with a chuckle*] Cheah up, nigger, de worst is yet to come. [*He lifts his head and stares at the forest. His chuckle peters out abruptly. In a tone of awe*] My goodness, look at dem woods, will you? Dat no-count Smithers said dey'd be black an' he sho' called de turn. [*Turning away from them quickly and looking down at his feet, he snatches at a chance to change the subject – solicitously.*] Feet, you is holdin' up yo' end fine an' I sutinly hopes you ain't blisterin'. It's time you git a rest. [*He takes off his shoes, his eyes studiously avoiding the forest. He feels the soles of his feet gingerly.*] You is still in de pink – on'y a little mite feverish. Cool yo'selfs. Remember you got a long journey yit before you. [*He sits in a weary attitude, listening to the rhythmic beating of the tom-tom. He grumbles in a loud tone to cover up a growing uneasiness.*] Bush niggers! Wonder dey wouldn' git sick o' beatin' dat drum. Sounds louder, seem like. I wonder if dey's startin' after me? [*He scrambles to his feet, looking back across the plain.*] Couldn't see dem now, nohow, if dey was hundred feet away. [*Then shaking himself like a wet dog to get rid of these depressing thoughts*] Sho', dey's miles an' miles behind. What you gittin' fidgety about? [*But he sits down and begins to lace up his shoes in great haste, all the time muttering reassuringly.*] You know what? Yo' belly is empty, dat's what's de matter wid you. Come time to eat! Wid nothin' but wind on yo' stumach, o' course you feels jiggedy. Well, we eats right heah an' now soon's I gits dese here shoes laced up. [*He finishes lacing up his shoes.*] Dere! Now le's see! [*Gets on his hands and knees and searches the ground around him with his eyes.*] White stone, white stone, where is you? [*He sees the first white stone and crawls to it – with satisfaction.*] Heah you is! I knowed dis was de right place. Box of grub, come to me. [*He turns over the stone and feels in under it – in a tone of dismay.*] Ain't heah! Gorry, is I in de right place or isn't I? Dere's 'nother stone. Guess dat's it. [*He scrambles to the next stone and turns it over.*] Ain't heah, neither! Grub, whar is you? Ain't heah. Gorry, has I got to go hungry into dem woods – all de night? [*While he is talking he scrambles from one stone to another, turning them over in frantic haste. Finally he jumps to his feet excitedly.*] Is I lost de place? Must have! But how dat happen when I was followin' de trail across de plain in broad daylight? [*Almost plaintively*] I'se hungry, I is! I gotta git my feed. Whar's my strength gonna come from if I doesn't? Gorry, I gotta find dat grub high an' low somehow! Why it come dark so quick like dat? Can't see nothin'. [*He scratches a match on his trousers and peers about him. The rate of the beat of the far-off tom-tom increases perceptibly as he does so. He mutters in a bewildered voice.*] How come all dese white stones come heah when I only remembers one? [*Suddenly, with a frightened gasp, he flings the match on the ground and stamps on it.*] Nigger, is you gone crazy mad? Is you lightin' matches to show dem whar you is? Fo' Lawd's sake, use yo' haid. Gorry, I'se got to be careful! [*He stares at the plain behind him apprehensively, his hand on his revolver.*] But how come all dese white stones? And whar's dat tin box o' grub I hid all wrapped up in oil cloth?

[*While his back is turned, the* LITTLE FORMLESS FEARS *creep out from the deeper blackness of the forest. They are black, shapeless, only their glittering little eyes can be seen. If they have any describable form at all it is that of a grubworm about the size of a creeping child. They move noiselessly, but with deliberate, painful effort, striving to raise themselves on end, failing and sinking prone again.* JONES *turns about to face the forest. He stares up at the tops of the trees, seeking vainly to discover his whereabout by their conformation.*]

JONES: Can't tell nothin' from dem trees! Gorry, nothin' 'round heah look like I evah seed it befo'. I'se gone lost de place sho' 'nuff. [*With mournful foreboding*] It's mighty queer! It's mighty queer! [*With sudden forced defiance – in an angry tone*] Woods, is you tryin' to put somethin' ovah on me? [*From the formless creatures on the ground in front of him comes a tiny gale of low mocking laughter like a rustling of leaves. They squirm upward towards him in twisted attitudes.* JONES *looks down, leaps backwards with a yell of terror, pulling out his revolver as he does so – in a quavering voice.*] What's dat? Who's dar? What is you? Git away from me befo' I shoots! You don't? –

[*He fires. There is a flash, a loud report, then silence broken only by the far-off quickened throb of the tom-tom. The formless creatures have scurried back into the forest.* JONES *remains fixed in his position listening intently. The sound of the shot, the reassuring feel of the revolver in his hand, have somewhat restored his shaken nerve. He addresses himself with renewed confidence.*]

JONES: Dey're gone. Dat shot fix 'em. Dey was only little animals – little wild pigs, I reckon. Dey've maybe rooted out yo' grub an' eat it. Sho', you fool nigger, what you think dey is – ha'nts. [*Excitedly*] Gorry, you give de game away when you fire dat shot. Dem niggers heah dat fo' su'tin! Time you beat it in de woods widout no long waits. [*He starts for the forest – hesitates before the plunge – then urging himself in with manful resolution.*] Git in, nigger! What you skeered at? Ain't nothin' dere but de trees! Git in! [*He plunges boldly into the forest.*]

SCENE THREE

Nine o'clock. In the forest. The moon has just risen. Its beams, drifting through the canopy of leaves, make a barely perceptible, suffused, eerie glow. A dense low wall of underbrush and creepers is in the nearer forground, fencing in a small triangular clearing. Beyond this is the massed blackness of the forest like an encompassing barrier. A path is dimly discerned leading down to the clearing from left, rear, and winding away from it again towards the right.

[*As the scene opens nothing can be distinctly made out. Except for the beating of the tom-tom, which is a trifle louder and quicker than in the previous scene, there is silence, broken every few seconds by a queer, clicking sound. Then gradually the figure of the Negro,* JEFF, *can be discerned crouching on his haunches at the rear of the triangle He is middle-aged, thin, brown in colour, is dressed in a Pullman porter's uniform, cap, etc. He is throwing a pair of dice on the ground before him, picking them up, shaking them, casting them out with the regular, rigid, mechanical movements of an automaton. The heavy, plodding footsteps of someone approaching along the trail from the left are heard and* JONES'S *voice, pitched in a slightly higher key and strained in a cheering effort to overcome its own tremors.*]

JONES: De moon's rizen. Does you heah dat, nigger? You gits more light from dis forrard. No mo' buttin' yo' fool head agin' de trunks an' scratchin' de hide off yo' legs in de bushes. Now you sees whar you'se gwine. So cheer up! From now on you has it easy. [*He steps just to the rear of the triangular clearing and mops off his face on his sleeve. He has lost his Panama hat. His face is scratched, his brilliant uniform shows several large rents.*] What time's it gittin' to be, I wonder? I dassent light no match to find out. Phoo'. It's wa'm an' dat's a fac'! [*Wearily*] How long I been makin' trampin' dese woods? Must be hours an' hours. Seems like fo'evah! Yit can't be, when de moon's jes' riz. Dis am a long night fo' yo', yo' Majesty! [*With a mournful chuckle*] Majesty! Der ain't much majesty 'bout dis baby now. [*With attempted cheerfulness*] Never min'. It's all part o' de game. Dis night come to an end like everything else. And when you gits dar safe and has dat bankroll in yo' hands you laughs at all dis. [*He starts to whistle, but checks himself abruptly.*] What yo' whistlin' for, you po' fool! Want all de worl' to heah you? [*He stops talking to listen.*] Heah dat ole drum! Sho' gits nearer from de sound. Dey're takin' it along wid 'em. Time fo' me to move. [*He takes a step forward, then stops – worriedly.*] What's dat odder queer clickety sound I heah? Dere it is! Sound close! Sound like – sound like – Fo' God sake, sound like some nigger was shootin' dice! [*Frightenedly*] I better get on quick when I gits dem notions. [*He walks quickly into the clear space – then stands transfixed as he sees* JEFF *– in a terrified gasp*] Who dar? Who dat? Is dat you, Jeff? [*Starting towards the other, forgetful for a moment of his surroundings and really believing it is a living man that he sees – in a tone of happy relief.*] Jeff! I'se sho' mighty glad to see you! Dey tol' me you done died from dat razor cut I give you. [*Stopping suddenly, bewildered*] But how you come to be heah, nigger? [*He stares fascinatedly at the other who continues his mechanical play with the dice.* JONES'S *eyes begin to roll wildly. He stutters.*] Ain't you gwine – look up – can't you speak to me? Is you – is you – a ha'nt? [*He jerks out his revolver in a frenzy of terrified rage.*] Nigger, I kills you dead once. Has I got to kill you agin? You take it den. [*He fires. When the smoke clears away* JEFF *has disappeared.* JONES *stands trembling – then with a certain reassurance.*] He's gone, anyway. Ha'nt or no ha'nt, dat shot fix him. [*The beat of the far-off tom-tom is perceptibly louder and more rapid.* JONES *becomes conscious of it – with a start, looking back over his* *shoulder.*] Dey's gittin' near! Dey'se comin' fast! And heah I is shootin' shots to let 'em know jes' whar I is. Oh, Gorry, I'se got to run. [*Forgetting the path he plunges wildly into the underbrush in the rear and disappears in the shadow.*]

SCENE FOUR

Eleven o'clock. In the forest. A wide dirt road runs diagonally from right, front, to left, rear. Rising sheer on both sides the forest walls it in. The moon is now up. Under its light the road glimmers ghastly and unreal. It is as if the forest has stood aside momentarily to let the road pass through and accomplish its veiled purpose. This done, the forest will fold in upon itself again and the road will be no more.

[JONES *stumbles in from the forest on the right. His uniform is ragged and torn. He looks about him with numbed surprise when he sees the road, his eyes blinking in the bright moonlight. He flops down exhaustedly and pants heavily for a while. Then with sudden anger.*]

JONES: I'm meltin' wid heat! Runnin' an' runnin' an' runnin'! Damn dis heah coat! Like a strait-jacket! [*He tears off his coat and flings it away from him, revealing himself stripped to the waist.*] Dere! Dat's better! Now I kin breathe! [*Looking down at his feet, the spurs catch his eye*] And to hell wid dese high-fangled spurs. Dey're what's been a-trippin' me up an' breakin' me neck. [*He unstraps them and flings them away disgustedly.*] Dere! I gits rid o' dem frippety Emperor trappin's an' I travels lighter. Lawd! I'se tired! [*After a pause, listening to the insistent beat of the tom-tom in the distance*] I must 'a put some distance between myself an' dem – runnin' like dat – and yit – dat damn drum sound jes' de same – nearer, even. Well, I guess I a'most holds my lead anyhow. Dey won't never catch up. [*With a sigh*] If on'y my fool legs stands up. Oh, I'se sorry I evah went in for dis. Dat Emperor job is sho' hard to shake. [*He looks around him suspiciously.*] How'd dis road evah git heah? Good level road, too. I never remembers seein' it befo'. [*Shaking his head apprehensively*] Dese woods is sho' full o' de queerest things at night.

[*With a sudden terror*] Lawd God, don't let me see no more o' dem ha'nts! Dey gits me scared! [*Then trying to talk himself into confidence*] Ha'nts! You fool nigger, dey ain't no such things! Don't de Baptist parson tell you dat many time? Is you civilized, or is you like dese ign'rent black niggers heah? Sho'! Dat was all in yo' own head. Wasn't nothin' dere. Wasn't no Jeff! Know what? You jus' get seein' dem things 'cause yo' belly's empty and you's sick wid hunger inside. Hunger 'fects yo' head and yo' eyes. Any fool know dat. [*Then pleading fervently*] But bless God, I don't come across no more o' dem, whatever dey is! [*Then cautiously*] Rest! Don't talk! Rest! You needs it. Den you gits on yo' way again. [*Looking at the moon*] Night's half gone a'most. You hits de coast in de mawning! Den you'se all safe.

[*From the right forward a small gang of Negroes enter. They are dressed in striped convict suits, their heads are shaven, one leg drags limpingly, shackled to a heavy ball and chain. Some carry picks, the others shovels. They are followed by a white man dressed in the uniform of a* PRISON GUARD. *A Winchester rifle is slung across his shoulders and he carries a heavy whip. At a signal from the guard they stop on the road opposite where* JONES *is sitting.* JONES, *who has been staring up at the sky, unmindful of their noiseless approach, suddenly looks down and sees them. His eyes pop out, he tries to get to his feet and fly, but sinks back, too numbed by fright to move. His voice catches in a choking prayer*]

JONES: Lawd Jesus!

[*The* PRISON GUARD *cracks his whip – noiselessly – and at that signal all the* CONVICTS *start at work on the road. They swing their picks, they shovel, but not a sound comes from their labour. Their movements, like those of* JEFF *in the preceding scene, are those of automatons – rigid, slow, and mechanical. The* PRISON GUARD *points sternly at* JONES *with his whip, motions him to take his place among the other shovellers.* JONES *gets to his feet in a hypnotized stupor. He mumbles subserviently*]

JONES: Yes, suh! Yes, suh! I'se comin'.

[*As he shuffles, dragging one foot, over to his place, he curses under his breath with rage and hatred*]

JONES: God damn yo' soul, I gits even wid you yit, some time.

[*As if there were a shovel in his hands he goes through weary, mechanical gestures of digging up dirt, and throwing it to the roadside. Suddenly the* GUARD *approaches him angrily, threateningly. He raises his whip and lashes* JONES *viciously across the shoulders with it.* JONES *winces with pain and cowers abjectly. The* GUARD *turns his back on him and walks away contemptuously. Instantly* JONES *straightens up. With arms upraised as if his shovel were a club in his hands he springs murderously at the unsuspecting guard. In the act of crashing down his shovel on the white man's skull,* JONES *suddenly becomes aware that his hands are empty. He cries despairingly*]

JONES: Whar's my shovel? Gimme my shovel 'till I splits his damn head! [*Appealing to his fellow* CONVICTS] Gimme a shovel, one o' you, fo' God's sake!

[*They stand fixed in motionless attitudes, their eyes on the ground. The* GUARD *seems to wait expectantly, his back turned to the attacker.* JONES *bellows with baffled, terrified rage, tugging frantically at his revolver*]

JONES: I kills you, you white debil, if it's de last thing I evah does! Ghost or debil, I kill you agin!

[*He frees the revolver and fires point blank at the* GUARD'S *back. Instantly the walls of the forest close in from both sides, the road and the figures of the* CONVICT GANG *are blotted out in an enshrouding darkness. The only sounds are a crashing in the underbrush as* JONES *leaps away in mad flight and the throbbing of the tom-tom, still far distant, but increased in volume of sound and rapidity of beat.*]

SCENE FIVE

One o'clock. A large circular clearing, enclosed by the serried ranks of gigantic trunks of tall trees whose tops are lost to view. In the centre is a big dead stump worn by time into a curious resemblance to an auction block. The moon floods the clearing with a clear light.

[JONES *forces his way in through the forest on the left. He looks wildly about the clearing with hunted, fearful glances. His trousers are in tatters, his shoes cut and misshapen, flapping about his feet. He slinks cautiously to the stump in the centre and sits down in a tense position, ready for instant flight. Then he holds his head in his hands and rocks back and forth, moaning to himself miserably.*]

JONES: Oh Lawd, Lawd! Oh Lawd, Lawd! [*Suddenly he throws himself on his knees and raises his clasped hands to the sky – in a voice of agonized pleading.*] Lawd Jesus, heah my prayer! I'se a po' sinner, a po' sinner! I knows I done wrong, I knows it! When I cotches Jeff cheatin' wid loaded dice my anger overcomes me and I kills him dead! Lawd, I done wrong! When dat guard hits me wid de whip, my anger overcomes me, and I kills him dead. Lawd, I done wrong! And down heah whar dese fool bush niggers raises me up to the seat o' de mighty, I steals all I could grab. Lawd, I done wrong! I knows it! I'se sorry! Forgive me, Lawd! Forgive dis po' sinner! [*Then beseeching terrifiedly*] And keep dem away, Lawd! Keep dem away from me! And stop dat drum soundin' in my ears! Dat begin to sound ha'nted, too. [*He gets to his feet, evidently slightly reassured by his prayer – with attempted confidence.*] De Lawd'll preserve me from dem ha'nts after dis. [*Sits down on the stump again.*] I ain't skeered o' real men. Let dem come. But dem odders – [*He shudders – then looks down at his feet, working his toes inside the shoes –*

with a groan.] Oh, my po' feet! Dem shoes ain't no use no more 'ceptin' to hurt. I'se better off widout dem. [*He unlaces them and pulls them off – holds the wrecks of the shoes in his hands and regards them mournfully.*] You was real, A-one patin' leather, too. Look at you now. Emperor, you'se gittin' mighty low!

[*He sighs dejectedly and remains with bowed shoulders, staring down at the shoes in his hands as if reluctant to throw them away. While his attention is thus occupied, a crowd of figures silently enter the clearing from all sides. All are dressed in Southern costumes of the period of the fifties of the last century. There are middle-aged men who are evidently well-to-do* PLANTERS. *There is one spruce, authoritative individual – the* AUCTIONEER. *There are a crowd of curious spectators, chiefly young belles and dandies who have come to the slave-market for diversion. All exchange courtly greetings in dumb show and chat silently together. There is something stiff, rigid, unreal, marionettish about their movements. They group themselves about the stump. Finally a batch of slaves are led in from the left by an attendant – three men of different ages, two women, one with a baby in her arms, nursing. They are placed to the left of the stump, beside* JONES.

The WHITE PLANTERS *look them over appraisingly as if they were cattle. The dandies point their fingers and make witty remarks. The belles titter bewitchingly. All this in silence save for the ominous throb of the tom-tom. The* AUCTIONEER *holds up his hand, taking his place at the stump. The groups strain forward. He touches* JONES *on the shoulder peremptorily, motioning for him to stand on the stump – the auction block.*

JONES *looks up, sees the figures on all sides, looks wildly for some opening to escape, sees none, screams, and leaps madly to the top of the stump to get as far away from them as possible. He stands there, cowering, paralysed with horror. The* AUCTIONEER *begins his silent speech. He points to* JONES, *appeals to the planters to see for themselves. Here is a good field hand, sound in wind and limb as they can see. Very strong still in spite of his being middle-aged. Look at that back. Look at those shoulders. Look at the muscles in his arms and his sturdy legs. Capable of any amount of hard labour. Moreover of a good disposition, intelligent and tractable. Will any gentleman start the bidding? The planters raise their fingers, make their bids. They are apparently all eager to possess* JONES. *The bidding is lively, the crowd interested. While this has been going on,* JONES *has been seized by the courage of desperation. He dares to look down and around him. Over his face abject terror gives way to mystification, to gradual realization – stutteringly.*]

JONES: What you all doin', white folks? What's all dis? What you all lookin' at me fo'? What you doin' wid me, anyhow? [*Suddenly convulsed with raging hatred and fear*] Is dis a auction? Is you sellin' me like dey uster befo' de war? [*Jerking out his revolver just as the* AUCTIONEER *knocks him down to one of the planters – glaring from him to the purchaser*] And *you* sells me? And *you* buys me? I shows you I'se a free nigger, damn yo' souls!

[*He fires at the* AUCTIONEER *and at the* PLANTER *with such rapidity that the two shots are almost simultaneous. As if this were a signal the walls of the forest fold in. Only blackness remains and silence broken by* JONES *as he rushes off, crying with fear – and by the quickened, ever louder beat of the tom-tom.*]

SCENE SIX

Three o'clock. A cleared space in the forest. The limbs of the trees meet over it forming a low ceiling about five feet from the ground. The interlocked ropes of creepers reaching upward to entwine the tree trunks give an arched appearance to the sides. The space thus enclosed is like the dark, noisome hold of some ancient vessel. The moonlight is almost completely shut out and only a vague, wan light filters through.

[*There is the noise of someone approaching from the left, stumbling and crawling through the undergrowth.* JONES'S *voice is heard between chattering moans.*]

JONES: Oh, Lawd, what I gwine do now? Ain't got no bullet left on'y de silver one. If mo' o' dem ha'nts come after me, how I gwine skeer dem away? Oh, Lawd, on'y de silver one left – an' I gotta save dat fo' luck. If I shoots dat one I'm a goner sho'! Lawd, it's black heah! Whar's de moon? Oh, Lawd, don't dis night evah come to an end? [*By the sounds, he is feeling his way cautiously forward.*] Dere! Dis feels like a clear space. I gotta lie down an' rest. I don't care if dem niggers does cotch me. I gotta rest.

[*He is well forward now where his figure can be dimly made out. His trousers have been so torn away that what is left of them is no better than a loin-cloth. He flings himself full length, face downward on the ground, panting with exhaustion. Gradually it seems to grow lighter in the enclosed space and two rows of seated figures can be seen behind* JONES. *They are sitting in crumpled, despairing attitudes, hunched, facing one another with their backs touching the forest walls as if they were shackled to them. All are Negroes naked save for loin-cloths. At first they are silent and motionless. Then they begin to sway slowly forward toward each and back again in unison, as if they were laxly letting themselves follow the long roll of a ship at sea. At the same time a low, melancholy murmur rises among them, increasing gradually by rhythmic degrees which seem to be directed and controlled by the throb of the tom-tom in the distance, to a long, tremulous wail of despair that reaches a certain pitch, unbearably acute, then falls by slow gradations of tone into silence and is taken up again.* JONES *starts, looks up, sees the figures, and throws himself down again to shut out the sight. A shudder of terror shakes his whole body as the wail rises up about him again. But the next time his voice, as if under some uncanny compulsion, starts with the others. As their chorus lifts he rises to a sitting posture similar to the others, swaying back and forth. His voice reaches the highest pitch of sorrow, of desolation. The light fades out, the other voices cease, and only darkness is left.* JONES *can be heard scrambling to his feet and running off, his voice sinking down the scale and receding as he moves farther and farther away in the forest. The tom-tom beats louder, quicker, with a more insistent, triumphant pulsation.*]

SCENE SEVEN

Five o'clock. The foot of a gigantic tree by the edge of a great river. A rough structure of boulders, like an altar, is by the tree. The raised river bank is in the nearer background. Beyond this the surface of the river spreads out, brilliant and unruffled in the moonlight, blotted out and merged in a veil of bluish mist in the d stance.

[JONES'S *voice is heard from the left rising and falling in the long, despairing wail of the chained slaves, to the rhythmic beat of the tom-tom. As his voice sinks into silence, he enters the open space. The expression of his face is fixed and stony, his eyes have an obsessed glare, he moves with a strange delibera- tion like a sleep-walker or one in a trance. He looks around at the tree, the rough stone altar, the moonlit surface of the river beyond, and passes his hand over his head with a vague gesture of puzzled bewilderment. Then, as if in obedience to some obscure impulse, he sinks into a kneeling, devotional posture before the altar. Then he seems to come to himself partly, to have an uncertain realization of what he is doing, for he straightens up and stares about him horrifiedly – in an in- coherent mumble*]

JONES: What – what is I doin'? What is – dis place? Seems like – seems like I know dat tree – an' dem stones – an' de river. I remember – seems like I been heah befo'. [*Trem- blingly*] Oh, Gorry, I'se skeered in dis place! I'se skeered! Oh, Lawd, pertect dis sinner!

[*Crawling away from the altar, he cowers close to the ground, his face hidden, his shoulders heaving with sobs of hysterical fright. From behind the trunk of the tree, as if he had sprung out of it, the figure of the Congo* WITCH-DOCTOR *appears. He is wizened and old, naked except for the fur of some small animal tied about his waist, its bushy tail hanging down in front. His body is stained all over a bright red. Antelope horns are on each side of his head, branching upward. In one hand he carries a bone rattle, in the other a charm stick with a bunch of white cockatoo feathers tied to the end. A great number of glass beads and bone ornaments are about his neck, ears, wrists, and ankles. He struts noiselessly with a queer prancing step to a position in the clear ground between* JONES *and the altar. Then with a preliminary, summoning stamp of his foot on the earth, he begins to dance and to chant. As if in response to his summons the beating of the tom-tom grows to a fierce, exultant boom whose throbs seem to fill the air with vibrating rhythm.* JONES *looks up, starts to spring to his feet, reaches a half-kneeling, half-squatting position and remains rigidly fixed there, paralysed with awed fascination by this new apparition. The* WITCH-DOCTOR *sways, stamping with his foot, his bone rattle clicking the time. His voice rises and falls in a weird, monotonous croon, without articulate word divisions. Gradually his dance becomes clearly one of a narrative in pantomime, his croon is an incantation, a charm to allay the fierceness of some implacable deity demanding sacrifice. He flees, he is pursued by devils, he hides, he flees again. Ever wilder and wilder becomes his flight, nearer and nearer draws the pursuing evil, more and more the spirit of terror gains possession of him. His croon, rising to intensity, is punctuated by shrill cries.* JONES *has become completely hypnotized. His voice joins in the incantation, in the cries, he beats time with his hands and sways his body to and fro from the waist. The whole spirit and meaning of the dance has entered into him, has become his spirit. Finally the theme of the pantomime halts on a howl of despair, and is taken up again in a note of savage hope. There is a salvation. The forces of evil demand sacrifice. They must be appeased. The* WITCH-DOCTOR *points with his wand to the sacred tree, to the river beyond, to the altar, and finally to* JONES *with a ferocious command.* JONES *seems to sense the meaning of this. It is he who must offer himself for sacrifice.*

He beats his forehead abjectly to the ground, moaning hysterically.]

JONES: Mercy, oh Lawd! Mercy! Mercy on dis po' sinner.

[*The* WITCH-DOCTOR *springs to the river bank. He stretches out his arms and calls to some god within its depths. Then he starts backward slowly, his arms remaining out. A huge head of a crocodile appears over the bank and its eyes, glittering greenly, fasten upon* JONES. *He stares into them fascinatedly. The* WITCH-DOCTOR *prances up to him, touches him with his wand, motions with hideous command towards the waiting monster.* JONES *squirms on his belly nearer and nearer, moaning continually.*]

JONES: Mercy, Lawd! Mercy!

[*The crocodile heaves more of his enormous hulk on to the land.* JONES *squirms toward him. The* WITCH-DOCTOR'S *voice shrills out in furious exultation, the tom-tom beats madly.* JONES *cries out in a fierce, exhausted spasm of anguished pleading.*]

JONES: Lawd, save me! Lawd Jesus, heah my prayer!

[*Immediately, in answer to his prayer, comes the thought of the one bullet left him. He snatches at his hip, shouting defiantly.*]

JONES: De silver bullet! You don't git me yit!

[*He fires at the green eyes in front of him. The head of the crocodile sinks back behind the river bank, the* WITCH-DOCTOR *springs behind the sacred tree and disappears.* JONES *lies with his face to the ground, his arms outstretched, whimpering with fear as the throb of the tom-tom fills the silence about him with a sombre pulsation, a baffled but revengeful power.*]

SCENE EIGHT

Dawn. Same as Scene Two, the dividing line of forest and plain. The nearest tree trunks are dimly revealed, but the forest behind them is still a mass of glooming shadow. The tom-tom seems on the very spot, so loud and continuously vibrating are its beats.

[LEM *enters from the left, followed by a small squad of his* SOLDIERS, *and by the Cockney trader,* SMITHERS. LEM *is a heavy-set, ape-faced old savage of the extreme African type, dressed only in a loin-cloth. A revolver and cartridge belt are about his waist. His* SOLDIERS *are in different degrees of rag-concealed nakedness. All wear broad palm-leaf hats. Each one carries a rifle.* SMITHERS *is the same as in Scene One. One of the soldiers, evidently a tracker, is peering about keenly on the ground. He grunts and points to the spot where* JONES *entered the forest.* LEM *and* SMITHERS *come to look.*]

SMITHERS [*after a glance, turns away in disgust*]: That's where 'e went in right enough. Much good it'll do yer. 'E's miles orf by this an' safe to the coast, damn 's 'ide! I tole yer yer'd lose 'im, didn't I? – wastin' the 'ole bloomin' night beatin' yer bloody drum and castin' yer silly spells! Gawd blimey, wot a pack!

LEM [*gutturally*]: We cotch him. You see. [*He makes a motion to his soldiers who squat down on their haunches in a semi-circle.*]

SMITHERS [*exasperatedly*]: Well, ain't yer goin' in an' 'unt 'im in the woods? What the 'ell's the good of waitin'?

LEM [*imperturbably – squatting down himself*]: We cotch him.

SMITHERS [*turning away from him contemptuously*]: Aw! Garn! 'E's a better man than the lot o' you put together. I 'ates the sight o' 'im, but I'll say that for 'im.

[*A sound of snapping twigs comes from the forest. The* SOLDIERS *jump to their feet, cocking their rifles alertly.*

LEM remains sitting with an imperturbable expression, but listening intently. The sound from the woods is repeated. LEM makes a quick signal with his hand. His followers creep quickly but noiselessly into the forest, scattering so that each enters at a different spot.]

SMITHERS [*in the silence that follows – in a contemptuous whisper*]: You ain't thinkin' that would be 'im, I 'ope?

LEM [*calmly*]: We cotch him.

SMITHERS: Blarsted fat 'eads! [*Then after a second's thought – wonderingly*] Still, after all, it might 'appen. If 'e lost 'is bloody way in these stinkin' woods 'e'd likely turn in a circle without 'is knowin' it. They all does.

LEM [*peremptorily*]: Ssshh! [*The reports of several rifles sound from the forest, followed a second later by savage, exultant yells. The beating of the tom-tom abruptly ceases. LEM looks up at the white man with a grin of satisfaction.*] We cotch him. Him dead.

SMITHERS [*with a snarl*]: 'Ow d'yer know it's 'im, an' 'ow d'yer know 'e's dead?

LEM: My mens dey got 'um silver bullets. Dey kill him shure.

SMITHERS [*astonished*]: They got silver bullets?

LEM: Lead bullet no kill him. He got um strong charm. I cook um money, make um silver bullet, make um strong charm, too.

SMITHERS [*light breaking upon him*]: So that's wot you was up to all night, wot? You was scared to put after 'im till you'd moulded silver bullets, eh?

LEM [*simply stating a fact*]: Yes. Him got strong charm. Lead no good.

SMITHERS [*slapping his thigh and guffawing*]: Haw-haw! If yer don't beat all 'ell! [*Then recovering himself – scornfully*] I'll bet yer it ain't 'im they shot at all, yer bleedin' looney!

LEM [*calmly*]: Dey come bring him now. [*The SOLDIERS come out of the forest, carrying JONES's limp body. There is a little reddish-purple hole under his left breast. He is dead. They carry him to LEM, who examines his body with great satisfaction.*]

SMITHERS [*leans over his shoulder – in a tone of frightened awe*]: Well, they did for yer right enough, Jonesy, me lad! Dead as a bloater! [*Mockingly*] Where's yer 'igh an' mighty airs now, yer bloomin' Majesty? [*Then with a grin*] Silver bullets! Gawd blimey, but yer died in the 'eighth o' style, any'ow! [LEM *makes a motion to the soldiers to carry the body out, left.* SMITHERS *speaks to him sneeringly.*] And I s'pose you think it's yer bleedin' charms and yer silly beatin' the drum that made 'im run in a circle when 'e'd lost 'imself, don't yer? [*But* LEM *makes no reply, does not seem to hear the question, walks out, left, after his men.* SMITHERS *looks after him with contemptuous scorn.*] Stupid as 'ogs, the lot of 'em! Blarsted niggers!

THE CURTAIN FALLS

DESIRE UNDER THE ELMS

A Play in Three Parts

CHARACTERS

EPHRAIM CABOT

SIMEON } His sons
PETER }
EBEN }

ABBIE PUTNAM

Young Girl; Two Farmers; the Fiddler; a Sheriff; and other people from the surrounding farms.

DESIRE UNDER THE ELMS

THE action of the entire play takes place in, and immediately outside of, the Cabot farm-house in New England, in the year 1850. The south end of the house faces a stone wall with a wooden gate at centre opening on a country road. The house is in good condition, but in need of paint. Its walls are a sickly greyish, the green of the shutters faded. Two enormous elms are on each side of the house. They bend their trailing branches down over the roof – they appear to protect and at the same time subdue; there is a sinister maternity in their aspect, a crushing, jealous absorption. When the wind does not keep them astir, they develop from their intimate contact with the life of man in the house an appalling humanness. They brood oppressively over the house, they are like exhausted women resting their sagging breasts and hands and hair on its roof, and when it rains their tears trickle down monotonously and rot on the shingles.

There is a path running from the gate around the right corner of the house to the front door. A narrow porch is on this side. The end wall facing us has two windows in its upper story, two larger ones on the floor below. The two upper are those of the father's bedroom and that of the brothers. On the left, ground floor, is the kitchen – on the right, the parlour, the blinds of which are always pulled down.

PART ONE

SCENE 1

Exterior of the farm-house. It is sunset of a day at the beginning of summer in the year 1850. There is no wind and everything is still. The sky above the roof is suffused with deep colours, the green of the elms glows, but the house is in shadow, seeming pale and washed out by contrast.

[*A door opens and* EBEN CABOT *comes to the end of the porch and stands looking down the road to the right. He has a large bell in his hand and this he swings mechanically, awakening a deafening clangour. Then he puts his hands on his hips and stares up at the sky. He sighs with a puzzled awe and blurts out with halting appreciation.*]

EBEN: God! Purty!

[*His eyes fall and he stares about him frowningly. He is twenty-five, tall, and sinewy. His face is well formed, good-looking, but its expression is resentful and defensive. His defiant dark eyes remind one of a wild animal's in captivity. Each day is a cage in which he finds himself trapped, but inwardly unsubdued. There is a fierce repressed vitality about him. He has black hair, moustache, a thin curly trace of beard. He is dressed in rough farm clothes.*

He spits on the ground with intense disgust, turns and goes back into the house.

SIMEON *and* PETER *come in from their work in the fields. They are tall men, much older than their half-brother* (SIMEON *is thirty-nine and* PETER *thirty-seven*)*, built on a squarer, simpler model, fleshier in body, more bovine and homelier in face, shrewder, and more practical. Their shoulders stoop a bit* *from years of farm work. They clump heavily along in their clumsy thick-soled boots caked with earth. Their clothes, their faces, hands, bare arms and throats are earth-stained. They smell of earth. They stand together for a moment in front of the house and, as if with the one impulse, stare dumbly up at the sky, leaning on their hoes. Their faces have a compressed, unresigned expression. As they look upward, this softens.*]

SIMEON [*grudgingly*]: Purty.

PETER: Ay-eh.

SIMEON [*suddenly*]: Eighteen year ago.

PETER: What?

SIMEON: Jenn. My woman. She died.

PETER: I'd fergot.

SIMEON: I rec'lect – now an' agin. Makes it lonesome. She'd hair long's a hoss's tail – an' yaller like gold!

PETER: Waal – she's gone. [*This with indifferent finality – then after a pause*] They's gold in the West, Sim.

SIMEON [*still under the influence of sunset – vaguely*]: In the sky?

PETER: Waal – in a manner o' speakin' – thar's the promise. [*Growing excited*] Gold in the sky – in the west – Golden Gate – Californi-a! – Golden West! – fields o' gold!

SIMEON [*excited in his turn*]: Fortunes layin' just atop o' the ground waitin' t' be picked! Solomon's mines, they says! [*For a moment they continue looking up at the sky – then their eyes drop.*]

PETER [*with sardonic bitterness*]: Here – it's stones atop o' the ground – stones atop o' stones – makin' stone walls – year atop o' year – him 'n' yew 'n' me 'n' then Eben – makin' stone walls fur him to fence us in!

SIMEON: We've wuked. Give our strength. Give our years. Ploughed 'em under in the ground [*he stamps rebelliously*] – rottin' – makin' soil for his crops! [*A pause*] Waal – the farm pays good for hereabouts.

PETER: If we ploughed in Californi-a, they'd be lumps o' gold in the furrow –!

SIMEON: Californi-a's t'other side o' earth, a'most. We got t' calc'late –

PETER [*after a pause*]: 'Twould be hard fur me, too, to give up what we've 'arned here by our sweat. [*A pause.* EBEN *sticks his head out of the dining-room window, listening.*]

SIMEON: Ay-eh. [*A pause*] Mebbe – he'll die soon.

PETER [*doubtfully*]: Mebbe.

SIMEON: Mebbe – fur all we knows – he's dead now.

PETER: Ye'd need proof –

SIMEON: He's been gone two months – with no word.

PETER: Left us in the fields an evenin' like this. Hitched up an' druv off into the West. That's plumb onnateral. He hain't never been off this farm 'ceptin' t' the village in thirty year or more, not since he married Eben's maw. [*A pause. Shrewdly*] I calc'late we might git him declared crazy by the court.

SIMEON: He skinned 'em too slick. He got the best o' all on 'em. They'd never b'lieve him crazy. [*A pause*] We got t' wait – till he's under ground.

EBEN [*with a sardonic chuckle*]: Honour thy father! [*They turn, startled, and stare at him. He grins, then scowls.*] I pray he's died. [*They stare at him. He continues matter-of-factly.*] Supper's ready.

SIMEON *and* PETER [*together*]: Ay-eh.

EBEN [*gazing up at the sky*]: Sun's downin' purty.

SIMEON *and* PETER [*together*]: Ay-eh. They's gold in the West.

EBEN: Ay-eh. [*Pointing*] Yonder atop o' the hill pasture, ye mean?

SIMEON *and* PETER [*together*]: In Californi-a!

EBEN: Hunh? [*Stares at them indifferently for a second, then drawls.*] Waal – supper's gittin' cold. [*He turns back into kitchen.*]

SIMEON [*startled – smacks his lips*]. I air hungry!

PETER [*sniffing*]: I smells bacon!

SIMEON [*with hungry appreciation*]: Bacon's good!

PETER [*in same tone*]: Bacon's bacon!

[*They turn, shouldering each other, their bodies bumping and rubbing together as they hurry clumsily to their food, like two friendly oxen toward their evening meal. They disappear around the right corner of house and can be heard entering the door.*]

CURTAIN

SCENE 2

The colour fades from the sky. Twilight begins. The interior of the kitchen is now visible. A pine table is at centre, a cooking-stove in the right rear corner, four rough wooden chairs, a tallow candle on the table. In the middle of the rear wall is fastened a big advertising poster with a ship in full sail and the word 'California' in big letters. Kitchen utensils hang from nails. Everything is neat and in order, but the atmosphere is of a men's camp kitchen rather than that of a home.

[*Places for three are laid.* EBEN *takes boiled potatoes and bacon from the stove and puts them on the table, also a loaf of bread and a crock of water.* SIMEON *and* PETER *shoulder in, slump down in their chairs without a word.* EBEN *joins them. The three eat in silence for a moment, the two elder as naturally unrestrained as beasts of the field,* EBEN *picking at his food without appetite, glancing at them with a tolerant dislike.*]

SIMEON [*suddenly turns to* EBEN]: Looky here! Ye'd oughtn't t' said that, Eben.

PETER: 'Twa'n't righteous.

EBEN: What?

SIMEON: Ye prayed he'd die.

EBEN: Waal – don't yew pray it? [*A pause*]

PETER: He's our Paw.

EBEN [*violently*]: Not mine!

SIMEON [*dryly*]: Ye'd not let no one else say that about yer Maw! Ha! [*He gives one abrupt sardonic guffaw.* PETER *grins.*]

EBEN [*very pale*]: I meant – I hain't his'n – I hain't like him – he hain't me –

PETER [*dryly*]: Wait till ye've growed his age!

EBEN [*intensely*]: I'm Maw – every drop of blood! [*A pause. They stare at him with indifferent curiosity.*]

PETER [*reminiscently*]: She was good t' Sim 'n' me. A good step-maw's scurse.

SIMEON: She was good t' every one.

EBEN [*greatly moved, gets to his feet and makes an awkward bow to each of them – stammering*]: I be thankful t' ye. I'm her. Her heir. [*He sits down in confusion.*]

PETER [*after a pause – judicially*]: She was good even t' him.

EBEN [*fiercely*]: An' fur thanks he killed her!

SIMEON [*after a pause*]: No one never kills nobody. It's allus somethin'. That's the murderer.

EBEN: Didn't he slave Maw t' death?

PETER: He's slaved himself t' death. He's slaved Sim 'n' me 'n' yew t' death – on'y none o' us hain't died – yit.

SIMEON: It's somethin' – drivin' him – t' drive us –

EBEN [*vengefully*]: Waal – I hold him t' jedgement! [*Then scornfully*] Somethin'! What's somethin'?

SIMEON: Dunno.

EBEN [*sardonically*]: What's drivin' yew to Californi-a, mebbe? [*They look at him in surprise.*] Oh, I've heerd ye! [*Then, after a pause*] But ye'll never go t' the gold-fields!

PETER [*assertively*]: Mebbe!

EBEN: Whar'll ye git the money?

PETER: We kin walk. It's an a'mighty ways – Californi-a – but if yew was t' put all the steps we've walked on this farm end t' end we'd be in the moon!

EBEN: The Injuns'll skulp ye on the plains.

SIMEON [*with grim humour*]: We'll mebbe make 'em pay a hair fur a hair!

EBEN [*decisively*]: But 'tain't that. Ye won't never go because ye'll wait here fur yer share o' the farm, thinkin' allus he'll die soon.

SIMEON [*after a pause*]: We've a right.

PETER: Two-thirds belongs t' us.

EBEN [*jumping to his feet*]: Ye've no right! She wa'n't yewr Maw! It was her farm! Didn't he steal it from her? She's dead. It's my farm.

SIMEON [*sardonically*]: Tell that t' Paw – when he comes! I'll bet ye a dollar he'll laugh – fur once in his life. Ha! [*He laughs himself in one single mirthless bark.*]

PETER [*amused in turn, echoes his brother*]: Ha!

SIMEON [*after a pause*]: What've ye got held agin us, Eben? Year arter year it's skulked in yer eye – somethin'.

PETER: Ay-eh.

EBEN: Ay-eh. They's somethin'. [*Suddenly exploding*] Why didn't ye never stand between him 'n' my Maw when he was slavin' her to her grave – t' pay her back fur the kindness she done t' yew? [*There is a long pause. They stare at him in surprise.*]

SIMEON: Waal – the stock'd got t' be watered.

PETER: 'R they was woodin' t' do.

SIMEON: 'R ploughin'.

PETER: 'R hayin'.

SIMEON: 'R spreadin' manure.

PETER: 'R weedin'.

SIMEON: 'R prunin'.

PETER: 'R milkin'.

EBEN [*breaking in harshly*]: An' makin' walls – stone atop o' stone – makin' walls till yer heart's a stone ye heft up out o' the way o' growth on to a stone wall t' wall in yer heart!

SIMEON [*matter-of-factly*]: We never had no time t' meddle.

PETER [*to* EBEN]: Yew was fifteen afore yer Maw died – an' big fur yer age. Why didn't ye never do nothin'?

EBEN [*harshly*]: They was chores t' do, wa'n't they? [*A pause – then slowly*] It was on'y arter she died I come to think o' it. Me cookin' – doin' her work – that made me know her, suffer her sufferin' – she'd come back t' help – come back t' bile potatoes – come back t' fry bacon – come back t' bake biscuits – come back all cramped up t' shake the fire, an' carry ashes, her eyes weepin' an' bloody with smoke an' cinders same's they used t' be. She still comes back – stands by the stove thar in the evenin' – she can't find it nateral sleepin' an' restin' in peace. She can't git used t' bein' free – even in her grave.

SIMEON: She never complained none.

EBEN: She'd got too tired. She'd got too used t' bein' too tired. That was what he done. [*With vengeful passion*] An' sooner'r later, I'll meddle. I'll say the thin's I didn't say then t' him! I'll yell 'em at the top o' my lungs. I'll see t' it my Maw gits some rest an' sleep in her grave! [*He sits down again, relapsing into a brooding silence. They look at him with a queer indifferent curiosity.*]

PETER [*after a pause*]: Whar in tarnation d'ye s'pose he went, Sim?

SIMEON: Dunno. He druv off in the buggy, all spick an' span, with the mare all breshed an' shiny, druv off clackin' his tongue an' wavin' his whip. I remember it right well. I was finishin' ploughin', it was spring an' May an' sunset, an' gold in the West, an' he druv off into it. I yells 'Whar ye goin', Paw?' an' he hauls up by the stone wall a jiffy. His old snake's eyes was glitterin' in the sun like he'd been drinkin' a jugful an' he says with a mule's grin: 'Don't ye run away till I come back!'

PETER: Wonder if he knowed we was wantin' fur Californi-a?

SIMEON: Mebbe. I didn't say nothin' and he says, lookin' kinder queer an' sick: 'I been hearin' the hens cluckin' an' the roosters crowin' all the durn day. I been listenin' t' the cows lowin' an' everythin' else kickin' up till I can't stand it no more. It's spring an' I'm feelin' damned,' he says. 'Damned like an old bare hickory tree fit on'y fur burnin',' he says. An' then I calc'late I must've looked a mite hopeful, fur he adds real spry and vicious: 'But don't git no fool idee I'm dead. I've sworn t' live a hundred an' I'll do it, if on'y t' spite yer sinful greed! An' now I'm ridin' out t' learn God's message t' me in the spring, like the prophets done. An' yew git back t' yer ploughin',' he says. An' he druv off singin' a hymn. I thought he was drunk – 'r I'd stopped him goin'.

EBEN [*scornfully*]: No, ye wouldn't! Ye're scared o' him. He's stronger – inside – than both o' ye put together!

PETER [*sardonically*]: An' yew – be yew Samson?

EBEN: I'm gittin' stronger. I kin feel it growin' in me – growin' an' growin' – till it'll bust out –! [*He gets up and puts on his coat and a hat. They watch him, gradually breaking into grins.* EBEN *avoids their eyes sheepishly.*] I'm goin' out fur a spell – up the road.

PETER: T' the village?

SIMEON: T' see Minnie?

EBEN [*defiantly*]: Ay-eh!

PETER [*jeeringly*]: The Scarlet Woman!

SIMEON: Lust – that's what's growin' in ye!

EBEN: Waal – she' s purty!

PETER: She's been purty fur twenty year!

SIMEON: A new coat o' paint'll make a heifer out of forty.

EBEN: She hain't forty!

PETER: If she hain't, she's teeterin' on the edge.

EBEN [*desperately*]: What d'yew know –?

PETER: All they is . . . Sim knew her – an' then me arter –

SIMEON: An' Paw kin tell yew somethin', too! He was fust!

EBEN: D'ye mean t' say he –?

SIMEON [*with a grin*]: Ay-eh! We air his heirs in everythin'!

EBEN [*intensely*]: That's more to it! That grows on it! It'll bust soon! [*Then violently*] I'll go smash my fist in her face! [*He pulls open the door in rear violently.*]

SIMEON [*with a wink at* PETER – *drawlingly*]: Mebbe – but the night's wa'm – purty – by the time ye git thar mebbe ye'll kiss her instead!

PETER: Sart'n he will!

[*They both roar with coarse laughter.* EBEN *rushes out and slams the door – then the outside front door – comes around the corner of the house and stands still by the gate, staring up at the sky.*]

SIMEON [*looking after him*]: Like his Paw!

PETER: Dead spit an' image!

SIMEON: Dog'll eat dog!

PETER: Ay-eh. [*Pause. With yearning*] Mebbe a year from now we'll be in Californi-a.

SIMEON: Ay-eh. [*A pause. Both yawn.*] Let's git t' bed.

[*He blows out the candle. They go out door in rear.* EBEN *stretches his arms up to the sky – rebelliously.*]

EBEN: Waal – thar's a star, an' somewhar's they's him, an' here's me, an' thar's Min up the road – in the same night. What if I does kiss her? She's like t'night, she's soft 'n' wa'm, her eyes kin wink like a star, her mouth's wa'm, her arms're wa'm, she smells like a wa'm ploughed field, she's purty.... Ay-eh! By God A'mighty she's purty, an' I don't give a damn how many sins she's sinned afore mine or who she's sinned 'em with, my sin's as purty as any one on 'em! [*He strides off down the road to the left.*]

SCENE 3

It is the pitch darkness just before dawn.

[EBEN *comes in from the left and goes around to the porch, feeling his way, chuckling bitterly and cursing half-aloud to himself.*]

EBEN: The cussed old miser! [*He can be heard going in the front door. There is a pause as he goes upstairs, then a loud knock on the bedroom door of the brothers.*] Wake up!

SIMEON [*startled*]: Who's thar?

EBEN [*pushing open the door and coming in, a lighted candle in his hand. The bedroom of the brothers is revealed. Its ceiling is the sloping roof. They can stand upright only close to the centre dividing wall of the upstairs.* SIMEON *and* PETER *are in a double bed, front.* EBEN'S *cot is to the rear.* EBEN *has a mixture of silly grin and vicious scowl on his face*]: I be!

PETER [*angrily*]: What in hell fire –?

EBEN: I got news fur ye! Ha! [*He gives one abrupt sardonic guffaw.*]

SIMEON [*angrily*]: Couldn't ye hold it 'till we'd got our sleep?

EBEN: It's nigh sun up. [*Then explosively*] He's gone an' married agen!

SIMEON *and* PETER [*explosively*]: Paw?

EBEN: Got himself hitched to a female 'bout thirty-five – an' purty, they says –

SIMEON [*aghast*]: It's a durn lie!

PETER: Who says?

SIMEON: They been stringin' ye!

EBEN: Think I'm a dunce, do ye? The hull village says. The preacher from New Dover, he brung the news – told it t' our preacher – New Dover, that's whar the old loon got himself hitched – that's whar the woman lived –

PETER [*no longer doubting – stunned*]: Waal . . .!

SIMEON [*the same*]: Waal . . .!

EBEN [*sitting down on a bed – with vicious hatred*]: Ain't he a devil out o' hell? It's jest t' spite us – the damned old mule!

PETER [*after a pause*]: Everythin'll go t' her now.

SIMEON: Ay-eh. [*A pause – dully*] Waal – if it's done –

PETER: It's done us. [*Pause – then persuasively*] They's gold in the fields o' Californi-a, Sim. No good a-stayin' here now.

SIMEON: Jes what I was a-thinkin'. [*Then with decision*] 'S well fust's last! Let's lightout and git this mornin'.

PETER: Suits me.

EBEN: Ye must like walkin'.

SIMEON [*sardonically*]: If ye'd grow wings on us we'd fly thar!

EBEN: Ye'd like ridin' better – on a boat, wouldn't ye? [*Fumbles in his pocket and takes out a crumpled sheet of foolscap.*] Waal, if ye sign this ye kin ride on a boat. I've had it writ out an' ready in case ye'd ever go. It says fur three hundred dollars t' each ye agree yewr shares o' the farm is sold t' me. [*They look suspiciously at the paper. A pause.*]

SIMEON [*wonderingly*]: But if he's hitched agen –

PETER: An' whar'd yew git that sum o' money, anyways?

EBEN [*cunningly*]: I know whar it's hid. I been waitin' – Maw told me. She knew whar it lay fur years, but she was waitin'. . . . It's her'n – the money he hoarded from her farm an' hid from Maw. It's my money by rights now.

PETER: Whar's it hid?

EBEN [*cunningly*]: Whar yew won't never find it without me. Maw spied on him – 'r she'd never knowed. [*A pause. They look at him suspiciously, and he at them.*] Waal, is it fa'r trade?

SIMEON: Dunno.

PETER: Dunno.

SIMEON [*looking at window*]: Sky's greyin'.

PETER: Ye better start the fire, Eben.

SIMEON: An' fix some vittles.

EBEN: Ay-eh. [*Then with a forced jocular heartiness*] I'll git ye a good one. If ye're startin' t' hoof it t' California ye'll need somethin' that'll stick t' yer ribs. [*He turns to the door, adding meaningly*] But ye kin ride on a boat if ye'll swap. [*He stops at the door and pauses. They stare at him.*]

SIMEON [*suspiciously*]: Whar was ye all night?

EBEN [*defiantly*]: Up t' Min's. [*Then slowly*] Walkin' thar, fust I felt 's if I'd kiss her; then I got a-thinkin' o' what ye'd said o' him an' her an' I says, I'll bust her nose fur that! Then I got t' the village an' heerd the news an' I got madder'n hell an' run all the way t' Min's not knowin' what I'd do – [*He pauses – then sheepishly but more defiantly*] Waal – when I seen her, I didn't hit her – nor I didn't kiss her nuther – I begun t' beller like a calf an' cuss at the same time, I was so durn mad – an' she got scared – an' I jest grabbed holt an' tuk her! [*Proudly*] Yes, sirree! I tuk her. She may've been his'n – an' your'n, too – but she's mine now!

SIMEON [*dryly*]: In love, air yew?

EBEN [*with lofty scorn*]: Love! I don't take no stock in sech slop!

PETER [*winking at* SIMEON]: Mebbe Eben's aimin' t' marry, too.

SIMEON: Min'd make a true faithful he'pmeet – fur the army! [*They snicker.*]

EBEN: What do I care fur her – 'ceptin' she's round an' wa'm? The p'int is she was his'n – an' now she b'longs t' me! [*He goes to the door – then turns – rebelliously.*] An' Min hain't sech a bad un. They's worse'n Min in the world, I'll bet ye! Wait'll we see this cow the Old Man's hitched t'! She'll beat Min, I got a notion! [*He starts to go out.*]

SIMEON [*suddenly*]: Mebbe ye'll try t' make her your'n, too?

PETER: Ha! [*He gives a sardonic laugh of relish at this idea.*]

EBEN [*spitting with disgust*]: Her – here – sleepin' with him – stealin' my Maw's farm! I'd as soon pet a skunk 'r kiss a snake! [*He goes out. The two stare after him suspiciously. A pause. They listen to his steps receding.*]

PETER: He's startin' the fire.

SIMEON: I'd like t' ride t' Californi-a – but –

PETER: Min might 'a' put some scheme in his head.

SIMEON: Mebbe it's all a lie 'bout Paw marryin'. We'd best wait an' see the bride.

PETER: An' don't sign nothin' till we does –

SIMEON: Nor till we've tested it's good money! [*Then with a grin*] But if Paw's hitched we'd be sellin' Eben somethin' we'd never git nohow!

PETER: We'll wait an' see. [*Then with sudden vindictive anger*] An' till he comes, let's yew 'n' me not wuk a lick, let Eben tend to thin's if he's a mind t', let's us jest sleep an' eat an' drink likker, an' let the hull damned farm go t' blazes!

SIMEON [*excitedly*]: By God, we've 'arned a rest! We'll play rich fur a change. I hain't agoin' to stir outa bed till breakfast's ready.

PETER: An' on the table!

SIMEON [*after a pause – thoughtfully*]: What d'ye calc'late she'll be like – our new Maw? Like Eben thinks?

PETER: More'n likely.

SIMEON [*vindictively*]: Waal – I hope she's a she-devil that'll make him wish he was dead an' livin' in the pit o' hell fur comfort!

PETER [*fervently*]: Amen!

SIMEON [*imitating his father's voice*]: 'I'm ridin' out t' learn God's message t' me in the spring like the prophets done,' he says. I'll bet right then an' thar he knew plumb well he was goin' whorin', the stinkin' old hypocrite!

SCENE 4

Same as Scene 2 – shows the interior of the kitchen, with a lighted candle on table. It is grey dawn outside.

[SIMEON *and* PETER *are just finishing their breakfast.* EBEN *sits before his plate of untouched food, brooding frowningly.*]

PETER [*glancing at him rather irritably*]: Lookin' glum don't help none.

SIMEON [*sarcastically*]: Sorrowin' over his lust o' the flesh.

PETER [*with a grin*]: Was she yer fust?

EBEN [*angrily*]: None o' yer business. [*A pause*] I was thinkin' o' him. I got a notion he's gittin' near – I kin feel him comin' on like yew kin feel malaria chill afore it takes ye.

PETER: It's too early yet.

SIMEON: Dunno. He'd like t' catch us nappin' – jest t' have somethin' t' hoss us 'round over.

PETER [*mechanically gets to his feet.* SIMEON *does the same*]: Waal – let's git t' wuk. [*They both plod mechanically toward the door before they realize. Then they stop short.*]

SIMEON [*grinning*]: Ye're a cussed fool, Pete – and I be wuss! Let him see we hain't wukin'! We don't give a durn!

PETER [*as they go back to the table*]: Not a damned durn! It'll serve t' show him we're done with him. [*They sit down again.* EBEN *stares from one to the other with surprise.*]

SIMEON [*grins at him*]: We're aimin' t' start bein' lilies o' the field.

PETER: Nary a toil 'r spin 'r lick o' wuk do we put in!

SIMEON: Ye're sole owner – till he comes – that's what ye wanted. Waal, ye got t' be sole hand, too.

PETER: The cows air bellerin'. Ye better hustle at the milkin'.

EBEN [*with excited joy*]: Ye mean ye'll sign the paper?

SIMEON [*dryly*]: Mebbe.

PETER: Mebbe.

SIMEON: We're considerin'. [*Peremptorily*] Ye better git t' wuk.

EBEN [*with queer excitement*]: It's Maw's farm agen! It's my farm! Them's my cows! I'll milk my durn fingers off fur cows o' mine! [*He goes out door in rear, they stare after him indifferently.*]

SIMEON: Like his Paw.

PETER: Dead spit 'n' image!

SIMEON: Waal – let dog eat dog!

[EBEN *comes out of front door and around the corner of the house. The sky is beginning to grow flushed with sunrise.* EBEN *stops by the gate and stares around him with glowing, possessive eyes. He takes in the whole farm with his embracing glance of desire.*]

EBEN: It's purty! It's damned purty! It's mine! [*He suddenly throws his head back boldly and glares with hard, defiant eyes at the sky.*] Mine, d'ye hear? Mine! [*He turns and walks quickly off left, rear, toward the barn. The two brothers light their pipes.*]

SIMEON [*putting his muddy boots up on the table, tilting back his chair, and puffing defiantly*]: Waal – this air solid comfort – fur once.

PETER: Ay-eh. [*He follows suit. A pause. Unconsciously they both sigh.*]

SIMEON [*suddenly*]: He never was much o' a hand at milkin', Eben wa'n't.

PETER [*with a snort*]: His hands air like hoofs! [*A pause*]

SIMEON: Reach down the jug thar! Let's take a swaller. I'm feelin' kind o' low.

PETER: Good idee! [*He does so – gets two glasses – they pour out drinks of whisky.*] Here's t' gold in Californi-a!

SIMEON: An' luck t' find it! [*They drink – puff resolutely – sigh – take their feet down from the table.*]

PETER: Likker don't 'pear t' sot right.

SIMEON: We hain't used t' it this early. [*A pause. They become very restless.*]

PETER: Gittin' close in this kitchen.

SIMEON [*with immense relief*]: Let's git a breath o' air.

[*They arise briskly and go out rear – appear around house and stop by the gate. They stare up at the sky with a numbed appreciation.*]

PETER: Purty!

SIMEON: Ay-eh. Gold's t' the East now.

PETER: Sun's startin' with us fur the Golden West.

SIMEON [*staring around the farm, his compressed lips tightened, unable to conceal his emotion*]: Waal – it's our last mornin' – mebbe.

PETER [*the same*]: Ay-eh.

SIMEON [*stamps his foot on the earth and addresses it desperately*]: Waal – ye've thirty year o' me buried in ye – spread out over ye – blood an' bone an' sweat – rotted away – fertilizin' ye – richin' yer soul – prime manure, by God, that's what I been t' ye!

PETER: Ay-eh! An' me!

SIMEON: An' yew, Peter. [*He sighs – then spits.*] Waal – no use'n cryin' over spilt milk.

PETER: They's gold in the West – an' freedom mebbe. We been slaves t' stone walls here.

SIMEON [*defiantly*]: We hain't nobody's slaves from this out – nor no thin's slaves nuther. [*A pause – restlessly*] Speakin' o' milk, wonder how Eben's managin'?

PETER: I s'pose he's managin'.

SIMEON: Mebbe we'd ought t' help – this once.

PETER: Mebbe. The cows knows us.

SIMEON: An' likes us. They don't know him much.

PETER: An' the hosses, an' pigs, an' chickens. They don't know him much.

SIMEON: They knows us like brothers – an' likes us! [*Proudly*] Hain't we raised 'em t' be fust-rate, number one prize stock?

PETER: We hain't – not no more.

SIMEON [*dully*]: I was fergittin'. [*Then resignedly*] Waal, let's go help Eben a spell an' git waked up.

PETER: Suits me.

[*They are starting off down left, rear, for the barn when* EBEN *appears from there hurrying toward them, his face excited.*]

EBEN [*breathlessly*]: Waal – har they be! The old mule an the bride! I seen 'em from the barn down below at the turnin'.

PETER: How could ye tell that far?

EBEN: Hain't I as far-sight as he's near-sight? Don't I know the mare 'n' buggy, an' two people settin' in it? Who else . . .? An' I tell ye I kin feel 'em a-comin', too! [*He squirms as if he had the itch.*]

PETER [*beginning to be angry*]: Waal – let him do his own unhitchin'!

SIMEON [*angry in his turn*]: Let's hustle in an' git our bundles an' be a-goin' as he's a-comin'. I don't want never t' step inside the door agen arter he's back.

[*They both start back around the corner of the house.* EBEN *follows them.*]

EBEN [*anxiously*]: Will ye sign it afore ye go?

PETER: Let's see the colour o' the old skinflint's money an' we'll sign.

[*They disappear left. The two brothers clump upstairs to get their bundles.* EBEN *appears in the kitchen, runs to window, peers out, comes back and pulls up a strip of flooring under stove, takes out a canvas bag and puts it on table, then sets the floor-board back in place. The two brothers appear a moment after. They carry old carpet bags.*]

EBEN [*puts his hand on bag guardingly*]: Have ye signed?

SIMEON [*shows paper in his hand*]: Ay-eh. [*Greedily*] Be that the money?

EBEN [*opens bag and pours out pile of twenty-dollar gold pieces*]: Twenty-dollar pieces – thirty on 'em. Count 'em. [PETER *does so, arranging them in stacks of five, biting one or two to test them.*]

PETER: Six hundred. [*He puts them in bag and puts it inside his shirt carefully.*]

SIMEON [*handing paper to* EBEN]: Har ye be.

EBEN [*after a glance, folds it carefully and hides it under his shirt – gratefully*]: Thank yew.

PETER: Thank yew fur the ride.

SIMEON: We'll send ye a lump o' gold fur Christmas. [*A pause. He stares at them and they at him.*]

PETER [*awkwardly*]: Waal – we're a-goin'.

SIMEON: Comin' out t' the yard?

EBEN: No. I'm waitin' in here a spell. [*Another silence. The brothers edge awkwardly to door in rear – then turn and stand.*]

SIMEON: Waal – good-bye.

PETER: Good-bye.

EBEN: Good-bye.

[*They go out. He sits down at the table, faces the stove, and pulls out the paper. He looks from it to the stove. His face, lighted up by the shaft of sunlight from the window, has an expression of trance. His lips move. The two brothers come out to the gate.*]

PETER [*looking off toward barn*]: Thar he be – unhitchin'.

SIMEON [*with a chuckle*]: I'll bet ye he's riled!

PETER: An' thar she be.

SIMEON: Let's wait 'n' see what our new Maw looks like.

PETER [*with a grin*]: An' give him our partin' cuss!

SIMEON [*grinning*]: I feel like raisin' fun. I feel light in my head an' feet.

PETER: Me, too. I feel like laffin' till I'd split up the middle.

SIMEON: Reckon it's the likker?

PETER: No. My feet feel itchin' t' walk an' walk – an' jump high over thin's – an' –

SIMEON: Dance? [*A pause*]

PETER [*puzzled*]: It's plumb onnateral.

SIMEON [*a light coming over his face*]: I calc'late it's 'cause school's out. It's holiday. Fur once we're free!

PETER [*dazedly*]: Free?

SIMEON: The halter's broke – the harness is busted – the fence bars is down – the stone walls air crumblin' an' tumblin'! We'll be kickin' up an' tearin' away down the road!

PETER [*drawing a deep breath – oratorically*]: Anybody that wants this stinkin' old rock-pile of a farm kin hev it. 'Tain't our'n, no sirree!

SIMEON [*takes the gate off its hinges and puts it under his arm*]: We harby 'bolishes shet gates, an' open gates, an' all gates, by thunder!

PETER: We'll take it with us fur luck an' let 'er sail free down some river.

SIMEON [*as a sound of voices comes from left, rear*]: Har they comes!

[*The two brothers congeal into two stiff, grim-visaged statues.* EPHRAIM CABOT *and* ABBIE PUTNAM *come in.* CABOT *is seventy-five, tall and gaunt, with great, wiry, concentrated power, but stoop-shouldered from toil. His face is as hard as if it were hewn out of a boulder, yet there is a weakness in it, a petty pride in its own narrow strength. His eyes are small, close together, and extremely near-sighted, blinking continually in the effort to focus on objects, their stare having a straining, in-growing quality. He is dressed in his dismal black Sunday suit.* ABBIE *is thirty-five, buxom, full of vitality. Her round face is pretty, but marred by its rather gross sensuality. There is strength and obstinacy in her jaw, a hard determination in her eyes, and about her whole personality the same unsettled, untamed, desperate quality which is so apparent in* EBEN.]

CABOT [*as they enter – a queer strangled emotion in his dry cracking voice*]: Har we be t' hum, Abbie.

ABBIE [*with lust for the word*]: Hum! [*Her eyes gloating on the house without seeming to see the two stiff figures at the gate.*] It's purty – purty! I can't b'lieve it's r'ally mine.

CABOT [*sharply*]: Yewr'n? Mine! [*He stares at her penetratingly. She stares back. He adds relentingly.*] Our'n – mebbe! It was lonesome too long. I was growin' old in the spring. A hum's got t' hev a woman.

ABBIE [*her voice taking possession*]: A woman's got t' hev a hum!

CABOT [*nodding uncertainly*]: Ay-eh. [*Then irritably*] Whar be they? Ain't thar nobody about – 'r wukin' – 'r nothin'?

ABBIE [*sees the brothers. She returns their stare of cold appraising contempt with interest – slowly*]: Thar's two men loafin' at the gate an' starin' at me like a couple o' strayed hogs.

CABOT [*straining his eyes*]: I kin see 'em – but I can't make out –

SIMEON: It's Simeon.

PETER: It's Peter.

CABOT [*exploding*]: Why hain't ye wukin'?

SIMEON [*dryly*]: We're waitin' t' welcome ye hum – yew an' the bride!

CABOT [*confusedly*]: Hunh? Waal – this be yer new Maw, boys. [*She stares at them and they at her.*]

SIMEON [*turns away and spits contemptuously*]: I see her!

PETER [*spits also*]: An' I see her!

ABBIE [*with the conqueror's conscious superiority*]: I'll go in an' look at *my* house. [*She goes slowly around to porch.*]

SIMEON [*with a snort*]: *Her* house!

PETER [*calls after her*]: Ye'll find Eben inside. Ye better not tell him it's *yewr* house.

ABBIE [*mouthing the name*]: Eben. [*Then quietly*] I'll tell Eben.

CABOT [*with a contemptuous sneer*]: Ye needn't heed Eben. Eben's a dumb fool – like his Maw – soft an' simple!

SIMEON [*with his sardonic burst of laughter*]: Ha! Eben's a chip o' yew – spit 'n' image – hard 'n' bitter's a hickory tree! Dog'll eat dog. He'll eat ye yet, old man!

CABOT [*commandingly*]: Ye git t' wuk!

SIMEON [*as* ABBIE *disappears in house – winks at* PETER *and says tauntingly*]: So that thar's our new Maw, be it? Whar in hell did ye dig her up? [*He and* PETER *laugh.*]

PETER: Ha! Ye'd better turn her in the pen with the other sows. [*They laugh uproariously, slapping their thighs.*]

CABOT [*so amazed at their effrontery that he stutters in confusion*]: Simeon! Peter! What's come over ye? Air ye drunk?

SIMEON: We're free, old man – free o' yew an' the hull damned farm! [*They grow more and more hilarious and excited.*]

PETER: An' we're startin' out fur the gold-fields o' Californi-a!

SIMEON: Ye kin take this place an' burn it!

PETER: An' bury it – fur all we cares!

SIMEON: We're free, old man! [*He cuts a caper.*]

PETER: Free! [*He gives a kick in the air.*]

SIMEON [*in a frenzy*]: Whoop!

PETER: Whoop! [*They do an absurd Indian war dance about the old man, who is petrified between rage and the fear that they are insane.*]

SIMEON: We're free as Injuns! Lucky we don't skulp ye!

PETER: An' burn yer barn an' kill the stock!

SIMEON: An' rape yer new woman! Whoop! [*He and* PETER *stop their dance, holding their sides, rocking with wild laughter.*]

CABOT [*edging away*]: Lust fur gold – fur the sinful, easy gold o' Californi-a! It's made ye mad!

SIMEON [*tauntingly*]: Wouldn't ye like us to send ye back some sinful gold, ye old sinner?

PETER: They's gold besides what's in Californi-a! [*He retreats back beyond the vision of the old man and takes the bag of money and flaunts it in the air about his head, laughing.*]

SIMEON: And sinfuller, too!

PETER: We'll be voyagin' on the sea! Whoop! [*He leaps up and down.*]

SIMEON: Livin' free! Whoop! [*He leaps in turn.*]

CABOT [*suddenly roaring with rage*]: My cuss on ye!

SIMEON: Take our'n in trade fur it! Whoop!

CABOT: I'll hev ye both chained up in the asylum!

PETER: Ye old skinflint! Good-bye!

SIMEON: Ye old blood-sucker! Good-bye!

CABOT: Go afore I –!

PETER: Whoop! [*He picks a stone from the road.* SIMEON *does the same.*]

SIMEON: Maw'll be in the parlour.

PETER: Ay-eh! One! Two!

CABOT [*frightened*]: What air ye – ?

PETER: Three! [*They both throw, the stones hitting the parlour window with a crash of glass, tearing the shade.*]

SIMEON: Whoop!

PETER: Whoop!

CABOT [*in a fury now, rushing toward them*]: If I kin lay hand on ye – I'll break yer bones fur ye!

[*But they beat a capering retreat before him,* SIMEON *with the gate still under his arm.* CABOT *comes back, panting with impotent rage. Their voices as they go off take up the song of the gold-seekers to the old tune of* '*Oh, Susannah!*']

'I jumped aboard the Liza ship,
And travelled on the sea,
And every time I thought of home
I wished it wasn't me!
Oh! Californi-a,
That's the land fur me!
I'm off to Californi-a!
With my wash-bowl on my knee.'

[*In the meantime the window of the upper bedroom on right is raised and* ABBIE *sticks her head out. She looks down at* CABOT *– with a sigh of relief.*]

ABBIE: Waal – that's the last o' them two, hain't it? [*He doesn't answer. Then in possessive tones*] This here's a nice bedroom, Ephraim. It's a r'al nice bed. Is it my room, Ephraim?

CABOT [*grimly – without looking up*]: Our'n! [*She cannot control a grimace of aversion and pulls back her head slowly and shuts the window. A sudden horrible thought seems to enter* CABOT'S *head.*] They been up to somethin'! Mebbe – mebbe they've pizened the stock – 'r somethin'!

[*He almost runs off down toward the barn. A moment later the kitchen door is slowly pushed open and* ABBIE *enters. For a moment she stands looking at* EBEN. *He does not notice her at first. Her eyes take him in penetratingly with a calculating appraisal of his strength as against hers. But under this her desire is dimly awakened by his youth and good looks. Suddenly he becomes conscious of her presence and looks up. Their eyes meet. He leaps to his feet, glowering at her speechlessly.*]

ABBIE [*in her most seductive tones which she uses all through this scene*]: Be you – Eben? I'm Abbie – [*She laughs.*] I mean, I'm yer new Maw.

EBEN [*viciously*]: No, damn ye!

ABBIE [*as if she hadn't heard – with a queer smile*]: Yer Paw's spoke a lot o' yew –

EBEN: Ha!

ABBIE: Ye mustn't mind him. He's an old man. [*A long pause. They stare at each other.*] I don't want t' pretend playin' Maw t' ye, Eben. [*Admiringly*] Ye're too big an' too strong fur that. I want t' be fren's with ye. Mebbe with me fur a fren' ye'd find ye'd like livin' here better. I kin make it easy fur ye with him, mebbe. [*With a scornful sense of power*] I calc'late I kin git him t' do most anythin' fur me.

EBEN [*with bitter scorn*]: Ha! [*They stare again,* EBEN *obscurely moved, physically attracted to her – in forced stilted tones.*] Yew kin go t' the devil!

ABBIE [*calmly*]: If cussin' me does ye good, cuss all ye've a mind t'. I'm all prepared t' have ye agin me – at fust. I don't blame ye nuther. I'd feel the same at any stranger comin' t' take my Maw's place. [*He shudders. She is watching him carefully.*] Yew must've cared a lot fur yewr Maw, didn't ye? My Maw died afore I'd growed. I don't remember her none. [*A pause*] But yew won't hate me long, Eben. I'm not the wust in the world – an' yew an' me've got a lot in common. I kin tell that by lookin' at ye. Waal – I've had a hard life, too – oceans o' trouble an' nuthin' but wuk fur reward. I was a' orphan early an' had t' wuk fur others in others' hums. Then I married, an' he turned out a drunken spreer an' so he had to wuk for others an' me too agen in others' hums, an' the baby died, an' my husband got sick an' died too, an' I was glad, sayin' now I'm free fur once, on'y I diskivered right away all I was free fur was t' wuk agen in others' hums, doin' others' wuk in others' hums till I'd most give up hope o' ever doin' my own wuk in my own hum, an' then your Paw come –

[CABOT *appears, returning from the barn. He comes to the gate and looks down the road the brothers have gone. A faint strain of their retreating voices is heard;* 'Oh Californi-a! That's the place for me.' *He stands glowering, his fist clenched, his face grim with rage.*]

EBEN [*fighting against his growing attraction and sympathy – harshly*]: An' bought yew – like a harlot! [*She is stung and flushes angrily. She has been sincerely moved by the recital of her troubles. He adds furiously*] An' the price he's payin' ye – this farm – was my Maw's, damn ye! – an' mine now!

ABBIE [*with a cool laugh of confidence*]: Yewr'n? We'll see 'bout that! [*Then strongly*] Waal – what if I did need a hum? What else'd I marry an old man like him fur?

EBEN [*maliciously*]: I'll tell him ye said that!

ABBIE [*smiling*]: I'll say ye're lyin' a-purpose – an' he'll drive ye off the place!

EBEN: Ye devil!

ABBIE [*defying him*]: This be my farm – this be my hum – this be my kitchen –!

EBEN [*furiously, as if he were going to attack her*]: Shut up, damn ye!

ABBIE [*walks up to him – a queer coarse expression of desire in her face and body – slowly*]: An' upstairs – that be my bedroom – an' my bed! [*He stares into her eyes, terribly confused and torn. She adds softly.*] I hain't bad nor mean – 'ceptin' fur an enemy – but I got t' fight fur what's due me out o' life, if I ever 'spect t' git it. [*Then putting her hand on his arm – seductively*] Let's yew 'n' me be fren's, Eben.

EBEN [*stupidly – as if hypnotized*]: Ay-eh. [*Then furiously flinging off her arm*] No, ye durned old witch! I hate ye! [*He rushes out the door.*]

ABBIE [*looks after him, smiling satisfiedly – then half to herself, mouthing the words*]: Eben's nice. [*She looks at the table, proudly.*] I'll wash up *my* dishes now. [EBEN *appears outside, slamming the door behind him. He comes around corner, stops on seeing his father, and stands staring at him with hate.*]

CABOT [*raising his arms to Heaven in the fury he can no longer control*]: Lord God o' Hosts, smite the undutiful sons with Thy wust cuss.

EBEN [*breaking in violently*]: Yew 'n' yewr God! Allus cussin' folks – allus naggin' em!

CABOT [*oblivious to him – summoningly*]: God o' the old! God o' the lonesome!

EBEN [*mockingly*]: Naggin' His sheep t' sin! T' hell with yewr God!

CABOT [*wrathfully*]: 'The days air prolonged and every vision faileth!'

EBEN [*spitting*]: Good enuf fur ye! [CABOT *turns. He and* EBEN *glower at each other.*]

CABOT [*harshly*]: So it's yew. I might've knowed it. [*Shaking his finger threateningly at him*] Blasphemin' fool! [*Then quickly*] Why hain't ye t' wuk?

EBEN: Why hain't yew? They've went. I can't wuk it all alone.

CABOT [*contemptuously*]: Nor noways! I'm wuth ten o' ye yit, old's I be! Ye'll never be more'n half a man! [*Then, matter-of-factly*] Waal – let's git t' the barn.

[*They go. A last faint note of the* 'Californi-a' *song is heard from the distance.* ABBIE *is washing the dishes.*]

CURTAIN

PART TWO

SCENE 1

The exterior of the farm-house, as in Part One – a hot Sunday afternoon two months later.

[ABBIE, *dressed in her best, is discovered sitting in a rocker at the end of the porch. She rocks listlessly, enervated by the heat, staring in front of her with bored, half-closed eyes.*

EBEN *sticks his head out of his bedroom window. He looks around furtively and tries to see – or hear – if anyone is on the porch, but although he has been careful to make no noise,* ABBIE *has sensed his movement. She stops rocking, her face grows animated and eager, she waits attentively.* EBEN *seems to feel her presence, he scowls back his thoughts of her and spits with exaggerated disdain – then withdraws back into the room.* ABBIE *waits, holding her breath as she listens with passionate eagerness for every sound within the house.*

EBEN *comes out. Their eyes meet. His falter, he is confused, he turns away and slams the door resentfully. At this gesture,* ABBIE *laughs tantalizingly, amused, but at the same time piqued and irritated. He scowls, strides off the porch to the path and starts to walk past her to the road with a grand swagger of ignoring her existence. He is dressed in his store suit, spruced up, his face shines from soap and water.* ABBIE *leans forward on her chair, her eyes hard and angry now, and, as he passes her, gives a sneering, taunting chuckle.*]

EBEN [*stung – turns on her furiously*]: What air yew cacklin' 'bout?

ABBIE [*triumphant*]: Yew!

EBEN: What about me?

ABBIE: Ye look all slicked up like a prize bull.

EBEN [*with a sneer*]: Waal – ye hain't so durned purty yerself, be ye? [*They stare into each other's eyes, his held by hers in spite of himself, hers glowingly possessive. Their physical attraction becomes a palpable force quivering in the hot air.*]

ABBIE [*softly*]: Ye don't mean that, Eben. Ye may think ye mean it, mebbe, but ye don't. Ye can't. It's agin nature, Eben. Ye been fightin' yer nature ever since the day I come – tryin' t' tell yerself I hain't purty t' ye. [*She laughs a low humid laugh without taking her eyes from his. A pause – her body squirms desirously – she murmurs languorously*] Hain't the sun strong an' hot? Ye kin feel it burnin' into the earth – Nature – makin' thin's grow – bigger 'n' bigger – burnin' inside ye – makin' ye want t' grow – into somethin' else – till ye're jined with it – an' it's your'n – but it owns ye, too – an' makes ye grow bigger – like a tree – like them elums – [*She laughs again softly, holding his eyes. He takes a step toward her, compelled against his will.*] Nature'll beat ye, Eben. Ye might's well own up t' it fust 's last.

EBEN [*trying to break from her spell – confusedly*]: If Paw'd hear ye goin' on . . . [*Resentfully*] But ye've made such a damned idjit out o' the old devil . . . [ABBIE *laughs.*]

ABBIE: Waal – hain't it easier fur yew with him changed softer?

EBEN [*defiantly*]: No. I'm fightin' him – fightin' yew – fightin' fur Maw's rights t' her hum! [*This breaks her spell for him. He glowers at her.*] An' I'm on to ye. Ye hain't foolin' me a mite. Ye're aimin' t' swaller up everythin' an' make it your'n. Waal, you'll find I'm a heap sight bigger hunk nor yew kin chew! [*He turns from her with a sneer.*]

ABBIE [*trying to regain her ascendancy – seductively*]: Eben!

EBEN: Leave me be! [*He starts to walk away.*]

ABBIE [*more commandingly*]: Eben!

EBEN [*stops – resentfully*]: What d'ye want?

ABBIE [*trying to conceal a growing excitement*]: Whar air ye goin'?

EBEN [*with malicious nonchalance*]: Oh – up the road a spell.

ABBIE: T' the village?

EBEN [*airily*]: Mebbe.

ABBIE [*excitedly*]: T' see that Min, I s'pose?

EBEN: Mebbe.

ABBIE [*weakly*]: What d'ye want t' waste time on her fur?

EBEN [*revenging himself now – grinning at her*]: Ye can't beat Nature, didn't ye say? [*He laughs and again starts to walk away.*]

ABBIE [*bursting out*]: An ugly old hake!

EBEN [*with a tantalizing sneer*]: She's purtier'n yew be!

ABBIE: That every wuthless drunk in the country has . . .

EBEN [*tauntingly*]: Mebbe – but she's better'n yew. She owns up fa'r 'n' squar' t' her doin's.

ABBIE [*furiously*]: Don't ye dare compare –

EBEN: She don't go sneakin' an' stealin' – what's mine.

ABBIE [*savagely seizing on his weak point*]: Your'n? Yew mean – my farm?

EBEN: I mean the farm yew sold yerself fur like any other old whore – my farm!

ABBIE [*stung – fiercely*]: Ye'll never live t' see the day when even a stinkin' weed on it 'll belong t' ye! [*Then in a scream*] Git out o' my sight! Go on t' yer slut – disgracin' yer Paw 'n' me! I'll git yer Paw t' horsewhip ye off the place if I want t'! Ye're only livin' here 'cause I tolerate ye! Git along! I hate the sight o' ye! [*She stops, panting and glaring at him.*]

EBEN [*returning her glance in kind*]: An' I hate the sight o' yew! [*He turns and strides off up the road. She follows his retreating figure with concentrated hate. Old* CABOT *appears coming up from the barn. The hard, grim expression of his face has changed. He seems in some queer way softened, mellowed. His eyes have taken on a strange, incongruous dreamy quality. Yet there is no hint of physical weakness about him – rather he looks more robust and younger.* ABBIE *sees him and turns away quickly with unconcealed aversion. He comes slowly up to her.*]

CABOT [*mildly*]: War yew an' Eben quarrellin' agin?

ABBIE [*shortly*]: No.

CABOT: Ye was talkin' a'mighty loud. . . . [*He sits down on the edge of porch.*]

ABBIE [*snappishly*]: If ye heerd us they hain't no need askin' questions.

CABOT: I didn't hear what ye said.

ABBIE [*relieved*]: Waal – it wa'n't nothin' t' speak on.

CABOT [*after a pause*]: Eben's queer.

ABBIE [*bitterly*]: He's the dead spit 'n' image o' yew!

CABOT [*queerly interested*]: D'ye think so, Abbie? [*After a pause, ruminatingly*] Me 'n' Eben's allus fit 'n' fit. I never could b'ar him noways. He's so thunderin' soft – like his Maw.

ABBIE [*scornfully*]: Ay-eh! 'Bout as soft as yew be!

CABOT [*as if he hadn't heard*]: Mebbe I been too hard on him.

ABBIE [*jeeringly*]: Waal – ye're gittin' soft now – soft as slop! That's what Eben was sayin'.

CABOT [*his face instantly grim and ominous*]: Eben was sayin'? Waal, he'd best not do nothin' t' try me 'r he'll soon diskiver . . . [*A pause. She keeps her face turned away. His gradually softens. He stares up at the sky.*] Purty, hain't it?

ABBIE [*crossly*]: I don't see nothin' purty.

CABOT: The sky. Feels like a warm field up thar.

ABBIE [*sarcastically*]: Air yew aimin' t' buy up over the farm, too? [*She snickers contemptuously.*]

CABOT [*strangely*]: I'd like t' own my place up thar. [*A pause*] I'm getting old, Abbie. I'm gittin' ripe on the bough. [*A pause. She stares at him mystified. He goes on.*] It's allus lonesome cold in the house – even when it's bilin' hot outside. Hain't yew noticed?

ABBIE: No.

CABOT: It's warm down t' the barn – nice smellin' an' warm – with the cows. [*A pause*] Cows is queer.

ABBIE: Like yew!

CABOT: Like Eben. [*A pause*] I'm gittin' t' feel resigned t' Eben – jest as I got t' feel 'bout his Maw. I'm gittin' t' learn to b'ar his softness – jest like her'n. I calc'late I c'd a'most take t' him – if he wa'n't sech a dumb fool! [*A pause*] I s'pose it's old age a-creepin' in my bones.

ABBIE [*indifferently*]: Waal – ye hain't dead yet.

CABOT [*roused*]: No, I hain't, yew bet – not by a hell of a sight – I'm sound 'n' tough as hickory! [*Then moodily*] But arter three score and ten the Lord warns ye t' prepare. [*A pause*] That's why Eben's come in my head. Now that his cussed sinful brothers is gone their path t' hell, they's no one left but Eben.

ABBIE [*resentfully*]: They's me, hain't they? [*Agitatedly*] What's all this sudden likin' ye've tuk to Eben? Why don't ye say nothin' 'bout me? Hain't I yer lawful wife?

CABOT [*simply*]: Ay-eh. Ye be. [*A pause – he stares at her desirously – his eyes grow avid – then with a sudden movement he seizes her hands and squeezes them, declaiming in a queer camp-meeting preacher's tempo.*] Yew air my Rose o' Sharon! Behold, yew air fair; yer eyes air doves; yer lips air like scarlet; yer two breasts air like two fawns; yer navel be like a round goblet; yer belly be like a heap o' wheat . . . [*He covers her hand with kisses. She does not seem to notice. She stares before her with hard angry eyes.*]

ABBIE [*jerking her hands away – harshly*]: So ye're plannin' t' leave the farm t' Eben, air ye?

CABOT [*dazedly*]: Leave . . .? [*Then with resentful obstinacy*] I hain't a-givin' it t' no one!

ABBIE [*remorselessly*]: Ye can't take it with ye.

CABOT [*thinks a moment – then reluctantly*]: No, I calc'late not. [*After a pause – with a strange passion*] But if I could, I would, by the Etarnal! 'R if I could, in my dyin' hour, I'd set it afire an' watch it burn – this house an' every ear o' corn an' every tree down t' the last blade o' hay! I'd sit an' know it was all a-dying with me an' no one else'd ever own what was mine, what I'd made out o' nothin' with my own sweat 'n' blood! [*A pause – then he adds with a queer affection.*] 'Ceptin' the cows. Them I'd turn free.

ABBIE [*harshly*]: An' me?

CABOT [*with a queer smile*]: Ye'd be turned free, too.

ABBIE [*furiously*]: So that's the thanks I git fur marryin' ye – t' have ye change kind to Eben who hates ye, an' talk o' turnin' me out in the road.

CABOT [*hastily*]: Abbie! Ye know I wa'n't. . . .

ABBIE [*vengefully*]: Just let me tell ye a thing or two 'bout Eben! Whar's he gone? T' see that harlot, Min! I tried fur t' stop him. Disgracin' yew an' me – on the Sabbath, too!

CABOT [*rather guiltily*]: He's a sinner – nateral-born. It's lust eatin' his heart.

ABBIE [*enraged beyond endurance – wildly vindictive*]: An' his lust fur me! Kin ye find excuses fur that?

CABOT [*stares at her – after a dead pause*]: Lust – fur yew?

ABBIE [*defiantly*]: He was tryin' t' make love t' me – when ye heerd us quarrellin'.

CABOT [*stares at her – then a terrible expression of rage comes over his face – he springs to his feet shaking all over*]: By the A'mighty God – I'll end him!

ABBIE [*frightened now for* EBEN]: No! Don't ye!

CABOT [*violently*]: I'll git the shotgun an' blow his soft brains t' the top o' them elums!

ABBIE [*throwing her arms around him*]: No, Ephraim!

CABOT [*pushing her away violently*]: I will, by God!

ABBIE [*in a quieting tone*]: Listen, Ephraim. T'wa'n't nothin' bad – on'y a boy's foolin' – t'wa'n't meant serious – jest jokin' an' teasin' . . .

CABOT: Then why did ye say – lust?

ABBIE: It must hev sounded wusser'n I meant. An' I was mad at thinkin' – ye'd leave him the farm.

CABOT [*quieter, but still grim and cruel*]: Waal then, I'll horse-whip him off the place if that much'll content ye.

ABBIE [*reaching out and taking his hand*]: No. Don't think o' me! Ye mustn't drive him off. T'ain't sensible. Who'll ye get to help ye on the farm? They's no one hereabouts.

CABOT [*considers this – then nodding his appreciation*]: Ye got a head on ye. [*Then irritably*] Waal, let him stay. [*He sits down on the edge of the porch. She sits beside him. He murmurs contemptuously.*] I oughtn't t' git riled so – at that 'ere fool calf. [*A pause*] But har's the p'int. What son o' mine'll keep on here t' the farm – when the Lord does call me? Simeon an' Peter air gone t' hell – an Eben's follerin' 'em –

ABBIE: They's me.

CABOT: Ye're on'y a woman.

ABBIE: I'm yewr wife.

CABOT: That hain't me. A son is me – my blood – mine. Mine ought t' git mine. An' then it's still mine – even though I be six foot under. D'ye see?

ABBIE [*giving him a look of hatred*]: Ay-eh. I see. [*She becomes very thoughtful, her face growing shrewd, her eyes studying* CABOT *craftily.*]

CABOT: I'm gittin' old – ripe on the bough. [*Then with a sudden forced reassurance*] Not but what I hain't a hard nut t' crack even yet – an' fur many a year t' come! By the Etarnal, I kin break most o' the young fellers' backs at any kind o' work any day o' the year!

ABBIE [*suddenly*]: Mebbe the Lord'll give *us* a son.

CABOT [*turns and stares at her eagerly*]: Ye mean – a son – t' me 'n' yew?

ABBIE [*with a cajoling smile*]: Ye're a strong man yet, hain't ye? 'Tain't noways impossible, be it? We know that. Why d'ye stare so? Hain't ye never thought o' that afore? I been thinkin' o' it all along. Ay-eh – an' I been prayin' it'd happen, too.

CABOT [*his face growing full of joyous pride and a sort of religious ecstasy*]: Ye been prayin', Abbie? – fur a son? – t' us?

ABBIE: Ay-eh. [*With a grim resolution*] I want a son now.

CABOT [*excitedly clutching both of her hands in his*]: It'd be the blessin' o' God, Abbie – the blessin' o' God A'mighty on me – in my old age – in my lonesomeness! They hain't nothin' I wouldn't do fur ye then, Abbie. Ye'd hev on'y t' ask it – anythin' ye'd a mind t' –

ABBIE [*interrupting*]: Would ye will the farm t' me then – t' me an' it – ?

CABOT [*vehemently*]: I'd do anythin' ye axed, I tell ye! I swear it! May I be everlastin' damned t' hell if I wouldn't! [*He sinks to his knees, pulling her down with him. He trembles all over with the fervour of his hopes.*] Pray t' the Lord agin, Abbie. It's the Sabbath! I'll jine ye! Two prayers air better nor one. 'An' God hearkened unto Rachel an' she conceived an' bore a son.' An' God hearkened unto Abbie! Pray, Abbie! Pray fur Him to hearken! [*He bows his head, mumbling. She pretends to do likewise, but gives him a side glance of scorn and triumph.*]

SCENE 2

About eight in the evening. The interior of the two bedrooms on the top floor is shown.

[EBEN *is sitting on the side of his bed in the room on the left. On account of the heat he has taken off everything but his undershirt and pants. His feet are bare. He faces front, brooding moodily, his chin propped on his hands, a desperate expression on his face.*

In the other room CABOT *and* ABBIE *are sitting side by side on the edge of their bed, an old fourposter with feather mattress. He is in his nightshirt, she in her nightdress. He is still in the queer excited mood into which the notion of a son has thrown him. Both rooms are lighted dimly and flickeringly by tallow candles.*]

CABOT: The farm needs a son.

ABBIE: I need a son.

CABOT: Ay-eh. Sometimes ye air the farm an' sometimes the farm be yew. That's why I clove t' ye in my lonesomeness. [*A pause. He pounds his knee with his fist.*] Me an' the farm has got t' beget a son!

ABBIE: Ye'd best go t' sleep. Ye're gittin' thin's all mixed.

CABOT [*with an impatient gesture*]: No, I hain't. My mind's clear's a well. Ye don't know me, that's it. [*He stares hopelessly at the floor.*]

ABBIE [*indifferently*]: Mebbe.

[*In the next room* EBEN *gets up and paces up and down distractedly.* ABBIE *hears him. Her eyes fasten on the intervening wall with concentrated attention.* EBEN *stops and stares. Their hot glances seem to meet through the wall. Unconsciously he stretches out his arms for her and she half-rises. Then aware, he mutters a curse at himself and flings himself face downward on the bed, his clenched fists above his head, his face buried in the pillow.* ABBIE *relaxes with a faint sigh, but her eyes remain fixed on the wall, she listens with all her attention for some movement from* EBEN.]

CABOT [*suddenly raises his head and looks at her – scornfully*]: Will ye ever know me – 'r will any man 'r woman? [*Shaking his head*] No. I calc'late 't wa'n't t' be. [*He turns away.* ABBIE *looks at the wall. Then, evidently unable to keep silent about his thoughts, without looking at his wife, he puts out his hand and clutches her knee. She starts violently, looks at him, sees he is not watching her, concentrates again on the wall and pays no attention to what he says.*] Listen, Abbie. When I come here fifty-odd year ago – I was jest twenty an' the strongest an' hardest ye ever seen – ten times as strong an' fifty times as hard as Eben. Waal – this place was nothin' but fields o' stones. Folks laughed when I tuk it. They couldn't know what I knowed. When ye kin make corn sprout out o' stones, God's livin' in yew. They wa'n't strong enuf fur that! They reckoned God was easy. They laughed. They don't laugh no more. Some died hereabouts. Some went West an' died. They're all under ground – fur follerin' arter an easy God. God hain't easy. [*He shakes his head slowly.*] An' I growed hard. Folks kept allus sayin', 'He's a hard man,' like 'twas sinful t' be hard, so's at last I said back at 'em, 'Waal then, by thunder, ye'll git me hard an' see how ye like it!' [*Then suddenly*] But I give in t' weakness once. 'Twas arter I'd been here two year. I got weak – despairful – they was so many stones. They was a party leavin', givin' up, goin' West. I jined 'em. We tracked on 'n' on. We come t' broad medders, plains, whar the soil was black an' rich as gold. Nary a stone. Easy. Ye'd on'y to plough an' sow an' then set an' smoke yer pipe an' watch thin's grow. I could o' been a rich man – but somethin' in me fit me an' fit me – the voice o' God sayin', 'This hain't wuth nothin' t' Me. Git ye back t' hum!' I got afeered o' that voice an' I lit out back t' hum here, leavin' my claim an' crops t' whoever'd a mind t' take 'em. Ay-eh. I actooly give up what was rightful mine! God's hard, not easy! God's in the stones! Build My church on a rock – out o' stones an' I'll be in them. That's what He meant t' Peter! [*He sighs heavily – a pause*] Stones. I picked 'em up an' piled 'em into walls. Ye kin read the years o' my life in them walls, every day a hefted stone, climbin' over the hills up and down, fencing in the fields that was mine, whar I'd made thin's grow out o' nothin' – like the will o' God, like the servant o' His hand. It wa'n't easy. It was hard an' He made me hard fur it. [*He pauses.*] All the time I kept gittin' lonesomer. I tuk a wife. She bore Simeon an' Peter. She was a good woman. She wuked hard. We was married twenty year. She never knowed me. She helped, but she never knowed what she was helpin'. I was allus lonesome. She died. After that it wa'n't so lonesome fur a spell. [*A pause*] I lost count o' the years. I had no time t' fool away countin' 'em. Sim an' Peter helped. The farm growed. It was all mine! When I thought o' that I didn't feel lonesome. [*A pause*] But ye can't hitch yer mind t' one thin' day an' night. I tuk another wife – Eben's Maw. Her folks was contestin' me at law over my deeds t' the farm – my farm! That's why Eben keeps a-talkin' his fool talk o' this bein' his Maw's farm. She bore Eben. She was purty – but soft. She tried t' be hard. She couldn't. She never knowed me nor nothin'. It was lonesomer 'n hell with her. After a matter o' sixteen-odd years, she died. [*A pause*] I lived with the boys. They hated me 'cause I was hard. I hated them 'cause they was soft. They coveted the farm without knowin' what it meant. It made me bitter 'n wormwood. It aged me – them coveting what I'd made fur mine. Then this spring the call come – the voice o' God cryin' in my wilderness, in my lonesomeness – t' go out an' seek an' find! [*Turning to her with strange passion*] I sought ye an' I found ye! Yew air my Rose o' Sharon! Yer eyes air like . . . [*She has turned a blank face, resentful eyes to his. He stares at her for a moment – then harshly*] Air ye any the wiser fur all I've told ye?

ABBIE [*confusedly*]: Mebbe.

CABOT [*pushing her away from him – angrily*]: Ye don't know nothin' – nor never will. If ye don't hev a son t' redeem ye . . . [*This in a tone of cold threat*]

ABBIE [*resentfully*]: I've prayed, hain't I?

CABOT [*bitterly*]: Pray agin – fur understandin'!

ABBIE [*a veiled threat in her tone*]: Ye'll have a son out o' me I promise ye.

CABOT: How can ye promise?

ABBIE: I got second-sight, mebbe. I kin foretell. [*She gives a queer smile.*]

CABOT: I believe ye have. Ye give me the chills sometimes. [*He shivers.*] It's cold in this house. It's oneasy. They's thin's pokin' about in the dark – in the corners. [*He pulls on his trousers, tucking in his night-shirt, and pulls on his boots.*]

ABBIE [*surprised*]: Whar air ye goin'?

CABOT [*queerly*]: Down whar it's restful – whar it's warm – down t' the barn. [*Bitterly*] I kin talk t' the cows. They know. They know the farm an' me. They'll give me peace. [*He turns to go out the door*]

ABBIE [*a bit frighteningly*]: Air ye ailin' tonight, Ephraim?

CABOT: Growin'. Growin' ripe on the bough. [*He turns and goes, his boots clumping down the stairs.* EBEN *sits up with a start, listening.* ABBIE *is conscious of his movement and stares at the wall.* CABOT *comes out of the house around the corner and stands by the gate, blinking at the sky. He stretches up his hands in a tortured gesture.*] God A'mighty, call from the dark!

[*He listens as if expecting an answer. Then his arms drop, he shakes his head and plods off toward the barn.* EBEN *and* ABBIE *stare at each other through the wall.* EBEN *sighs heavily and* ABBIE *echoes it. Both become terribly nervous, uneasy. Finally* ABBIE *gets up and listens, her ear to the wall. He acts as if he saw every move she was making; he becomes resolutely still. She seems driven into a decision – goes out the door in rear determinedly. His eyes follow her. Then as the door of his room is opened softly, he turns away, waits in an attitude of strained fixity.* ABBIE *stands for a second staring at him, her eyes burning with desire. Then with a little cry she runs over and throws her arms about his neck, she pulls his head back and covers his mouth with kisses. At first, he submits dumbly; then he puts his arms about her neck and returns her kisses, but finally, suddenly aware of his hatred, he hurls her away from him, springing to his feet. They stand speechless and breathless, panting like two animals.*]

ABBIE [*at last – painfully*]: Ye shouldn't, Eben – ye shouldn't – I'd make ye happy!

EBEN [*harshly*]: I don't want happy – from yew!

ABBIE [*helplessly*]: Ye do, Eben! Ye do! Why d'ye lie?

EBEN [*viciously*]: I don't take t' ye, I tell ye! I hate the sight o' ye!

ABBIE [*with an uncertain troubled laugh*]: Waal, I kissed ye anyways – an' ye kissed back – yer lips was burnin' – ye can't lie 'bout that! [*Intensely*] If ye don't care, why did ye kiss me back – why was yer lips burnin'?

EBEN [*wiping his mouth*]: It was like pizen on 'em. [*Then tauntingly*] When I kissed ye back, mebbe I thought 'twas someone else.

ABBIE [*wildly*]: Min?

EBEN: Mebbe.

ABBIE [*torturedly*]: Did ye go t' see her? Did ye r'ally go? I thought ye mightn't. Is that why ye throwed me off jest now?

EBEN [*sneeringly*]: What if it be?

ABBIE [*raging*]: Then ye're a dog, Eben Cabot!

EBEN [*threateningly*]: Ye can't talk that way t' me!

ABBIE [*with a shrill laugh*]: Can't I? Did ye think I was in love with ye – a weak thin' like yew? Not much! I on'y wanted ye fur a purpose o' my own – an' I'll hev ye fur it yet 'cause I'm stronger'n yew be!

EBEN [*resentfully*]: I knowed well it was on'y part o' yer plan t' swaller everythin'!

ABBIE [*tauntingly*]: Mebbe!

EBEN [*furious*]: Git out o' my room!

ABBIE: This air my room an' ye're on'y hired help!

EBEN [*threateningly*]: Git out afore I murder ye!

ABBIE [*quite confident now*]: I hain't a mite afeerd. Ye want me, don't ye? Yes, ye do! An yer Paw's son'll never kill what he wants! Look at yer eyes! They's lust fur me in 'em, burnin' 'em up! Look at yer lips now! They're tremblin' an' longin' t' kiss me, an' yer teeth t' bite! [*He is watching her now with a horrible fascination. She laughs a crazy triumphant laugh.*] I'm a-goin' t' make all o' this hum my hum! They's one room hain't mine yet, but it's a-goin' t' be tonight. I'm a-goin' down now an' light up! [*She makes him a mocking bow.*] Won't ye come courtin' me in the best parlour, Mister Cabot?

EBEN [*staring at her – horribly confused – dully*]: Don't ye dare! It hain't been opened since Maw died an' was laid out thar! Don't ye . . . [*But her eyes are fixed on his so burningly that his will seems to wither before hers. He stands swaying toward her helplessly.*]

ABBIE [*holding his eyes and putting all her will into her words as she backs out the door*]: I'll expect ye afore long, Eben.

EBEN [*stares after her for a while, walking toward the door. A light appears in the parlour window. He murmurs*]: In the parlour? [*This seems to arouse connexions, for he comes back and puts on his white shirt, collar, half-ties the tie mechanically, puts on coat, takes his hat, stands barefooted looking about him in bewilderment, mutters wonderingly.*] Maw! Whar air yew? [*Then goes slowly toward the door in rear.*]

SCENE 3

A few minutes later. The interior of the parlour is shown. A grim, repressed room like a tomb in which the family has been interred alive.

[ABBIE *sits on the edge of the horsehair sofa. She has lighted all the candles and the room is revealed in all its preserved ugliness. A change has come over the woman. She looks awed and frightened now, ready to run away.*

The door is opened and EBEN *appears. His face wears an expression of obsessed confusion. He stands staring at her, his arms hanging disjointedly from his shoulders, his feet bare, his hat in his hand.*]

ABBIE [*after a pause – with a nervous, formal politeness*]: Won't ye set?

EBEN [*dully*]: Ay-eh. [*Mechanically he places his hat carefully on the floor near the door and sits stiffly beside her on the edge of the sofa. A pause. They both remain rigid, looking straight ahead with eyes full of fear.*]

ABBIE: When I fust come in – in the dark – they seemed somethin' here.

EBEN [*simply*]: Maw.

ABBIE: I kin still feel – somethin' –

EBEN: It's Maw.

ABBIE: At fust I was feered o' it. I wanted t' yell an' run. Now – since yew come – seems like it's growin' soft an' kind t' me. [*Addressing the air – queerly*] Thank yew.

EBEN: Maw allus loved me.

ABBIE: Mebbe it knows I love ye, too. Mebbe that makes it kind t' me.

EBEN [*dully*]: I dunno. I should think she'd hate ye.

ABBIE [*with certainty*]: No. I kin feel it don't – not no more.

EBEN: Hate ye fur stealin' her place – here in her hum – settin' in her parlour whar she was laid. . . . [*He suddenly stops, staring stupidly before him.*]

ABBIE: What is it, Eben?

EBEN [*in a whisper*]: Seems like Maw didn't want me t' remind ye.

ABBIE [*excitedly*]: I knowed, Eben! It's kind t' me. It don't b'ar me no grudges fur what I never knowed an' couldn't help!

EBEN: Maw b'ars him a grudge.

ABBIE: Waal, so does all o' us.

EBEN: Ay-eh. [*With passion*] I does, by God!

ABBIE [*taking one of his hands in hers and patting it*]: Thar! Don't git riled thinkin' o' him. Think o' yer Maw who's kind t' us. Tell me about yer Maw, Eben.

EBEN: They hain't nothin' much. . . . She was kind. She was good.

ABBIE [*putting one arm over his shoulder. He does not seem to notice – passionately*]: I'll be kind an' good t' ye!

EBEN: Sometimes she used t' sing fur me.

ABBIE: I'll sing fur ye!

EBEN: This was her hum. This was her farm.

ABBIE: This is my hum. This is my farm.

EBEN: He married her t' steal 'em. She was soft an' easy. He couldn't 'preciate her.

ABBIE: He can't 'preciate me!

EBEN: He murdered her with his hardness.

ABBIE: He's murderin' me!

EBEN: She died. [*A pause*] Sometimes she used to sing fur me. [*He bursts into a fit of sobbing.*]

ABBIE [*both her arms around him – with wild passion*]: I'll sing fur ye! I'll die fur ye! [*In spite of her overwhelming desire for him, there is a sincere maternal love in her manner and voice – a horribly frank mixture of lust and mother-love.*] Don't cry, Eben! I'll take yer Maw's place! I'll be everythin' she was t' ye! Let me kiss ye, Eben! [*She pulls his head around. He makes a bewildered pretence of resistance. She is tender.*] Don't be afeered! I'll kiss ye pure, Eben – same 's if I was a Maw t' ye – an' ye kin kiss me back 's if yew was my son – my boy – sayin' good night t' me! Kiss me, Eben. [*They kiss in restrained fashion. Then suddenly wild passion overcomes her. She kisses him lustfully again and again and he flings his arms about her and returns her kisses. Suddenly, as in the bedroom, he frees himself from her violently and springs to his feet. He is trembling all over, in a strange state of terror.* ABBIE *strains her arms toward him with fierce pleading.*] Don't ye leave me, Eben! Can't ye see it hain't enuf – lovin' ye like a Maw – can't ye see it's got t' be that an' more – much more – a hundred times more – fur me t' be happy – fur yew t' be happy?

EBEN [*to the presence he feels in the room*]: Maw! Maw! What d'ye want? What air ye tellin' me?

ABBIE: She's tellin' ye t' love me. She knows I love ye an' I'll be good t' ye. Can't ye feel it? Don't ye know? She's tellin ye t' love me, Eben!

EBEN: Ay-eh. I feel – mebbe she – but – I can't figger out – why – when ye've stole her place – here in her hum – in the parlour whar she was . . .

ABBIE [*fiercely*]: She knows I love ye!

EBEN [*his face suddenly lighting up with a fierce triumphant grin*]: I see it! I sees why. It's her vengeance on him – so's she kin rest quiet in her grave!

ABBIE [*wildly*]: Vengeance o' her on him! Vengeance o' her on me – an' mine on yew – an' yourn on me – an' ourn on him! Vengeance o' God on the hull o' us! What d' we give a durn? I love ye, Eben! God knows I love ye! [*She stretches out her arms for him.*]

EBEN [*throws himself on his knees beside the sofa and grabs her in his arms – releasing all his pent-up passion*]: An' I love yew, Abbie! – now I kin say it! I been dyin' fur want o' ye – every hour – since ye come! I love ye! [*Their lips meet in a fierce, bruising kiss.*]

SCENE 4

Exterior of the farm-house. It is just dawn.

[*The front door at right is opened and* EBEN *comes out and walks around to the gate. He is dressed in his working clothes. He seems changed. His face wears a bold and confident expression, he is grinning to himself with evident satisfaction. As he gets near the gate, the window of the parlour is heard opening and the shutters are flung back and* ABBIE *sticks her head out. Her hair tumbles over her shoulders in disarray, her face is flushed, she looks at* EBEN *with tender, languorous eyes and calls softly.*]

ABBIE: Eben. [*As he turns – playfully*] Jest one more kiss afore ye go. I'm goin' t' miss ye fearful all day.

EBEN: An me yew, ye kin bet! [*He goes to her. They kiss several times. He draws away, laughingly.*] Thar. That's enuf, hain't it? Ye won't hev none left fur next time.

ABBIE: I got a million 'on 'em left fur ye! [*Then a bit anxiously*] D'ye r'ally love me, Eben?

EBEN [*emphatically*]: I like ye better'n any gal I ever knowed! That's gospel!

ABBIE: Likin' hain't lovin'.

EBEN: Waal then – I love ye. Now air yew satisfied?

ABBIE: Ay-eh, I be. [*She smiles at him adoringly.*]

EBEN: I better git t' the barn. The old critter's liable t' suspicion an' come sneakin' up.

ABBIE [*with a confident laugh*]: Let him! I kin allus pull the wool over his eyes. I'm goin' t' leave the shutters open and let in the sun 'n' air. This room's been dead long enuf. Now it's goin' t' be my room.

EBEN [*frowning*]: Ay-eh.

ABBIE [*hastily*]: I meant – our room.

EBEN: Ay-eh.

ABBIE: We made it our'n last night, didn't we? We give it life – our lovin' did. [*A pause*]

EBEN [*with a strange look*]: Maw's gone back t' her grave. She kin sleep now.

ABBIE: May she rest in peace! [*Then tenderly rebuking*] Ye oughtn't t' talk o' sad thin's – this mornin'.

EBEN: It jest come up in my mind o' itself.

ABBIE: Don't let it. [*He doesn't answer. She yawns.*] Waal, I'm a-goin' t' steal a wink o' sleep. I'll tell the Old Man I hain't feelin' pert. Let him git his own vittles.

EBEN: I see him comin' from the barn. Ye better look smart an' git upstairs.

ABBIE: Ay-eh. Good-bye. Don't ferget me.

[*She throws him a kiss. He grins – then squares his shoulders and awaits his father confidently.* CABOT *walks slowly up from the left, staring up at the sky with a vague face.*]

EBEN [*jovially*]: Mornin', Paw. Star-gazin' in daylight?

CABOT: Purty, hain't it?

EBEN [*looking around him possessively*]: It's a durned purty farm.

CABOT: I mean the sky.

EBEN [*grinning*]: How d'ye know? Them eyes o' your'n can't see that fur. [*This tickles his humour and he slaps his thigh and laughs.*] Ho-ho! That's a good un!

CABOT [*grimly sarcastic*]: Ye're feelin' right chipper, hain't ye? Whar'd ye steal the likker?

EBEN [*good-naturedly*]: 'Tain't likker. Jest life. [*Suddenly holding out his hand – soberly*] Yew 'n' me is quits. Let's shake hands.

CABOT [*suspiciously*]: What's come over ye?

EBEN: Then don't. Mebbe it's jest as well. [*A moment's pause*] What's come over me? [*Queerly*] Didn't ye feel her passin' – goin' back t' her grave?

CABOT [*dully*]: Who?

EBEN: Maw. She kin rest now an' sleep content. She's quits with ye.

CABOT [*confusedly*]: I rested. I slept good – down with the cows. They know how t' sleep. They're teachin' me.

EBEN [*suddenly jovial again*]: Good fur the cows! Waal – ye better git t' work.

CABOT [*grimly amused*]: Air yew bossin' me, ye calf?

EBEN [*beginning to laugh*]: Ay-eh! I'm bossin' yew! Ha-ha-ha! See how ye like it! Ha-ha-ha! I'm the prize rooster o' this roost. Ha-ha-ha! [*He goes off toward the barn laughing.*]

CABOT [*looks after him with scornful pity*]: Soft-headed. Like his Maw. Dead spit 'n' image. No hope in him! [*He spits with contemptuous disgust.*] A born fool! [*Then matter-of-factly*] Waal – I'm gittin' peckish. [*He goes toward door.*]

PART THREE

SCENE 1

A night in late spring the following year. The kitchen and the two bedrooms upstairs are shown. The two bedrooms are dimly lighted by a tallow candle in each.

[EBEN *is sitting on the side of the bed in his room, his chin propped on his fists, his face a study of the struggle he is making to understand his conflicting emotions. The noisy laughter and music from below where a kitchen dance is in progress annoy and distract him. He scowls at the floor.*

In the next room a cradle stands beside the double bed.

In the kitchen all is festivity. The stove has been taken down to give more room to the dancers. The chairs, with wooden benches added, have been pushed back against the walls. On these are seated, squeezed in tight against one another, farmers and their wives and their young folks of both sexes from the neighbouring farms. They are all chattering and laughing loudly. They evidently have some secret joke in common. There is no end of winking, of nudging, of meaning nods of the head toward CABOT *who, in a state of extreme hilarious excitement increased by the amount he has drunk, is standing near the rear door where there is a small keg of whisky and serving drinks to all the men. In the left corner, front, dividing the attention with her husband,* ABBIE *is sitting in a rocking chair, a shawl wrapped about her shoulders. She is very pale, her face is thin and drawn, her eyes are fixed anxiously on the open door in rear as if waiting for someone.*

The musician is tuning up his fiddle, seated in the far right corner. He is a lanky young fellow with a long weak face. His pale eyes blink incessantly and he grins about him slyly with a greedy malice.]

ABBIE [*suddenly turning to a young girl on her right*]: Whar's Eben?

YOUNG GIRL [*eyeing her scornfully*]: I dunno, Mrs Cabot. I hain't seen Eben in ages. [*Meaningly*] Seems like he's spent most o' his time t' hum since yew come.

ABBIE [*vaguely*]: I tuk his Maw's place.

YOUNG GIRL: Ay-eh. So I've heerd.

[*She turns away to retail this bit of gossip to her mother sitting next to her.* ABBIE *turns to her left to a big stoutish middle-aged man whose flushed face and starting eyes show the amount of 'likker' he has consumed.*]

ABBIE: Ye hain't seen Eben, hev ye?

MAN: No, I hain't. [*Then he adds with a wink*] If yew hain't, who would?

ABBIE: He's the best dancer in the county. He'd ought t' come an' dance.

MAN [*with a wink*]: Mebbe he's doin' the dutiful an' walkin' the kid t' sleep. It's a boy, hain't it?

ABBIE [*nodding vaguely*]: Ay-eh – born two weeks back – purty's a picter –

MAN: They all is – t' their Maws. [*Then in a whisper with a nudge and a leer*] Listen, Abbie – if ye ever git tired o' Eben, remember me! Don't fergit now! [*He looks at her uncomprehending face for a second – then grunts disgustedly.*] Waal – guess I'll likker agin. [*He goes over and joins* CABOT, *who is arguing noisily with an old farmer over cows. They all drink.*]

ABBIE [*this time appealing to nobody in particular*]: Wonder what Eben's a-doin'? [*Her remark is repeated down the line with many a guffaw and titter until it reaches the fiddler. He fastens his blinking eyes on* ABBIE.]

FIDDLER [*raising his voice*]: Bet I kin tell ye, Abbie, what

Eben's doin'! He's down t' the church offerin' up prayers o' thanksgivin'. [*They all titter expectantly.*]

A MAN: What fur? [*Another titter*]

FIDDLER: 'Cause unto him a – [*he hesitates just long enough*] – brother is born!

[*A roar of laughter. They all look from* ABBIE *to* CABOT. *She is oblivious, staring at the door.* CABOT, *although he hasn't heard the words, is irritated by the laughter, and steps forward, glaring about him. There is an immediate silence.*]

CABOT: What're ye all bleatin' about – like a flock o' goats? Why don't ye dance, damn ye? I axed ye here t' dance – t' eat, drink an' be merry – an' thar ye set cacklin' like a lot o' wet hens with the pip! Ye've swilled my likker an' guzzled my vittles like hogs, hain't ye? Then dance fur me, can't ye? That's fa'r an' squar', hain't it? [*A grumble of resentment goes around, but they are all evidently in too much awe of him to express it openly.*]

FIDDLER [*slyly*]: We're waitin' fur Eben. [*A suppressed laugh*]

CABOT [*with a fierce exultation*]: T' hell with Eben! Eben's done fur now! I got a new son! [*His mood switching with drunken suddenness*] But ye needn't t' laugh at Eben, none o' ye! He's my blood, if he be a dumb fool. He's better nor any o' yew! He kin do a day's work a'most up t' what I kin – an' that'd put any o' yew pore critters t' shame!

FIDDLER: An' he kin do a good night's work, too! [*A roar of laughter*]

CABOT: Laugh, ye damn fools! Ye're right just the same, Fiddler. He kin work day an' night, too, like I kin, if need be!

OLD FARMER [*from behind the keg where he is weaving drunkenly back and forth – with great simplicity*]: They hain't many t' touch ye, Ephraim – a son at seventy-six. That's a hard man fur ye! I be on'y sixty-eight an' I couldn't do it. [*A roar of laughter, in which* CABOT *joins uproariously.*]

CABOT [*slapping him on the back*]: I'm sorry fur ye, Hi. I'd never suspicion sech weakness from a boy like yew!

OLD FARMER: An' I never reckoned yew had it in ye nuther, Ephraim. [*Another laugh*]

CABOT [*suddenly grim*]: I got a lot in me – a hell of a lot – folks don't know on. [*Turning to the* FIDDLER] Fiddle 'er up, durn ye! Give 'em somethin' t' dance t'! What air ye, an ornament? Hain't this a celebration? Then grease yer elbow an' go it!

FIDDLER [*seizes a drink which the* OLD FARMER *holds out to him and downs it*]: Here goes!

[*He starts to fiddle 'Lady of the Lake'. Four young fellows and four girls form in two lines and dance a square dance. The* FIDDLER *shouts directions for the different movements, keeping his words in the rhythm of the music and interspersing them with jocular personal remarks to the dancers themselves. The people seated along the walls stamp their feet and clap their hands in unison.* CABOT *is especially active in this respect. Only* ABBIE *remains apathetic, staring at the door as if she were alone in a silent room.*]

FIDDLER: Swing your partner t' the right! That's it, Jim! Give her a b'ar hug! Her Maw hain't lookin'. [*Laughter*] Change partners! That suits ye, don't it, Essie, now ye got Reub afore ye? Look at her redden up, will ye? Waal, life is short an' so's love, as the feller says. [*Laughter*]

CABOT [*excitedly, stamping his foot*]: Go it, boys! Go it, gals!

FIDDLER [*with a wink at the others*]: Ye're the spryest seventy-six ever I sees, Ephraim! Now, if ye'd on'y good eyesight . . .! [*Suppressed laughter. He gives* CABOT *no chance to retort, but roars*] Promenade! Ye're walkin' like a bride down the aisle, Sarah! Waal, while they's life they's allus hope, I've heerd tell. Swing your partner to the left! Gosh A'mighty, look at Johnny Cook high-steppin'! They hain't goin' t' be much strength left fur howin' in the corn lot t'morrow. [*Laughter*]

CABOT: Go it! Go it! [*Then suddenly, unable to restrain himself any longer, he prances into the midst of the dancers, scattering them, waving his arms about wildly.*] Ye're all hoofs! Git out o' my road! Give me room! I'll show ye dancin'. Ye're all too soft! [*He pushes them roughly away. They crowd back toward the walls, muttering, looking at him resentfully.*]

FIDDLER [*jeeringly*]: Go it, Ephraim! Go it! [*He starts 'Pop Goes the Weasel', increasing the tempo with every verse until at the end he is fiddling crazily as fast as he can go.*]

CABOT [*starts to dance, which he does very well and with tremendous vigour. Then he begins to improvise, cuts incredibly grotesque capers, leaping up and cracking his heels together, prancing around in a circle with body bent in an Indian war dance, then suddenly straightening up and kicking as high as he can with both legs. He is like a monkey on a string. And all the while he intersperses his antics with shouts and derisive comments*]: Whoop! Here's dancin' fur ye! Whoop! See that! Seventy-six, if I'm a day! Hard as iron yet! Beatin' the young 'uns like I allus done! Look at me! I'd invite ye t' dance on my hundredth birthday on'y ye'll all be dead by then. Ye're a sickly generation! Yer hearts air pink, not red. Yer veins is full o' mud an' water! I be the on'y man in the county! Whoop! See that! I'm a Injun! I've killed Injuns in the West afore ye was born – an' skulped 'em, too! They's a arrer wound on my backside I c'd show ye! The hull tribe chased me. I outrun 'em all – with the arrer stuck in me! An' I tuk vengeance on 'em. Ten eyes fur an eye, that was my motter! Whoop! Look at me! I kin kick the ceilin' off the room! Whoop!

FIDDLER [*stops playing – exhaustedly*]: God A'mighty, I got enuf. Ye got the devil's strength in ye.

CABOT [*delightedly*]: Did I beat yew, too? Waal, ye played smart. Hev a swig.

[*He pours whisky for himself and* FIDDLER. *They drink. The others watch* CABOT *silently with cold, hostile eyes. There is a dead pause. The* FIDDLER *rests.* CABOT *leans against the keg, panting, glaring around him confusedly. In the room above,*

EBEN *get to his feet and tiptoes out the door in rear, appearing a moment later in the other bedroom. He moves silently, even frightenedly, toward the cradle and stands there looking down at the baby. His face is as vague as his reactions are confused, but there is a trace of tenderness, of interested discovery. At the same moment that he reaches the cradle,* ABBIE *seems to sense something. She gets up weakly and goes to* CABOT.]

ABBIE: I'm goin' up t' the baby.

CABOT [*with real solicitation*]: Air ye able fur the stairs? D'ye want me t' help ye, Abbie?

ABBIE: No. I'm able. I'll be down agin soon.

CABOT: Don't ye git wore out! He needs ye, remember – our son does! [*He grins affectionately, patting her on the back. She shrinks from his touch.*]

ABBIE [*dully*]: Don't – tech me. I'm goin' – up. [*She goes.* CABOT *looks after her. A whisper goes around the room.* CABOT *turns. It ceases. He wipes his forehead streaming with sweat. He is breathing pantingly.*]

CABOT: I'm a-goin' out t' git fresh air. I'm feelin' a mite dizzy. Fiddle up thar! Dance, all o' ye! Here's likker fur them as wants it. Enjoy yerselves. I'll be back. [*He goes, closing the door behind him.*]

FIDDLER [*sarcastically*]: Don't hurry none on our account! [*A suppressed laugh. He imitates* ABBIE.] Whar's Eben? [*More laughter*]

A WOMAN [*loudly*]: What's happened in this house is plain as the nose on yer face! [ABBIE *appears in the doorway upstairs and stands looking in surprise and adoration at* EBEN, *who does not see her.*]

A MAN: Ssshh! He's li'ble t' be listenin' at the door. That'd be like him.

[*Their voices die to an intensive whispering. Their faces are concentrated on this gossip. A noise as of dead leaves in the wind comes from the room.* CABOT *has come out from the porch and stands by the gate, leaning on it, staring at the sky blinkingly.* ABBIE *comes across the room silently.* EBEN *does not notice her until quite near.*]

EBEN [*starting*]: Abbie!

ABBIE: Ssshh! [*She throws her arms around him. They kiss – then bend over the cradle together.*] Ain't he purty? – dead spit 'n' image o' yew!

EBEN [*pleased*]: Air he? I can't tell none.

ABBIE: E-zactly like!

EBEN [*frowningly*]: I don't like this. I don't like lettin' on what's mine's his'n. I been doin' that all my life. I'm gittin' t' the end o' b'arin' it!

ABBIE [*putting her finger on his lips*]: We're doin' the best we kin. We got t' wait. Somethin's bound t' happen. [*She puts her arms around him.*] I got t' go back.

EBEN: I'm goin' out. I can't b'ar it with the fiddle playin' an' the laughin'.

ABBIE: Don't git feelin' low. I love ye, Eben. Kiss me. [*He kisses her. They remain in each other's arms.*]

CABOT [*at the gate, confusedly*]: Even the music can't drive it out – somethin' – ye kin feel it droppin' off the elums, climbin' up the roof, sneakin' down the chimney, pokin' in the corners. . . . They's no peace in houses, they's no rest livin' with folks. Somethin's always livin' with ye. [*With a deep sigh*] I'll go t' the barn an' rest a spell. [*He goes wearily toward the barn.*]

FIDDLER [*tuning up*]: Let's celebrate the old skunk gittin' fooled! We kin have some fun now he's went. [*He starts to fiddle 'Turkey in the Straw'. There is real merriment now. The young folks get up to dance.*]

SCENE 2

[A half-hour later – exterior – EBEN *is standing by the gate looking up at the sky, an expression of dumb pain bewildered by itself on his face.* CABOT *appears, returning from the barn, walking wearily, his eyes on the ground. He sees* EBEN *and his whole mood immediately changes. He becomes excited, a cruel, triumphant grin comes to his lips, he strides up and slaps* EBEN *on the back. From within come the whining of the fiddle and the noise of stamping feet and laughing voices.]*

CABOT: So har ye be!

EBEN [*startled, stares at him with hatred for a moment – then dully*]: Ay-eh.

CABOT [*surveying him jeeringly*]: Why hain't ye been in t' dance? They was all axin' fur ye.

EBEN: Let 'em ax!

CABOT: They's a hull passel o' purty gals –

EBEN: T' hell with 'em!

CABOT: Ye'd ought t' be marryin' one o' 'em soon.

EBEN: I hain't marryin' no one.

CABOT: Ye might 'arn a share o' a farm that way.

EBEN [*with a sneer*]: Like yew did, ye mean? I hain't that kind.

CABOT [*stung*]: Ye lie! 'Twas yer Maw's folks aimed t' steal my farm from me.

EBEN: Other folks don't say so. [*After a pause – defiantly*] An' I got a farm, anyways!

CABOT [*derisively*]: Whar?

EBEN [*stamps a foot on the ground*]: Har.

CABOT [*throws his head back and laughs coarsely*]: Ho-ho! Ye hev, hev ye? Waal, that's a good 'un!

EBEN [*controlling himself – grimly*]: Ye'll see.

CABOT [*stares at him suspiciously, trying to make him out – a pause – then with scornful confidence*]: Ay-eh. I'll see. So'll ye. It's ye what's blind – blind as a mole underground. [EBEN *suddenly laughs, one short sardonic bark:* 'Ha.' *A pause.* CABOT *peers at him with renewed suspicion.*] What air ye hawin' 'bout? [EBEN *turns away without answering.* CABOT *grows angry.*] God A'mighty, yew air a dumb dunce! They's nothin' in that thick skull o' your'n but noise – like a empty keg it be! [EBEN *doesn't seem to hear.* CABOT'S *rage grows.*] Yewr farm! God A'mighty! If ye wa'n't a born donkey ye'd know ye'll never own stick nor stone on it, specially now arter him bein' born. It's his'n, I tell ye – his'n arter I die – but I'll live a hundred jest t' fool ye all – an' he'll be growed then – yewr age a'most! [EBEN *laughs again his sardonic* 'Ha'. *This drives* CABOT *into a fury.*] Ha? Ye think ye kin git 'round that someways, do ye? Waal, it'll be her'n, too – Abbie's – ye won't git 'round her – she knows yer tricks – she'll be too much fur ye – she wants the farm her'n – she was afeerd o' ye – she told me ye was sneakin' 'round tryin' t' make love t' her t' git her on yer side . . . ye . . . ye mad fool, ye! [*He raises his clenched fists threateningly.*]

EBEN [*is confronting him, choking with rage*]: Ye lie, ye old shunk! Abbie never said no sech thing!

CABOT [*suddenly triumphant when he sees how shaken* EBEN *is*]: She did. An' I says, I'll blow his brains t' the top o' them elums – an' she says no, that hain't sense, who'll ye git t' help ye on the farm in his place – an' then she says yew'n me ought t' have a son – I know we kin, she says – an' I says, if we do, ye kin have anythin' I've got ye've a mind t'. An' she says, I wants Eben cut off so's this farm'll be mine when ye die! [*With terrible gloating*] An' that's what's happened, hain't it? An' the farm's her'n! An' the dust o' the road – that's your'n! Ha! Now who's hawin'?

EBEN [*has been listening, petrified with grief and rage – suddenly laughs wildly and brokenly*]: Ha-ha-ha! So that's her sneakin' game – all along! – like I suspicioned at fust – t' swaller it all

– an' me, too . . .! [*Madly*] I'll murder her! [*He springs toward the porch, but* CABOT *is quicker and gets in between.*]

CABOT: No, ye don't!

EBEN: Git out o' my road!

[*He tries to throw* CABOT *aside. They grapple in what becomes immediately a murderous struggle. The old man's concentrated strength is too much for* EBEN. CABOT *gets one hand on his throat and presses him back across the stone wall. At the same moment,* ABBIE *comes out on the porch. With a stifled cry she runs toward them.*]

ABBIE: Eben! Ephraim! [*She tugs at the hand on* EBEN'S *throat.*] Let go, Ephraim! Ye're chokin' him!

CABOT [*removes his hand and flings* EBEN *sideways full length on the grass, gasping and choking. With a cry,* ABBIE *kneels beside him, trying to take his head on her lap, but he pushes her away.* CABOT *stands looking down with fierce triumph*]: Ye needn't t've fret, Abbie, I wa'n't aimin' t' kill him. He hain't wuth hangin' fur – not by a hell of a sight! [*More and more triumphantly*] Seventy-six an' him not thirty yit – an' look whar he be fur thinkin' his Paw was easy! No, by God, I hain't easy! An' him upstairs, I'll raise him t' be like me! [*He turns to leave them.*] I'm goin' in an' dance! – sing an' celebrate! [*He walks to the porch – then turns with a great grin.*] I don't calc'late it's left in him, but if he gits pesky, Abbie, ye jest sing out. I'll come a-runnin' an', by the Etarnal, I'll put him across my knee an' birch him! Ha-ha-ha! [*He goes into the house laughing. A moment later his loud* 'Whoop' *is heard.*]

ABBIE [*tenderly*]: Eben! Air ye hurt? [*She tries to kiss him, but he pushes her violently away and struggles to a sitting position.*]

EBEN [*gaspingly*]: T' hell – with ye!

ABBIE [*not believing her ears*]: It's me, Eben – Abbie – don't ye know me?

EBEN [*glowering at her with hatred*]: Ay-eh – I know ye – now! [*He suddenly breaks down, sobbing weakly.*]

ABBIE [*fearfully*]: Eben – what's happened t' ye – why did ye look at me 's if ye hated me?

EBEN [*violently, between sobs and gasps*]: I do hate ye! Ye're a whore – a damn trickin' whore!

ABBIE [*shrinking back horrified*]: Eben! Ye don't know what ye're sayin'!

EBEN [*scrambling to his feet and following her – accusingly*]: Ye're nothin' but a stinkin' passel o' lies. Ye've been lyin' t' me every word ye spoke, day an' night, since we fust – done it. Ye've kept sayin' ye loved me. . . .

ABBIE [*frantically*]: I do love ye! [*She takes his hand, but he flings hers away.*]

EBEN [*unheeding*]: Ye've made a fool o' me – a sick, dumb fool – a-purpose! Ye've been on'y playin' yer sneakin', stealin' game all along – gittin' me t' lie with ye so's ye'd hev a son he'd think was his'n, an' makin' him promise he'd give ye the farm and let me eat dust, if ye did git him a son! [*Staring at her with anguished, bewildered eyes*] They must be a devil livin' in ye! 'Tain't human t' be as bad as that be!

ABBIE [*stunned – dully*]: He told yew . . .?

EBEN: Hain't it true? It hain't no good in yew lyin'. . . .

ABBIE [*pleadingly*]: Eben, listen – ye must listen – it was long ago – afore we done nothin' – yew was scornin' me – goin' t' see Min – when I was lovin' ye – an' I said it t' him t' git vengeance on ye!

EBEN [*unheedingly. With tortured passion*]: I wish ye was dead! I wish I was dead along with ye afore this come! [*Ragingly*] But I'll git my vengeance, too! I'll pray Maw t' come back t' help me – t' put her cuss on yew an' him!

ABBIE [*brokenly*]: Don't ye, Eben! Don't ye! [*She throws herself on her knees before him, weeping.*] I didn't mean t' do bad t' ye! Fergive me, won't ye?

EBEN [*not seeming to hear her – fiercely*]: I'll git squar' with the old skunk – an' yew! I'll tell him the truth 'bout the son he's so proud o'! Then I'll leave ye here t' pizen each other –

with Maw comin' out o' her grave at nights – an' I'll go t' the gold-fields o' Californi-a whar Sim an' Peter be. . . .

ABBIE [*terrified*]: Ye won't – leave me? Ye can't!

EBEN [*with fierce determination*]: I'm a-goin', I tell ye! I'll get rich thar an' come back an' fight him fur the farm he stole – an' I'll kick ye both out in the road – t' beg an' sleep in the woods – an' yer son along with ye – t' starve an' die! [*He is hysterical at the end.*]

ABBIE [*with a shudder – humbly*]: He's yewr son, too, Eben.

EBEN [*torturedly*]: I wish he never was born! I wish he'd die this minit! I wish I'd never sot eyes on him! It's him – yew havin' him – a-purpose t' steal – that's changed everythin'!

ABBIE [*gently*]: Did ye believe I loved ye – afore he come?

EBEN: Ay-eh – like a dumb ox!

ABBIE: An' ye don't believe no more?

EBEN: B'lieve a lyin' thief! Ha!

ABBIE [*shudders – then humbly*]: An' did ye really love me afore?

EBEN [*brokenly*]: Ay-eh – an' ye was trickin' me!

ABBIE: An' ye don't love me no more!

EBEN [*violently*]: I hate ye, I tell ye!

ABBIE: An' ye're truly goin' West – goin' t' leave me – all on account o' him bein' born?

EBEN: I'm a-goin' in the mornin' – or may God strike me t' hell!

ABBIE [*after a pause – with a dreadful cold intensity – slowly*]: If that's what his comin's done t' me – killin' yewr love – takin' ye away – my on'y joy – the on'y joy I ever knowed – like heaven t' me – purtier'n heaven – then I hate him, too, even if I be his Maw!

EBEN [*bitterly*]: Lies! Ye love him! He'll steal the farm fur ye! [*Brokenly*] But 'tain't the farm so much – not no more – it's yew foolin' me – gittin' me t' love ye – lyin' yew loved me – jest t' steal . . .!

ABBIE [*distractedly*]: He won't steal! I'd kill him fust! I do love ye! I'll prove t' ye –

EBEN [*harshly*]: 'Tain't no use lyin' no more. I'm deaf t' ye! [*He turns away.*] I hain't seein' ye agen. Good-bye!

ABBIE [*pale with anguish*]: Hain't ye even goin' t' kiss me – not once – arter all we loved – ?

EBEN [*in a hard voice*]: I hain't wantin' t' kiss ye never again! I'm wantin' t' forgit I ever sot eyes on ye!

ABBIE: Eben! – ye mustn't – wait a spell – I want t' tell ye . . .

EBEN: I'm a-goin' in t' git drunk. I'm a-goin' t' dance.

ABBIE [*clinging to his arm – with passionate earnestness*]: If I could make it – 's if he'd never come up between us – if I could prove t' ye I wa'n't schemin' t' steal from ye – so's everythin' could be jest the same with us, lovin' each other jest the same, kissin' an' happy the same's we've been happy all along – if I could do it – ye'd love me agen, wouldn't ye? Ye'd kiss me agen? Ye wouldn't never leave me, would ye?

EBEN [*moved*]: I calc'late not. [*Then shaking her hand off his arm – with a bitter smile*] But ye hain't God, be ye?

ABBIE [*exultantly*]: Remember ye've promised! [*Then with strange intensity*] Mebbe I kin do one thin' God does!

EBEN [*peering at her*]: Ye're gittin' cracked, hain't ye? [*Then going toward door*] I'm a-goin' t' dance.

ABBIE [*calls after him intensely*]: I'll prove t' ye! I'll prove I love ye better'n . . . [*He goes in the door, not seeming to hear. She remains standing where she is, looking after him – then she finishes desperately.*] Better'n everythin' else put t'gether!

SCENE 3

Just before dawn in the morning – shows the kitchen and CABOT'S *bedroom.*

[*In the kitchen, by the light of a tallow candle on the table,* EBEN *is sitting, his chin propped on his hands, his drawn face blank and expressionless. His carpet bag is on the floor beside him. In the bedroom, dimly lighted by a small whale-oil lamp,* CABOT *lies asleep.* ABBIE *is bending over the cradle, listening, her face full of terror, yet with an undercurrent of desperate triumph. Suddenly, she breaks down and sobs, appears about to throw herself on her knees beside the cradle, but the old man turns restlessly, groaning in his sleep, and she controls herself, and, shrinking away from the cradle with a gesture of horror, backs swiftly toward the door in rear and goes out. A moment later she comes into the kitchen and, running to* EBEN, *flings her arms about his neck and kisses him wildly. He hardens himself, he remains unmoved and cold, he keeps his eyes straight ahead.*]

ABBIE [*hysterically*]: I done it, Eben! I told ye I'd do it! I've proved I love ye – better'n everythin' – so's ye can't never doubt me no more!

EBEN [*dully*]: Whatever ye done, it hain't no good now.

ABBIE [*wildly*]: Don't ye say that! Kiss me, Eben, won't ye? I need ye t' kiss me arter what I done! I need ye t' say ye love me!

EBEN [*kisses her without emotion – dully*]: That's fur good-bye. I'm a-goin' soon.

ABBIE: No! No! Ye won't go – not now!

EBEN [*going on with his own thoughts*]: I been a-thinkin' – an' I hain't goin' t' tell Paw nothin'. I'll leave Maw t' take vengeance on ye. If I told him, the old skunk'd jest be stinkin' mean enuf to take it out on that baby. [*His voice showing emotion in spite of him*] An' I don't want nothin' bad t' happen t' him. He hain't t' blame fur yew. [*He adds with a certain queer pride.*] An' he looks like me! An', by God, he's mine! An' some day I'll be a-comin' back an' –

ABBIE [*too absorbed in her own thoughts to listen to him – pleadingly*]: They's no cause fur ye t' go now – they's no sense – it's all the same's it was – they's nothin' come b'tween us now – arter what I done!

EBEN [*something in her voice arouses him. He stares at her a bit frightenedly*]: Ye look mad, Abbie. What did ye do?

ABBIE: I – I killed him, Eben.

EBEN [*amazed*]: Ye killed him?

ABBIE [*dully*]: Ay-eh.

EBEN [*recovering from his astonishment – savagely*]: An' serves him right! But we got t' do somethin' quick t' make it look 's if the old skunk'd killed himself when he was drunk. We kin prove by 'em all how drunk he got.

ABBIE [*wildly*]: No! No! Not him! [*Laughing distractedly*] But that's what I ought t' done, hain't it? I oughter killed him instead! Why didn't ye tell me?

EBEN [*appalled*]: Instead? What d'ye mean?

ABBIE: Not him.

EBEN [*his face grown ghastly*]: Not – not that baby!

ABBIE [*dully*]: Ay-eh!

EBEN [*falls to his knees as if he'd been struck – his voice trembling with horror*]: Oh, God A'mighty! A'mighty God! Maw, whar was ye, why didn't ye stop her?

ABBIE [*simply*]: She went back t' her grave that night we fust done it, remember! I hain't felt her about since. [*A pause.* EBEN *hides his head in his hands, trembling all over as if he had the ague. She goes on dully.*] I left the piller over his little face. Then he killed himself. He stopped breathin'. [*She begins to weep softly.*]

EBEN [*rage beginning to mingle with grief*]: He looked like me. He was mine, damn ye!

ABBIE [*slowly and brokenly*]: I didn't want t' do it. I hated myself fur doin' it. I loved him. He was so purty – dead spit 'n' image o' yew. But I loved yew more – an' yew was goin' away – far off whar I'd never see ye agen, never kiss ye, never feel ye pressed agin me agen – an' ye said ye hated me fur havin' him – ye said ye hated him an' wished he was dead – ye said if it hadn't been fur him comin' it'd be the same's afore between us.

EBEN [*unable to endure this, springs to his feet in a fury, threatening her, his twitching fingers seeming to reach out for her throat*]: Ye lie! I never said – I never dreamed ye'd – I'd cut off my head afore I'd hurt his finger!

ABBIE [*piteously, sinking on her knees*]: Eben, don't ye look at me like that – hatin' me – not after what I done fur ye – fur us – so's we could be happy agen –

EBEN [*furiously now*]: Shut up, or I'll kill ye! I see yer game now – the same old sneakin' trick – ye're aimin' t' blame me fur the murder ye done!

ABBIE [*moaning – putting her hands over her ears*]: Don't ye, Eben! Don't ye! [*She grasps his legs.*]

EBEN [*his mood suddenly changing to horror, shrinks away from her*]: Don't ye tech me! Ye're pizen! How could ye – t' murder a pore little critter – Ye must've swapped yer soul t' hell! [*Suddenly raging*] Ha! I kin see why ye done it! Not the lies ye jest told – but 'cause ye wanted t' steal agen – steal the last thin' ye'd left me – my part o' him – no, the hull o' him – ye saw he looked like me – ye knowed he was all mine – an' ye couldn't b'ar it – I know ye! Ye killed him fur bein' mine! [*All this has driven him almost insane. He makes a rush past her for the door – then turns –shaking both fists at her, violently.*] But I'll take vengeance now! I'll git the Sheriff! I'll tell him everythin'! Then I'll sing, 'I'm off to Californi-a!' an' go – gold – Golden Gate – gold sun – fields o' gold in the West! [*This last he half-shouts, half-croons incoherently, suddenly breaking off passionately.*] I'm a-goin' fur the Sheriff t' come an' git ye! I want ye tuk away, locked up from me! I can't stand t' luk at ye! Murderer an' thief 'r not, ye still tempt me! I'll give ye up t' the Sheriff!

[*He turns and runs out, around the corner of house, panting and sobbing, and breaks into a swerving sprint down the road.*]

ABBIE [*struggling to her feet, runs to the door, calling after him*]: I love ye, Eben! I love ye! [*She stops at the door weakly, swaying, about to fall.*] I don't care what ye do – if ye'll on'y love me agen! [*She falls limply to the floor in a faint.*]

SCENE 4

About an hour later. Same as Scene 3. Shows the kitchen and CABOT'S *bedroom. It is after dawn. The sky is brilliant with the sunrise.*

[*In the kitchen,* ABBIE *sits at the table, her body limp and exhausted, her head bowed down over her arms, her face hidden. Upstairs,* CABOT *is still asleep, but awakens with a start. He looks toward the window and gives a snort of surprise and irritation – throws back the covers and begins hurriedly pulling on his clothes. Without looking behind him, he begins talking to* ABBIE, *whom he supposes beside him.*]

CABOT: Thunder 'n' lightnin', Abbie! I hain't slept this late in fifty year! Looks 's if the sun was full riz a'most. Must've been the dancin' an' likker. Must be gittin' old. I hope Eben's t' wuk. Ye might've tuk the trouble t' rouse me, Abbie. [*He turns – sees no one there – surprised.*] Waal – whar air she? Gittin' vittles, I calc'late. [*He tiptoes to the cradle and peers down – proudly.*] Mornin', sonny. Purty's a picter! Sleepin' sound. He don't beller all night like most on 'em. [*He goes quietly out the door in rear – a few moments later enters kitchen – sees* ABBIE *– with satisfaction.*] So thar ye be. Ye got any vittles cooked?

ABBIE [*without moving*]: No.

CABOT [*coming to her, almost sympathetically*]: Ye feelin' sick?

ABBIE: No.

CABOT [*pats her on shoulder. She shudders*]: Ye'd best lie down a spell. [*Half-jocularly*] Yer son'll be needin' ye soon. He'd ought t' wake up with a gnashin' appetite, the sound way he's sleepin'.

ABBIE [*shudders – then in a dead voice*]: He hain't never goin' t' wake up.

CABOT [*jokingly*]: Takes after me this mornin'. I hain't slept so late in –

ABBIE: He's dead.

CABOT [*stares at her – bewilderedly*]: What –?

ABBIE: I killed him.

CABOT [*stepping back from her – aghast*]: Air ye drunk – 'r crazy – 'r – ?

ABBIE [*suddenly lifts her head and turns on him – wildly*]: I killed him, I tell ye! I smothered him. Go up an' see if ye don't b'lieve me!

[CABOT *stares at her a second, then bolts out the rear door, can be heard bounding up the stairs, and rushes into the bedroom and over to the cradle.* ABBIE *has sunk back lifelessly into her former position.* CABOT *puts his hand down on the body in the crib. An expression of fear and horror comes over his face.*]

CABOT [*shrinking away – trembling*]: God A'mighty! God A'mighty. [*He stumbles out the door – in a short while returns to the kitchen – comes to* ABBIE, *the stunned expression still on his face – hoarsely.*] Why did ye do it? Why? [*As she doesn't answer, he grabs her violently by the shoulder and shakes her.*] I ax ye why ye done it! Ye'd better tell me 'r –

ABBIE [*gives him a furious push which sends him staggering back and springs to her feet – with wild rage and hatred*]: Don't ye dare tech me! What right hev ye t' question me 'bout him? He wa'n't yewr son! Think I'd have a son by yew? I'd die fust! I hate the sight o' ye an' allus did! It's yew I should've murdered, if I'd had good sense! I hate ye! I love Eben. I did from the fust. An' he was Eben's son – mine an' Eben's – not your'n!

CABOT [*stands looking at her dazedly – a pause – finding his words with an effort – dully*]: That was it – what I felt – pokin' round the corners – while ye lied – holdin' yerself from me – sayin' ye'd a'ready conceived. . . . [*He lapses into crushed silence – then with a strange emotion.*] He's dead, sart'n. I felt his heart. Pore little critter! [*He blinks back one tear, wiping his sleeve across his nose.*]

ABBIE [*hysterically*]: Don't ye! Don't ye! [*She sobs unrestrainedly.*]

CABOT [*with a concentrated effort that stiffens his body into a rigid line and hardens his face into a stony mask – through his teeth to himself*]: I got t' be – like a stone – a rock o' jedgement! [*A pause. He gets complete control over himself – harshly.*] If he was Eben's, I be glad he air gone! An' mebbe I suspicioned it all along. I felt they was somethin' onnateral – somewhars – the house got so lonesome – an' cold – drivin' me down t' the barn – t' the beasts o' the field. . . . Ay-eh. I must've suspicioned – somethin'. Ye didn't fool me – not altogether, leastways – I'm too old a bird – growin' ripe on the bough. . . . [*He becomes aware he is wandering, straightens again, looks at* ABBIE *with a cruel grin.*] So ye'd liked t' hev murdered me 'stead 'o him, would ye? Waal, I'll live to a hundred! I'll live t' see ye hung! I'll deliver ye up t' the jedgement o' God an' the law! I'll git the Sheriff now. [*Starts for the door.*]

ABBIE [*dully*]: Ye needn't. Eben's gone fur him.

CABOT [*amazed*]: Eben – gone fur the Sheriff?

ABBIE: Ay-eh.

CABOT: T' inform agen ye?

ABBIE: Ay-eh.

CABOT [*considers this – a pause – then in a hard voice*]: Waal, I'm thankful fur him savin' me the trouble. I'll git t' wuk. [*He goes to the door – then turns – in a voice full of strange emotion.*] He'd ought t' been my son, Abbie. Ye'd ought t' loved me. I'm a man. If ye'd loved me, I'd never told no Sherif on ye, no matter what ye did, if they was t' brile me alive!

ABBIE [*defensively*]: They's more to it nor yew know, makes him tell.

CABOT [*dryly*]: Fur yewr sake, I hope they be. [*He goes out – comes around to the gate – stares up at the sky. His control relaxes. For a moment he is old and weary. He murmurs despairingly.*] God A'mighty, I be lonesomer'n ever! [*He hears running footsteps from the left, immediately is himself again.* EBEN *runs in, panting exhaustedly, wild-eyed and mad-looking. He lurches through the gate.* CABOT *grabs him by the shoulder.* EBEN *stares at him dumbly.*] Did ye tell the Sheriff?

EBEN [*nodding stupidly*]: Ay-eh.

CABOT [*gives him a push away that sends him sprawling – laughing with withering contempt*]: Good fur ye! A prime chip o' yer Maw ye be! [*He goes toward the barn, laughing harshly.* EBEN *scrambles to his feet. Suddenly* CABOT *turns – grimly threatening.*] Git off this farm when the Sheriff takes her – or, by God, he'll have t' come back an' git me fur murder, too!

[*He stalks off.* EBEN *does not appear to have heard him. He runs to the door and comes into the kitchen.* ABBIE *looks up with a cry of anguished joy.* EBEN *stumbles over and throws himself on his knees beside her – sobbing brokenly.*]

EBEN: Fergive me!

ABBIE [*happily*]: Eben! [*She kisses him and pulls his head over against her breast.*]

EBEN: I love ye! Fergive me!

ABBIE [*ecstatically*]: I'd fergive ye all the sins in hell fur sayin' that! [*She kisses his head, pressing it to her with a fierce passion of possession.*]

EBEN [*brokenly*]: But I told the Sheriff. He's comin' fur ye!

ABBIE: I kin b'ar what happens t' me – now!

EBEN: I woke him up. I told him. He says, 'Wait 'til I git dressed.' I was waiting. I got to thinkin' o' yew. I got to thinkin' how I'd loved ye. It hurt like somethin' was bustin' in my chest an' head. I got t' cryin'. I knowed sudden I loved ye yet, an' allus would love ye!

ABBIE [*caressing his hair – tenderly*]: My boy, hain't ye?

EBEN: I begun t' run back. I cut across the fields an' through the woods. I thought ye might have time t' run away – with me – an' –

ABBIE [*shaking her head*]: I got t' take my punishment – t' pay fur my sin.

EBEN: Then I want t' share it with ye.

ABBIE: Ye didn't do nothin'.

EBEN: I put it in yer head. I wisht he was dead! I as much as urged ye t' do it!

ABBIE: No. It was me alone!

EBEN: I'm as guilty as yew be! He was the child o' our sin.

ABBIE [*lifting her head as if defying God*]: I don't repent that sin! I hain't askin' even God t' fergive that!

EBEN: Nor me – but it led up t' the other – an' the murder ye did, ye did 'count o' me – an' it's my murder, too, I'll tell the Sheriff – an' if ye deny it, I'll say we planned it t'gether – an' they'll all b'lieve me, fur they suspicion everythin' we've done, an' it'll seem likely an' true to 'em. An' it is true – way down – I did help ye – somehow.

ABBIE [*laying her head on his – sobbing*]: No! I don't want yew t' suffer!

EBEN: I got t' pay fur my part o' the sin! An' I'd suffer wuss leavin' ye, goin' West, thinkin' o' ye day an' night, bein' out when yew was in . . . [*Lowering his voice*] 'R bein' alive when yew was dead. [*A pause*] I want t' share with ye, Abbie – prison 'r death 'r hell 'r anythin'! [*He looks into her eyes and forces a trembling smile.*] If I'm sharin' with ye, I won't feel lonesome, leastways.

ABBIE [*weakly*]: Eben! I won't let ye! I can't let ye!

EBEN [*kissing her – tenderly*]: Ye can't he'p yerself. I got ye beat fur once!

ABBIE [*forcing a smile – adoringly*]: I hain't beat – s'long's I got ye!

EBEN [*hears the sound of feet outside*]: Ssshh! Listen! They've come t' take us!

ABBIE: No, it's him. Don't give him no chance to fight ye, Eben. Don't say nothin' – no matter what he says. An' I won't, neither. [*It is* CABOT. *He comes up from the barn in a great state of excitement and strides into the house and then into the kitchen.* EBEN *is kneeling beside* ABBIE, *his arm around her, hers around him. They stare straight ahead.*]

CABOT [*stares at them, his face hard. A long pause – vindictively*]: Ye make a slick pair o' murderin' turtle-doves! Ye'd ought t' be both hung on the same limb an' left thar t' swing in the breeze an' rot – a warnin' t' old fools like me t' b'ar their lonesomeness alone – an' fur young fools like ye t' hobble their lust. [*A pause. The excitement returns to his face, his eyes snap, he looks a bit crazy.*] I couldn't work today. I couldn't take no interest. T' hell with the farm! I'm leavin' it! I've turned the cows an' other stock loose! I've druv 'em into the woods whar they kin be free! By freein' 'em, I'm freein' myself! I'm quittin' here today! I'll set fire t' house an' barn an' watch 'em burn, an' I'll leave yer Maw t' haunt the ashes, an' I'll will the fields back t' God, so that nothin' human kin never touch 'em! I'll be a-goin' to Californi-a – t' jine Simeon an' Peter – true sons o' mine if they be dumb fools – an' the Cabots 'll find Solomon's Mines t'gether! [*He suddenly cuts a mad caper.*] Whoop! What was the song they sung? 'Oh, Californi-a! That's the land fur me.' [*He sings this – then gets on his knees by the floor-board under which the money was hid.*] An' I'll sail thar on one o' the finest clippers I kin find! I've got the money! Pity ye didn't know whar this was hidden so's ye could steal . . . [*He has pulled up the board. He stares – feels – stares again. A pause of dead silence. He slowly turns, slumping into a sitting position on the floor, his eyes like those of a dead fish, his face the sickly green of an attack of nausea. He swallows painfully several times – forces a weak smile at last.*] So – ye did steal it!

EBEN [*emotionlessly*]: I swapped it t' Sim an' Peter fur their share o' the farm – t' pay their passage t' Californi-a.

CABOT [*with one sardonic laugh*]: Ha! [*He begins to recover. Gets slowly to his feet – strangely.*] I calc'late God give it to 'em – not yew! God's hard, not easy! Mebbe they's easy gold in the West, but it hain't God's gold. It hain't fur me. I kin hear His voice warnin' me agen t' be hard an' stay on my farm. I kin see His hand usin' Eben t' steal t' keep me from weakness. I kin feel I be in the palm o' His hand, His fingers guidin' me. [*A pause – then he mutters sadly.*] It's a-goin' t' be lonesomer now than ever it war afore – an' I'm gittin' old, Lord – ripe on the bough. . . . [*Then stiffening*] Waal – what d'ye want? God's lonesome, hain't He? God's hard an' lonesome! [*A pause. The* SHERIFF *with two men comes up the road from the left. They move cautiously to the door. The* SHERIFF *knocks on it with the butt of his pistol.*]

SHERIFF: Open in the name o' the law! [*They start.*]

CABOT: They've come fur ye. [*He goes to the rear door.*] Come in, Jim! [*The three men enter.* CABOT *meets them in doorway.*] Jest a minit, Jim. I got 'em safe here. [*The* SHERIFF *nods. He and his companions remain in the doorway.*]

EBEN [*suddenly calls*]: I lied this mornin', Jim. I helped her do it. Ye kin take me, too.

ABBIE [*brokenly*]: No!

CABOT: Take 'em both. [*He comes forward – stares at* EBEN *with a trace of grudging admiration.*] Purty good – fur yew! Waal, I got t' round up the stock. Good-bye.

EBEN: Good-bye.

ABBIE: Good-bye.

[CABOT *turns and strides past the men – comes out and around the corner of the house, his shoulders squared, his face stony, and stalks grimly toward the barn. In the meantime the* SHERIFF *and men have come into the room.*]

SHERIFF [*embarrassed*]: Waal – we'd best start.

ABBIE: Wait. [*Turns to* EBEN.] I love ye, Eben.

EBEN: I love ye, Abbie. [*They kiss. The three men grin and shuffle embarrassedly.*]

EBEN [*to the* SHERIFF]: Now. [*He takes* ABBIE'S *hand.*] Come. [*They go out the door in rear, the men following, and come from the house, walking hand-in-hand to the gate.* EBEN *stops there and points to the sunrise sky.*] Sun's a-risin'. Purty, hain't it?

ABBIE: Ay-eh. [*They both stand for a moment looking up raptly in attitudes strangely aloof and devout.*]

SHERIFF [*looking around at the farm enviously – to his companions*]: It's a jim-dandy farm, no denyin'. Wish I owned it!

CURTAIN

MORE ABOUT PENGUINS

If you have enjoyed reading this book you may wish to know that *Penguin Book News* appears every month. It is an attractively illustrated magazine containing a complete list of books published by Penguins and still in print, together with details of the month's new books. A specimen copy will be sent free on request.

Penguin Book News is obtainable from most bookshops; but you may prefer to become a regular subscriber at 3s. for twelve issues. Just write to Dept EP, Penguin Books Ltd, Harmondsworth, Middlesex, enclosing a cheque or postal order, and you will be put on the mailing list.

Some other books published by Penguins are described on the following pages.

Note: *Penguin Book News* is not available in the U.S.A., Canada or Australia

WHO'S AFRAID OF VIRGINIA WOOLF?

Edward Albee

'Frighteningly well-observed picture of a matrimonial *corrida*, with the scarred and bloody husband at last taking the cow by the horns after a long, liquor-logged evening' – Alan Brien in the *Sunday Telegraph*

'It has established Albee in the world's mind as the proper successor to Tennessee Williams and Arthur Miller' – Bamber Gascoigne in the *Observer Weekend Review*

'He is the most exciting American playwright of his generation' – *Vogue*

'Has an intensity, a demoniac misery, a ferocious humour, an ability to rend and tear and crucify to a degree unfamiliar in the English theatre . . . no one can remain indifferent to its power, its resilience of ideas and its range of language' – Harold Hobson in the *Sunday Times Weekend Review*

THREE PLAYERS OF A SUMMER GAME AND OTHER STORIES

Tennessee Williams

Tennessee Williams, author of *A Streetcar Named Desire*, *Cat on a Hot Tin Roof*, and other plays, has now written a collection of stories, his first ever to be published in England. It shows every facet of this author's remarkable talent – his capacity to shock, his tenderness, and his uncanny ability to get under the skins of abnormal people.

Also available

SWEET BIRD OF YOUTH

A STREETCAR NAMED DESIRE

THE GLASS MENAGERIE